The Word of a Woman

Feminist Dispatches 1968 – 1992

Also by Robin Morgan

Feminist
Dispatches

1968 – 1992

Robin
Morgan

The
Word
of a
Woman

W·W·Norton & Company

New York   London

The text of this book is composed
in 10.5/13 Linotype Walbaum
with the display set in
Walbaum and Walbaum Bold
Composition/Manufacturing by
The Maple-Vail Book Manufacturing Group.
Book design by Margaret M. Wagner

Library of Congress Cataloging-in-Publication Data
Morgan, Robin.
The word of a woman : feminist dispatches, 1968–1992 /
by Robin Morgan.
p.   cm.
Includes index.
1. Feminist theory.   2. Feminism.   3. Feminism—United
States.
I. Title.
HQ1190.M67   1993
305.42'01—dc20   92–7377

ISBN: 0-393-03427-5

W. W. Norton & Company, Inc.
500 Fifth Avenue, New York, N.Y. 10110
W. W. Norton & Company Ltd.
10 Coptic Street, London WC1A 1PU

    3 4 5 6 7 8 9 0

Contents

Foreword

Composing an introduction to a selection of one's early writings through one's recent work can provoke a state of mind somewhere between nostalgia and hilarity. Some would call this perspective.

I write this—on a wintery North American day in 1992—during what the mainstream media have proclaimed the "post-feminist" era. In the late 1960s, at the beginning of the current wave of feminist activism, that media had authoritatively declared that this movement would never get off the ground. During the intervening quarter-century, those same pundits announced with dependably annual regularity that the death of feminism was imminent. (*I* would call this period the beginning of the post-*patriarchal* era.)

Meanwhile, women all over the planet steadily continued to think, write, organize, and (O subversive act!) *compare notes,* pausing now and then in irritation, amusement, and incredulity, to gasp at how the reality in which we live can be so ignored or trivialized, at how most men seem able to go directly from a denial of our social existence to a declaration of our political demise without having passed through mere comprehension of "what women really want."

We are told, for instance, that feminism is a Western—and recent—novelty. That this overlooks such phenomena as the twelfth-century Turkish harem revolts, the forty "women's rights armies" of China's 1851 Taiping Rebellion, the founding of Indonesia's women's movement in 1904, the activism of the Argentinean National Feminist Party in 1918, and the contemporary worldwide Women's Movement, seems of little consequence. (I would term this willful myopia, plain old ahistoric ethnocentrism.)

We are told that younger women aren't interested in feminism. That this ignores the proliferation of newly militant campus-based women's groups and national young feminists' conferences, not to speak of such coalitions as The Third Wave and SOS (Students Organizing Students), seems not to count for much. Furthermore, those of us who lecture frequently at high schools and universities must be hallucinating when we address standard enthusiastic audiences of a thousand people—mostly female and all in their late teens or early twenties. (I would name such disinformation age-bigotry.)

We are told that the so-called men's movement, complete with such overnight millionaires as Robert Bly and his "wild men" drum-beaters, is a new (and solemnly important) development. That this disregards the intense dedication of many male people, from Cro-Magnon times through "men's sensitivity" trends, to focus on *anything* rather than relate to a dirty floor (or a child) seems not to matter. (I would identify such hoary, hairy stunts as reliable backlash.)

We are told that "feminist theory" (what's left of it, one presumes?) can emanate only from academia, complete with deconstructionist and "post-history" frilly obfuscation. That this attempts to obliterate the work of such feminist theorists as Nawal El Saadawi of Egypt, Hilkka Pietilä of Finland, Margarita Chant Papandreou of Greece, Marjorie Agosín of Chile, Kumari Jayarawenda of Sri Lanka, Tatyana Mamonova of Russia, and Gwendoline

Konie of Zambia—only a sampling—as well as that of thousands of other activists and writers in the United States and abroad, seems to disconcert few academics. That such a proprietary attitude also violates two feminist principles of the original women's studies' vision—that "the personal is political" and that "every woman is an expert about her own life"—seems of even less concern. (I would grade such theses with an "E" or an "O"—for elitism and opportunism.)

We in the United States are told how far female citizens have come, how the "revolution" has already been won. (I must have been in the shower when it happened.) That the year 1991 alone saw a flood of women's outrage—at the Senate, over the Clarence Thomas confirmation hearings; at the legal system, over the manipulations in the William Kennedy Smith rape trial; and at the government, over continued massive cutbacks in social services and the feminization of poverty—gets conveniently slighted. (I would say that such visible, articulate fury constitutes the warning of a revolution yet to come.)

We are told that "women's issues" are limited to such subjects as reproductive freedom, freedom of sexual choice, the rising tide of violence against women (including rape, battery, sexual molestation, and harassment), equal-opportunity access to education and employment, childcare, and so forth. (This in itself does, I grant, constitute a considerable "to do" list.) But at this writing, most world leaders are busy congratulating themselves and each other on the achievements of the past twenty-four months. These leaders are, to be sure, concerned about the intensifying environmental crisis and distressed about the state of the world's economy, but they console themselves by praising new growth industries dedicated to "pollution control," and by referring to a global depression in such Orwellian terms as "sluggish markets" or "stagflation."

All of the above—and more—are "women's issues."

The growing number of homeless people and those rioting in lines for bread in the former Soviet Union, are women. Those civilians most devastated by the civil wars in Eastern Europe (wars that would in racist terms be called "tribal" if they were occurring on the African continent) are women and children. Those most threatened by the outlawing of abortion in Poland and the flood of pornography in Hungary, are women. In the wake of the Gulf War, women in "liberated" Kuwait still are not permitted to vote; women in Saudi Arabia still are not permitted to drive; women in Iraq still are busy mourning, starving, and trying to save wounded, diseased, and malnutritive children; and women throughout the Muslim world are fighting a new wave of religious fundamentalism. In South Africa, Nelson Mandela and Prime Minister de Klerck meet and smile at photo-opportunities, while the women of both the African National Congress and Inkatha protest their non-inclusion in the new draft constitution. That there is less threat of superpower nuclear war (thanks to the initiative of Mikhail Gorbachev) does not diminish the specter of nuclear *accident,* as nuclear-power plants proliferate and as the armaments industry refocuses its sights on the Third World market—and it is no coincidence that the expanding global anti-nuclear and environmentalism movements were begun by women and remain largely peopled by women.

All this and more constitutes the news between the lines, the action behind the scenes—a *deeper reality.*

Meanwhile, in the tedious tradition of woman as object rather than subject, this feminist wave falls apparent prey to be written about, distorted, erased, simplified, analyzed, or compartmentalized by a new crop of "objective" historians with their own hidden political agendas— whether conservative, Marxist, male supremacist, or simply boring. So it becomes all the more crucial that we tell our own story, because, to paraphrase Walt Whitman: We were the women, we suffered, we were there.

This collection—the dispatches from one participatory observer—is, I hope, as volatile and versatile, as serious and funny, as energetic, eclectic, and elegantly nonlinear as the almost twenty-five years of feminist activism it reflects and describes. It includes some journalism, a number of theoretical articles, a bit of polemic, a few pieces that grew into book chapters and are here returned to their original core as intended essays, some meditations, one obituary, and one fable. When I have revised these pieces at all, it has been for the sake of clarity; I have made no revisionist changes in the politics or style, but have deliberately left intact all the contradictions and disagreements with myself that were (and are) part of this individual, literary, and historical process. The largest section is composed of new writings, almost all of them published here for the first time. For context, I have written short prefaces to each selection.

The choice of what to include in such a collection is ultimately a personal (which is to say, political) one.

Certain articles flatly refused exclusion: the piece covering the first Miss America Pageant protest in 1968 marks a watershed—the beginning of a grass-roots feminist explosion in North America; "Goodbye To All That" became famous (or infamous) as a classic example of women's rage at male-Left betrayal; "On Women as a Colonized People" and "Theory and Practice: Pornography and Rape" offered new metaphors and theories for women's previously unnamed and unspeakable experience. I have included some so-called meditative prose as well as "active" journalism, because the Women's Movement courageously and repeatedly defies the bifurcations of inner and outer, and because politics in the most profound sense is not restricted to deals made in the halls of the powerful or demonstrations marched in the streets of the powerless. "Politics" is also what a solitary woman does at 3 A.M., sitting at the kitchen table with a mug of tea and a damp handkerchief, thinking about how to change her life.

There is an undeniable hubris attendant on being a writer at all, particularly in an age of sound-bites. For someone blessed (or cursed) with a literary sensibility and also cursed (or blessed) with an ardor for political engagement, that hubris is heightened by a sense of omnipresent guilt (when one is writing, why isn't one "at the barricades"?; when one is at the barricades, why isn't one writing?). Add to the hubris and the guilt an awareness of irony—that one writes in a world where two-thirds of all illiterates are women—and you get an approximation of the moral predicament in which the writer who is a feminist lives and works. This collection mirrors such ambivalence.

I can't help noticing the shifts in *tone* in these pages. During the sixties, I was busy explaining (as fast as I discovered them) The Basics, and the tone was largely defensive and reactive. (We were all a bit nervous that we might alienate men "too much," that we might unlearn our appetite for male approval in its various protean and withheld forms.) In the seventies, new issues and theories surfaced in the work, but much energy was still spent re-explaining The Basics, although the tone moved away from reactive defensiveness and jargon into a clear, refreshing anger. The eighties witnessed a *re*-re-explaining of The Basics (this is the voice of an organizer, after all), but those basics had broadened, and the personal voice began to dare a style more metaphorical, philosophical, and lyrical.

Now, in the nineties, I notice that the voice in these writings is even more impassioned about the (continually expanding) issues, but far less concerned with explaining The Basics. There is, at times, some jostling for primacy between creative thinking and the lust to communicate in a useful manner, some crossing and recrossing of the bridge between intellectual exploration on the far bank and practical coaxing of the reader on the near one. But the language tightens (always a good sign) and rhetoric peels away (always a relief). Perhaps a maturation of the Movement and, hopefully, the self, accounts for this. Perhaps it is a taking to heart of feminist historian Gerda Lerner's excellent prescription, from her book *The Creation of Patriarchy**: "We must, as far as possible, leave patriarchal thought behind. ... [This requires] being skeptical toward every known system of thought: being critical of all assumptions, ordering values and definitions, ... developing intellectual courage, ... the challenge to move from the desire for safety and approval to the most 'unfeminine' quality of all—that of intellectual arrogance, the supreme hubris which asserts to itself the right to reorder the world."

Which brings us, full circle, back to hubris.

It is my hope that women of my generation will laugh and cry in recognition at many of the actions and consciousness-shifts preserved in these pages, that this personal journey—which reflects the history of this past quarter-century of feminist energy and vision—will grant us some perspective on where we came from, where we've been, what small and large miracles we've wrought, and what we have yet to accomplish.

It is also my hope that younger women—including those lovely, fierce feminists the newspapers insist I imagine exist—will encounter here some first-person truths about older sisters (some of whom are their mothers), some recognitions all their own, and some sturdy shoulders on which to stand, inspired to go not just "too far," but even further.

Last, it is my wish that those men who venture reading

*(New York and London: Oxford University Press, 1986).

this book may begin to understand some part of the deeper reality.

My own still-evolving consciousness of that reality is due in large part to the ongoing support of many women. But the struggle to describe that reality in words is a demanding one, and I am especially indebted to a few people who continue to see me through book after book, who tolerate my despair as well as my elation, and who proffer both loving criticism and critically important love. My gratitude goes to Mary Cunnane, my editor, for her good humor, her faith in my work, and her standards of excellence; to Edite Kroll, my literary agent, who generously shared in the activism described on many of these pages as well as in the writing about it; to Blake Morgan, whose ethical criteria about being human and being an artist continue to amaze, delight, and challenge me; and to Marilyn J. Waring, whose encouragement (and endurance) of much of the newest work in this book constitute a testament to her own passionate integrity.

In a world where "a man's word is his honor," and where female human beings have been both silenced and dishonored for millennia, the word of a woman seems a fragile thing. But to break silence is an act of audacity, with enormous implications. And given all the means by which silence is reinforced again and again, to break and re-break it one's whole life long, in newer and different ways, is an honorable and gratifying task, a humbling sort of hubris. I offer these pages, then, to the participatory reader—from a twentieth-century writer, with a love for women and a love for words.

Robin Morgan
New York City
1992

I

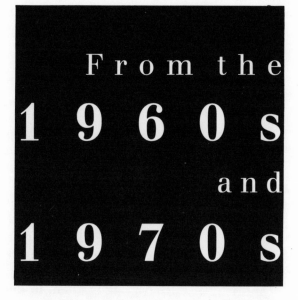

From the
1960s
and
1970s

Women *vs.* the Miss America Pageant

The following piece is based on an article that appeared in various New Left publications. I made no pretense at being an objective journalist (if such an animal ever existed); I had been one of the organizers of the demonstration, so my reporting was a perfect example of what then was proudly called "participatory journalism."

The 1968 women's demonstration against the Miss America Pageant in Atlantic City was the first major action of the current wave of feminism in the United States. But years of meetings, consciousness raising, thought, and plain old organizing had taken place before any of us set foot on the boardwalk.

It was an early group, New York Radical Women, that decided to protest the pageant. Almost all of us in that group had been active in civil-rights organizations, the student movement, anti-Vietnam War coalitions, or some such wing of the New Left, but not one of us had ever organized a demonstration on her own before. I can still remember the feverish excitement I felt: dickering with the company that chartered buses, wangling a permit from the mayor of Atlantic City, sleeping about three hours a night for days preceding the demonstration. The acid taste of coffee from paper containers and of cigarettes from crumpled packs

*was in my mouth; my eyes were bloodshot and my glasses
kept slipping down my nose; my feet hurt and my neck
ached and my voice had gone hoarse—and I was deliri-
ously happy. Each meeting was an excitement "high":
whether we were lettering posters or writing leaflets or
deciding who would deal with which reporter requesting
an interview, we were affirming our mutual feelings of
outrage, hope, and readiness to conquer the world. We also
all felt, well,* grown up; *we were doing this one for ourselves, and we were consequently getting to do those things
the men never let us do, like talk to the press and deal with
the mayor's office. We fought a lot and laughed a lot and
pretended we weren't extremely nervous.*

*Possibly the most enduring contribution of that protest
was our decision to recognize newswomen only. After much
discussion, we settled on refusing to speak to male reporters—not because we were so naive as to think that women
journalists would automatically give us more sympathetic
coverage but because taking this stand made a political
statement consistent with our beliefs. Furthermore, we estimated correctly that it would raise consciousness about
the position of women in the media—and help more women
get jobs there (as well as helping those who were already
there escape from the ghetto of "the women's pages"). It
was a risky but wise decision that shocked many but soon
set a precedent. Today, most networks, wire services, and
major newspapers across North America know without
being reminded that newswomen should be sent to cover
feminist demonstrations and press conferences. And this
has perceptibly helped to change the pre-1970s, all-but-
invisible status of women in media.*

*We also made certain Big Mistakes. Not so much the
tactical ones: we had women doctors, nurses, and lawyers
on stand-by, and local "turf" to which we could strategi-
cally flee if the going got too ugly. Our errors were more
in the area of consciousness about ourselves and other*

*women—who we really were and who we wanted to reach.
For example, our leaflets, press statements, and guerrilla-
theater actions didn't make clear that we were not dem-
onstrating against the pageant* contestants *(with whom,
on the contrary, we expressed solidarity as women exploited
by the male system), but that our adversaries were the
pageant organizers and the pageant concept and process
itself. The spontaneous appearance of various posters
spouting slogans like "Miss America Goes Down" and certain revised song lyrics (such as "Ain't she sweet / making
profit off her meat") didn't help matters. Another error,
with 20/20 hindsight, was our crowning of a live sheep on
the boardwalk. Not only was this (understandably) perceived as denigrating the contestants; it was, I now think,
rather unfair to the ewe. I'm glad that we organizers, well
before the days of animal-rights consciousness, took excellent care of the sheep (better care than we ensured ourselves), not out of any awareness of being "politically
correct," but out of simple compassion. We made sure the
animal had shade, water, and a stash of hay that had been
unceremoniously hauled along in one of the buses full of
demonstrators singing "We Shall Overcome." And the rented
sheep went back to her home, at a nearby New Jersey farm,
long before the human protestors left the fray. Yet from my
perspective now, renting, crowning, and parading her
before press and onlookers was not one of my finest hours.*

*Still: we came, we saw, and if we didn't conquer, we
learned. And other women learned that we existed; the week
before the demonstration there had been thirty women at
the New York Radical Women meeting; the week after, there
were approximately a hundred and fifty.*

*A year later, there was another demonstration in Atlan-
tic City; I went as a reluctant "old" organizer (based on
my vast experience from the previous year) to help and
advise those who were putting it together. I had given birth
less than two months earlier and was breast-feeding the*

baby, who was clearly too young to tolerate an all-day and most-of-the-night demonstration. Thus my memories of the 1969 protest are largely of worrying that the child would accept my husband's bottle-feeding, and my own keen discomfort with milk-full breasts—which I regularly emptied via a breast pump I had brought along for that purpose, quitting the picket line every two hours to dash to the nearest women's room and pump myself out. Such are the vicissitudes encountered by a feminist activist.

During the past two decades, some of us from that original small organizing group in 1968 have managed to stay in loose touch with one another. One got divorced and became an actress and drama teacher in California; one owns and runs a women's crafts shop with her woman lover and partner in Virginia; one teaches sociology and women's studies in Alabama, where she's raised her two children; one is an OWL (Older Women's Liberation) activist in upstate New York. But we've lost touch with the others, and two women are lost to us permanently. One died in her early forties after a brave struggle against cancer. The other—a European emigré, a classically trained violinist who had co-founded the first Women's Liberation Rock Band and later played bass with a male jazz combo—fought a long battle with drugs but died of an overdose, whether accidental or intentional no one could tell.

The pageant still exists, of course, but draws less of an audience each year. Meanwhile, the intervening twenty-plus years have seen feminist protests on both state and national levels become as much a tradition as the pageant itself. (The Santa Cruz demonstrations against the Miss California Pageant were so relentless and ingenious as to include full parades with floats, and the successful infiltration by a feminist "contestant" who almost won the Miss California crown—but who pulled a banner reading "Pageants Hurt All Women" from her bra on live TV; finally, the Santa Cruz city leaders capitulated and the state con-

test site was moved to another city.) The past decades have also witnessed pageant officials jettisoning the require-ment of virginity for contestants and admitting women of color as contestants—dubious victories, but changes reflecting feminist protest. The 1970s saw a finalist who publicly tore off her crown and denounced the whole com-petitive, objectifying process. The 1980s made note of the unfortunate fall in a corruption scandal of Bess Myerson, a public servant and much publicized Miss A. of the 1940s (always used as an example of how far a winner could go). And 1991 broke another first: former crownholder Marilyn Van Derbur's account (in People *magazine, June 10) of having been sexually abused by her father.*

Some things have not changed at all, however. In 1968 we protested the use of Miss America as an entertainer for the U.S. troops in Vietnam; in 1990, the winner entertained the U.S. troops in the Persian Gulf.

Still, the time will come when feminists automatically gearing themselves up for Atlantic City will find that there is no longer anything there about which to protest.

No matter how empathetic you are to another's oppres-sion, you become truly committed to radical change only when you realize your own oppression—it has to reach you on a gut level. This is what has been happening to American women, both in and out of the New Left.

Having functioned "underground" for a few years now, the Women's Liberation movement surfaced with its first major demonstration on September 7, 1968, in Atlantic City, New Jersey, at the Miss America Pageant. Women came from as far away as Canada, Florida, and Michigan, as well as from all over the Eastern seaboard. The pag-eant was chosen as a target for a number of reasons: it is patently degrading to women (in propagating the Mind-less Sex-Object Image); it has always been a lily-white, racist contest (there has never been a black finalist); the winner tours Vietnam, entertaining the troops as a mascot of murder; the whole gimmick of the million-dollar pageant corporation is one commercial shill-game to sell the sponsors' products. Where else could one find such perfect combination of American values—racism, militarism, capitalism—all packaged in one "ideal" symbol: a woman. This was the basic reason why the protesters disrupted the pageant—the contestants epitomize the role all women are forced to play in this society, one way or the other: apolitical, unoffending, passive, delicate (but delighted by drudgery) *things.*

About two hundred women descended on this tacky town and staged an all-day demonstration on the boardwalk in front of the Convention Hall (where the pageant was taking place), singing, chanting, and performing guerrilla theater nonstop throughout the day. The crowning of a live sheep as Miss America was relevant to where this society is at; the crowning of Miss Illinois as the "real" Miss America, her smile metaphorically blood-flecked from [Chicago political boss] Mayor Daley's kiss, was also relevant. The demonstrators mock-auctioned off a dummy of Miss America, and flung dishcloths, steno pads, girdles, and bras into a Freedom Trash Can. (This last was translated by the male-controlled media into the totally fabricated act of "bra-burning," a non-event upon which they have fixated constantly ever since.)

Most picket signs proclaimed solidarity with the pageant contestants, while condemning the pageant itself. An active solidarity has possibly been at work, for that matter: it has been rumored that one of the contestants decided to function as an infiltrator and was responsible for the scrambling of [master of ceremonies] Bert Parks's cue cards, temporarily melting his perfect plastic smile. At night, an "inside squad" of twenty brave sisters disrupted the live telecast of the pageant, yodeling the eerie

Berber Yell (from the film the *Battle of Algiers*) shouting "Freedom for Women!" and unfurling a huge banner reading WOMEN'S LIBERATION from the balcony rail—all of which stopped the nationwide-televised show cold for ten bloodcurdling seconds. One woman was arrested for "emitting a noxious odor"—spraying Toni hair conditioner (a vile-smelling sponsor of the pageant) near the mayor's box, although the sister-traveler among the contestants who shuffled Parks's cue cards was never apprehended. The upshot: The show may have to be taped in the future, possibly without an audience, and the action, widely covered in the press, brought excited new members into the Women's Movement. Who knows? There just might be two thousand of us liberating women from the Miss America image some year.* Women's Liberation immediately set up a Legal Defense Fund for those busted in Atlantic City—money and supportive letters poured in to help these sisters. One groovy by-product from the action is a film by women, to be used for organizing purposes.

Women's Liberation demanded the use of women reporters—much to the annoyance of the male-dominated media under- *and* over-ground, which like to keep "news chicks" covering flower and fashion shows. Some of the press were put through considerable changes by this insistence on recognizing only women reporters, but the press as a whole weren't prepared for anything as "heavy" as arrests; most of them had assumed that the protesters wouldn't be taken that seriously. This assumption came from not realizing that the real soft white underbelly of the American beast was being socked in Atlantic City. So seriously were the women taken, in fact,

---

*In September 1974, more than two thousand women demonstrated against the pageant, marching intrepidly in front of Convention Hall; this, according to the wire-service stories and the *New York Times*. The prophecy turned out to be not an empty rhetorical flourish.

that the original disorderly conduct charge for the militant use of hair spray was later escalated to an indictable offense with a possible two-to-three-year sentence (ultimately, the sentence was suspended). Reports are also coming back that the fears of the pageant officials are not completely lulled by the idea of taping future events without an audience—since what will they do for contestants, when they no longer can trust even "their own"?

Nevertheless, some male reactionaries in the Left still think Women's Liberation "frivolous" in the face of "larger, more important" revolutionary problems. But what is "frivolous" about rapping for four hours across police barricades with hecklers, trying to get through to the women in the crowd who smile surreptitiously but remain silent while their men scream vilification? What is frivolous, for that matter, about a woman who isn't rich enough to fly to Puerto Rico for an abortion and so must lie on some kitchen table watching cockroaches on the ceiling articulate the graph of her pain? What is frivolous about the young black woman, proud and beautiful and militant, whose spirit cracks when she hears Stokely Carmichael say that "the only position for women in SNCC* is prone"? What is frivolous about the welfare recipient who must smuggle her husband or boyfriend out of the house when the social worker arrives, denying her own sexuality or risking the loss of her sustenance (to say nothing of having her children taken away from her)? What is frivolous about the migrant-worker mother who must be yet one step lower than her oppressed husband, must endure his beating her up, impregnating her just after she's dropped her seventh child, and maybe disappearing for a year now and then so that he can exercise his "manhood"? And what is frivolous about the women in

*Student Nonviolent Coordinating Committee, a major black civil-rights organization of the period.

Fayerweather Hall at Columbia University last spring, new-minted revolutionaries ready to be tear-gassed and busted as well as anybody (and they were), ready to form a commune that would reflect alternative life styles to this whole sick culture, only to hear a male SDS* leader ask for "chicks to volunteer for cooking duty"?

Sexual mores lie at the heart of a society. Men will not be liberated until women are free—truly free, not tokenly equal. The Women's Liberation groups, already becoming a movement, take up this task of liberating themselves and their society on a new (although the oldest) front. Their plans include twenty-four-hour-open storefronts providing everything from birth-control and abortion information to child-care services, crash pads for women "running away from home," English lessons for Spanish-speaking women (and vice versa), judo lessons for all women, free food and coffee and liberation rapping. They are plotting actions against cosmetic and fashion empires for perpetuating ludicrous beauty standards; against male-supremacist, No Women Allowed public eating places; against debutante balls as well as the conditions in decrepit women's houses of detention.

The death of the concept of Miss America in Atlantic City (celebrated by a candlelight funeral dance on the boardwalk at midnight) was only the beginning. A sisterhood of free women is giving birth to a new lifestyle, and the throes of its labor are authentic stages in the Revolution.

—October 1968

---

*Students for a Democratic Society, a national coalition of radical campus-based groups.

The Wretched of
the Hearth

*This article was originally written as the token "Women's
Liberation piece" for an anthology representing the New
Left. All the other articles were by men. The anthology
wasn't ever published because the young male radical
compiling it never finished the job.*

*But the piece remains for me an interesting fossil of that
period. Because I wrote it for a mass audience who might
never have read anything but* Time *magazine's definition
of the Women's Movement, it contains more than a few
points I had made earlier in articles for Leftist media. Yet
something has changed in the tone; the author seems less
driven to convince herself.*

*I still use a somewhat pleading manner, however, per-
haps to convince Leftist "brothers" in the next room, who
might, in Virginia Woolf's memorable metaphor, over-
hear me and disapprove. How I wanted to convince them,
as if only their agreement would validate my political
reality! For their ears was meant the prediction that women
were a "potentially revolutionary vanguard." For their
approval did I harp on the differences between "revolutionary" and "reformist." It would be some years yet before
I would understand that women really stood altogether
outside those arbitrary and sometimes false distinctions;*

*before I would touch a banked, white-hot anger at realiz-
ing that the Left, the Right, and certainly the Center as we
know them are male defined—and have all exploited
women for their own purposes and then betrayed women
in their own fashions. But if, in this essay, I no longer
wanted any Daddy's blessing, I did still long for any (radical) Brother's respect.*

*So I adopted a sexual liberationist tone, citing men
(Freud through Norman O. Brown) to impress other men
with my hip erudition, and I pretended that dropping "acid"
was a liberating act. This, though my actual experience of
the so-called sexual revolution of the sixties and seventies—like that of most other women—felt depressingly more
like rape than revolution, and my LSD trips were mostly
journeys to a (justifiably) paranoid hell in what was
becoming an escalating struggle in my marriage. I still
shrank from saying, in this piece, that women should be
the priority for women. I was grovelingly grateful to SDS
for having thrown a crumb of recognition to the Women's
Movement, and I refrained, like a good girl, from noting
that the practice of anti-sexism in SDS was all but non-
existent. I still had an embarrassingly missionary attitude
toward Third World women and I looked for sisters in the
unpromising Leftward direction of the Black Panthers—
myopically unable to foresee that the National Black Feminist Organization might boast members who were housewives, college professors, welfare mothers, lesbians, poets,
legislators, editors, businesswomen, and ex-Panthers,
among others. I played Blame the Victim, in referring to
the "internalization" of roles, the "brainwashing" of
women—as if that act took place once, like the insertion of
an electrode into the skull, and as if it were our own fault
that we didn't just pluck the little bug out. I still made a
shallow attack on the family, reflexively advocating communes as the perfect alternative—despite the fact that my
own experience with even semi-communal "extended fam-*

ily" living had been miserable (this would not necessarily have to be the case, though it was so for me, in 1969). I still largely ignored the oppression of "housewives" and mothers, despite the title of the article.

But there are shifts in perception. I ventured a glimpse of the white, middle-class, educated woman as relatively powerless. I began to affirm her as a sister and was less guilty about articulating that (even if I did solve her problems abominably by having her, in my article, drop out of college and reject the tools of power inherent in education). I acknowledged lesbian suffering and supported lesbian pride. I advanced, tentatively, the need for the autonomous women's movement; I hinted at getting flashes about feminism being more than a "front" of any male-defined movement. I expressed a glimmer of consciousness about the connections between feminism and environmentalism (though with a naive reverance for technology), and about international feminism. Most important, I had begun to read again, unapologetically: anthropology, the history of the suffrage movement—the stuff of what would become women's studies.

In its own way, the male Left cheapened language as much as the male Establishment had, a codicil to the way the former's politics reacted to and reflected those of the latter. To break free of the politics and the means of communicating them—both content and form—was (and remains) a parallel task. In this article, the literary sensibility found more room to breathe as the political sensibility expanded. Not uncoincidentally, the verbs in this piece began to carry more weight than the adjectives, and the use of metaphor and mini-parables increased. I even devoted some (too few) lines to the subject of language itself, at a time when it was considered ridiculous merely to note that sexist and racist terminology was pervasive and pernicious. But it had not yet occurred to me that "America" was not a synonym for the United States but the geograph-

ical site of countries both to the north and to the south; or that "whites" were not the generic but simply European-Americans; or that the word "revolution," whether capitalized or not, was insufficient to describe the profound cultural and societal transformations feminism inherently requires.

I wish I could go back in time to where I sat writing this article. I wish I could embrace that young woman and encourage her and tell her what a long way there was ahead. After all, in this piece, I still mostly referred to women as "they."

But I was at least experimenting with the frightening word "we."

She is white, about nineteen, carefully made up with blush-on, adorned in the latest tights-and-miniskirt combo, her hair properly ironed for that long wild look. She wears a shy smile and a huge plastic ring on a non-engagement finger. She attends one of the Seven Sisters, the Ivy League colleges that originally were established as valid feminist institutions pledged to educate women—now dedicated to churning out the corporate wives of tomorrow's Big Business. She curls up in the corner of a sofa in her dorm lounge, and lights a Virginia Slim. Underneath her languor, she is angry. She knows she is insulated, but she reads the *New York Times:* Twelve teenage girls are in training to climb Mount Everest. A nineteen-year-old woman jockey braves rocks hurled at her by male jockeys defending their hegemony. A thirteen-year-old girl goes to court to desegregate an all-male public high school specializing in math and science, supposedly unfeminine subjects. Sarah Lawrence and Briarcliff students have seized buildings on their campuses.

These and certain other facts have penetrated her quiet campus and dented her consciousness. Although she seems barely awake politically, she still feels herself part of a generation pledged to radical change. Perhaps she's even more frustrated than her activist contemporaries, because she is so tightly leashed and because she cannot help but realize she is undergoing a four-year packaging program aimed at manufacturing "a certain kind of woman." Any recognition, let alone admission, of this— no matter how oblique—humiliates and hurts, so she must defend her situation:

"But *I'm* not oppressed."

At the largest woman's college in the United States, which has never had a woman president, and where there is no course in women's history, there is, on the other hand, a required course in "Basic Motor Skills"—how to enter and leave an automobile gracefully, how to pour tea, which foot to shift your weight to as you stand at a cocktail party. No birth-control information is available, but students who become pregnant are expelled in disgrace. (This is not a finishing school, but a college with a proudly defended "academic standing.") At a nearby, less social women's college, where the dorm rules are just as absurd (no drinking, no smoking, no men, no door keys except to seniors, and weekly housemother chats required), the emphasis is more on intellectual pursuits: a crypto-analysis course is good preparation for the CIA recruiters who appear frequently on campus. At the more demure schools, women may not wear slacks to dinner or even to class. At the "swinging" schools, there are still courses (often required) in "Preparation for Marriage." Women are discouraged from going on to graduate school—the proportion of Ph.D. degrees awarded to women has declined in the past fifty years. The emphasis now is on glorification of Women in the Home, the Creative Housewife, active (but not too active) in her community, focused on husband and children.

She knows all this. She finds forty such focused years

yawning ahead of her unattractive. But she has been carefully conditioned, and out come the proper pro-grammed defenses: "Women's place is in the home. Aggressive women are emasculating. A clever women never shows her brains. It is glorious to be the mother of mankind. Women like to be protected and treated like little girls. It's a women's duty to make herself attractive. Women aren't really interested in sex. Women love to be dominated. Women are basically passive, intuitive, and simple. It's *inherent.*"

The subtlest and most vicious aspect of women's oppression is that we have been conditioned to believe we are not oppressed, blinded so as not to see our own condition. But when a well-trained slave first encounters even the concept of injustice, let alone the notion of fight-ing against it, psychic sunbursts occur. How many of us have grown up with the lovingly nurtured fantasy of mar-rying the right guy and then helping him become great, powerful, famous, wealthy, or—the 1969 radical wom-an's version—a leader of the revolution? The initial jolt of consciousness raising comes as a profound shock: always the power behind the throne, the hand that rocks the cradle, the face that launches those bloody ships. Where is the sum of *my* parts? What are my plans for *myself?* Who am I?

She begins to think for herself. She uncurls herself from her kittenish pose and stretches her legs. She checks some books out of the library. She starts to question just what is inherent in being "womanly." She talks with other women. She dares to disagree with men. Perhaps her boyfriend wonders why she has become an aggressive bitch all of a sudden. She gets depressed, fears she is becoming a "man-hater." She begins to *listen* to other women, to respect some of their ideas, to even *like* other women. Shocking. One day she wears slacks to dinner, mortally offending her housemother. She becomes less interested in make-up, but is still afraid of looking like "a grind." She is also less interested in all the books available on women by men—an endless reading list of cultural assumptions by male psychologists, psychiatrists, historians. She starts turning on to anthropology, since it attempts to report cultural differences without value judgement; she notices that traits considered inherent in one culture do not exist in another. She experiences pressure from family, friends, the man in her life, to cut out what they term identity confusion and to return to her former state of blissful ignorance. She gets angrier.

She realizes that she is being schooled in a nineteenth-century institution—what does one do with such an artifact? Get out of it, or change it, or speed the dying process from within. She drops out of school and begins to organize women. She experiences a "freedom high." She begins to look at her own degraded position as related to that of others—the "underprivileged" she has been taught to pity and despise. She undergoes a mutation toward something human.

This imaginary woman is neither a stereotypical nor an atypical college student. She shares much in common with women at coed schools—even radical women—despite her wrapped-in-cotton-batting life. In fact, women in superficially freer atmospheres often take longer to realize their true situation.

At the time of this writing, in early 1969, when radicals all over the United States are in varying stages of depression, and when the most frequently asked question is, "Where does the Left go from here?" it becomes progressively apparent that the disheartened questioners are mostly white males. Black people are moving, not theorizing. And now there is another group—this time not a minority (albeit treated like one). It is a potential revolutionary vanguard: women. We have seen the consciousness that arises and the results that are born out of a growing awareness that race lines cut even deeper than class lines in a capitalist society—and that the two are inseparable. If we begin to think about sex lines and how these distinctions shore up the values of our culture, and begin to wake up to what could happen if these were challenged—the concept is mind-blowing.

First some historical background. The women's movement in the last century in the United States and England was originally a revolutionary movement (a little-known fact, since women's history, like that of black people, has been neatly edited away by white men). The winning of suffrage for women was more the compromise than the victory of that movement. Women had been the first abolitionists, which led them to relate their own oppression to that of the slaves. These women began to look around them, to see, denounce, and fight against the structure that had conceived such abominations; some denounced the concepts of private property, bourgeois marriage, and family structures, as well as expansionist foreign policy and domestic robber-baronism. And then the reaction hit. Riots. Insurrections. Civil War. And, finally, an early version of what social critic Herbert Marcuse would later call repressive tolerance. "See, we've freed the slaves (now we create segregation)." "Look, we'll give you the vote (which will become meaningless anyway)."

So radicalism gave way to reformism, and the women bound up their wounds, as well as everybody else's, and were silent for a while. The first decades of this century saw the beginnings of what has been amusingly referred to as the sexual liberation of women—culminating in the frenzy of the twenties and collapsing in the gloom of the thirties. Men began to admit that maybe all women didn't detest sex; that maybe women could smoke and drink and carry on an intellectual conversation—although, of course, they weren't quite "nice" if they did so. But with the Depression, the rise of the labor movement, and then the coming of World War II, the issue of women's status again got shunted to second (or third, or tenth) place. Radicals in the thirties were even more puritanical and culture-bound than we are today—which is saying something. But at least during the war years, with the need for labor in factories, women achieved some economic visibility and glimpsed some escape from the kitchen. Then, the war over, Rosie the Riveter was told to go back to the stove. A lot of women wouldn't go. Some began to make inroads into professions hitherto considered male territory: medicine, publishing, scientific research, business, and law. We're not now speaking of the already enghettoed women's professions, for which read service professions—nursing, teaching, garment-making, waiting on tables, etc.—those jobs with little prestige, low pay, and intensive labor. Also, women could now be active in the arts without being marked as "fallen." But engineering, architecture, positions of corporate, religious, military, or political power—the positions that control our lives—remained, and still remain, sealed to all but white males.

Women as Radicals: New Ideas, Old Roles

So now we're part of a growing number of radicals fighting for a just society, at first nonviolently, later on with whatever tactics are necessitated by the nature of the enemy. And what are we, as women, doing? We are doing, to put it delicately, shit jobs: bolstering the boys' egos and keeping the necessities of existence functioning while men go off to change the system. We're goddamn home-fire revolutionaries.

We still end up "supporting." Good god, supporting [Eugene] McCarthy the Second or Bobby [Kennedy] the Progenitor. Or moving past such expectable traps, supporting draft resisters, supporting (male-led) black groups, supporting (male-led) grape strikers, supporting (male) GI's. You'd think we were caryatids. Not that any of these actions are unimportant. On the contrary, they may have been valid tactics at one time, just as "Girls say yes to boys who say no" was a clever and workable, if degrading, slogan. But each of these roles reinforce the stereotype of women as sub-citizens, even sub-radicals—defining women only as they relate to men.

Stereotypes are crucial. The oppressor may, in fact, never really believe in the stereotype at all—what is important is that the oppressed do. Women have internalized the image of themselves as weak, incompetent, emotional, unintellectual, dependent. Who wants to dare speak out at a meeting and risk the labels: movement harridan, castrating bitch, frigid neurotic, unfeminine pushy bitch? That's one extreme reaction, of course. The other extreme is that she will simply be ignored: the Invisible Woman, since whatever she has to say couldn't possibly be relevant anyway, the dumb cunt. If she does grit her teeth and try to speak, she will be so uptight by this time that she will stutter, anecdotalize, and generally reinforce the image of her inarticulacy to the men's satisfaction and her own torment. Naturally, a few women have managed to overcome this, at high personal and emotional cost, and in fact are accepted as equals—for public view, at least. The Left has to have its tokens, too.

Feminine Radicals Become Radical Feminists

Starting in 1966, small caucuses of radical women were formed at SDS conventions, at campus meetings, at such nationwide actions as the March on the Pentagon. (Later, in the 1968 Battle of Chicago, cadres of women would be into actions all their own.) In November 1967, thousands of women participated in the Jeannette Rankin Brigade March against the Vietnam War in Washington. There, a group of radical women split off from the march and met to discuss the possibilities of a feminist movement. And over the next few months, brought into clearer focus by Women's Liberation meetings at the Columbia Liberation School during the summer of 1968, that movement began to come together. At present, there are women's groups in every major city in the United States. There are black, Puerto Rican, Mexican, and Native American women involved. Some female Black Panthers in California, tired of being referred to as Pantherettes, have been discussing starting a separate women's corps in the Panthers.

Women—black and white—are beginning to *act*. As Ethel Romm wrote: "For some time the underground has been railing against 'plastic' or phony commercial cultural events. It took the Women's Liberation groups to lead the way to action. They threw stink bombs in the auditorium at the Miss America contest, called the winner 'a military mascot, off to Vietnam'—to entertain the troops each year. ... The success of the venture has opened up new horizons in the Movement. Any film or rock festival is vulnerable."*

This, however, was only the beginning. NOW (National Organization for Women) forced the *New York Times* to desegregate its help-wanted ads, while WITCH (Women's International Terrorist Conspiracy from Hell) hexed Wall Street. Films, articles, guerrilla-theater skits began to be used by groups organizing on campuses and in high schools. All-male public-accommodations establishments were hit with a rash of challenges and, in some cases, sit-ins or even bricks. The provision on sex in the

---

*New York, October 14, 1968.

civil rights bill was inserted as a joke by a southern con-
gressman; the joke has proved to be a valuable loophole.
Individual women, taking courage from the solidarity
of a burgeoning movement, are becoming politicized
and reporting discriminatory practices to Human Rights
Bureaus, even going to court. As of this writing, the
National Association to Repeal Abortion Laws (NARAL)
has just been formed; meanwhile there are a number of
abortion test cases in the docket. Actions are being planned
against women's houses of detention as well as against
debutante balls. Ironically, it is only now, with such furious
challenge in so many areas, that one can really begin to
see the extent of the oppression of women.

The Real Issues, the Real Constituency

On the surface, it seems easy enough to chronicle the
process of dehumanization—even the most blatant male
supremacist will agree that in the past women have been
shunted aside. The male liberal will agree that birth-control and abortion laws created by men—pressured by a
male celibate clergy, to boot—are horrendous; the male
liberal will tell you this earnestly, not realizing that as he
does so, he is interrupting "his" woman who is trying to
say something from the depths of the sink where she is
doing dishes.

But what about the real constituency? The one based
on an oppression that recognizes no class and economic
lines, making the woman always the lowest within each
self-contained pecking order? What about the Puerto Rican
girl who suffers all the indignities that the men in her
family suffer, but who also bears knife scars on her body
as testimony to the machismo in the rage those men feel
for other men but direct against her? What about the

laborer's wife who is brutalized by a slow procession of days in which the only relief is a television soap opera? What about the knocked-up Italian Catholic kid who must fear for her immortal soul, feeling her screams aborted along with the fetus? What about the woman factory worker who does embittering, uncreative work all day, and then goes home to clean, cook, and pamper her equally embittered husband, who can at least be a "king in his castle"? What about the young mother who spends all day with kids and housework and then is accused of being uninformed by her newspaper-reading-leisured spouse? What about the middle-class woman whose family has died or grown up or moved away, whom society treats as a pitiable leper? What about the fourteen-year-old girl who is the victim of rape, who is then considered unmarriageable? And the single woman who is nothing, nowhere, unless she can find a man and thus her own identity? What about the few women in Congress, who are patronized despite the population proportions of their sex? And what about the lesbian woman, who is even less socially acceptable than the male homosexual—although (reputedly) less harassed legally, because whatever women do is less important than whatever men do?

From Resistance to Revolution

Some radicals wonder how women can relate to the rest of the Left, to the struggle taking place within America and against its tentacles of power all over the world. A few points seem obvious.

Women have been subjugated longer than any other people on earth. Empires rose and fell but one constant remained, except in a few civilized tribal pockets of the world: everyone could stomp on women. This knowledge is carried, even if only semiconsciously, by every woman.

It accounts for a cumulative rage that, once released, will make demands for Black Power look not only reasonable but eminently desirable by comparison.

Black activists once told idealistic, young Lord and Lady Bountiful whites in the civil-rights movement to turn around and look at their own lives. By god, *they* weren't free, even nice middle-class college-grad students were enslaved by the culture. From this awareness was born the New Left. Now, women—angels of mercy for so many other causes—have also awakened to their own cause. Radical women learned, from the same Black Liberation movement, that mere empathy for the suffering of others never makes for revolutionary thinking or motivates a passionate desire for change.

Nevertheless, the chameleonic so-called revolutionist male (who at first thought the Women's Movement ridiculous, later modified that to "frivolous in the face of larger issues," still later accepted it only as an "organizing tool," and now nervously finds it "valid") has dreamed up a new hypocritical twist: isn't a drive for equality of women ultimately reformist, eminently cooptable?

Of course. So is Black Power—into Black Capitalism. So are the initial demands of any oppressed group. When slammed up against the wall, the Man will liberalize abortion and birth-control laws and open up the professions to a few more token women, just as he once rigged up for us the already marked ballot. But we want something more: freedom. Equality in an unjust society is meaningless.

Students for a Democratic Society (SDS), until recently male dominated in action as well as male supremacist in attitude, passed their first resolution on the Women's Movement in December 1968, at their Ann Arbor National Conference. The statement, which takes almost no notice of the social, sexual, or emotional valences of women's oppression, nevertheless is cogent on the economic aspects, and how they relate, ultimately, to revolutionary commitment:

> The inability of the most advanced, technologically developed, etc. capitalist society to provide equality to [more than] half its citizens not only exposes the thorough hypocrisy of all that society's words about "justice" and "equality." It also shows that the struggle for equality of women is a revolutionary task. ... Male supremacy [in the Left] mirrors male supremacy in the capitalist society. [This fact] raises the issue that although no people's liberation can happen without a socialist revolution in this country, a socialist revolution could take place which maintains the secondary position of women in society. ... The fight for Women's Liberation is a concretization of the struggle of all peoples from oppression. ... Therefore, the liberation of women must become a conscious part of our struggle.

We have, indeed, seen the erosion of women's position in the Soviet Union, and have heard rumors of the same development in Algeria and even in Cuba. The day comes when women who fought and died on the barricades as bravely as men are told, "That phase is over, comrade. Back to the kitchen." Hell no, we won't go.

Meanwhile, back in the United States, the newly articulated demands of such a vast constituency are proving revolutionary. What we must all learn, this time, is not to repeat history, not to copy the ego-tripping of many male-movement "nonleaders," not to gain control in order to manipulate and exploit others as they have us, but rather to seize power over our own lives by any means necessary, including force of arms, and then to begin the Revolution—in our minds, hearts, guts, culture, daily lives. That is the difficult task. Imperialism begins at home. The Revolution begins at home.

"The Revolution Made Flesh"

How relatively simple the economics seem when compared to the cultural, psychological, emotional, and sexual problems. Naturally no one should lack medical care or food or shelter or the pleasures of challenging work (as opposed to debilitating toil, which technology could assume).

But why are we ready to reject most values of a depraved society, while still clinging to others? How pervasive the puritanical conditioning must have been, to make us still afraid of our bodies, to fear the mystery of the opposite sex, and to be even more terrified of the familiarity of our own sex in someone else's body! "Radical" men who declare that the whole political structure must be torn down in the next breath play their male-mystique roles to the full (cuff women, talk heavy, and never embrace another man except in a locker-room parody of affection). Radical women are used to having commie-dirty-punk-creep epithets thrown at them, but whisper "lesbian" and they cringe in agonized denial. Of what? Intelligent people who have read their Freud and Jung and Norman O. Brown and Masters and Johnson as well as their Marx, Marcuse, Mao, and Guevara, still flinch at the thought of a revolution in sexual mores.

Surely no one dare call oneself a revolutionary unless a continual attempt is made to create a revolution in one's own psyche—the ongoing struggle toward the deepening of one's humanity. Any acid trip will teach you that. It will also prove the absurdity of emphasizing purely genitally oriented sex, and it will prove the natural order of what could be termed omnisexuality.

Yet so basic a scientific revelation as that in *Human Sexual Response* (Masters and Johnson), talking about the female orgasm as clitoraly based, has hardly dented con-

sciousness two years after the publication of their best-
seller. Nor has Ann Koedt's feminist paper, "The Myth of
the Vaginal Orgasm," had any greater effect, although it
makes the ramifications of this revelation even clearer.
"The myths remain," wrote Sue Lydon in *Ramparts*
(December 14, 1968), "because a male-dominated American culture has a vested interest in this continuance.
Before Masters and Johnson, men defined female sexuality in a way as favorable to themselves as possible."

The earlier Victorians were at least honest about their
sexual repression. Women weren't supposed to have
orgasms at all—and one Dr. Isaac Baker Brown, suspect-
ing that some women were daring to enjoy themselves,
performed numerous clitoridectomies, claiming that
sexual excitement in women led to insanity, catalepsy,
and epileptic seizures.

Depraved, of course, yet no more so than modern legislators who refuse to change perverted laws about natural behavior. Food, shelter, medicine—these are
inalienable rights, hardly revolutionary demands. Yet even
as we require these obvious rights, we must also have
revolutionary goals: for a whole new concept of sexuality, for a new definition of what a woman is, what a man
is; for joy and fun and freedom.

An examination of the structure of the bourgeois family and the mental price it has extracted is causing many
people to think more in terms of the communal family,
where children are raised by men as well as by women,
and by more than one pair; where parenthood is more a
biological fact than a property-defined relationship. Where
else do we first learn the dynamics of domination but in
the family, in which the woman is treated as a distinct
inferior? Therefore, to eliminate political and economic
domination, we must simultaneously uproot sexual domination from that microcosm where the developing individual's view of human possibility is irrevocably formed.

Marriage as a bourgeois institution is beginning to fade slowly but surely from the needs of the under-twenty-five-year-olds.* No more need the bride be passed from her father to her husband in order to produce (let's face it) sons. No more need the mother "possess" her children, since she will have something of herself to call her own.

As for the myth of the sexual revolution: there is no such thing yet—for women. The double standard exists more powerfully and hypocritically than ever, among radicals and hippies as well as straights. A sexually free woman is still a lay guys can exchange stories about, while a woman who might *not* "want to" is considered hung-up: she has the Pill, so what's stopping her? (Conceivably, a sense of distaste.)

Surely it is because women have for so long been regarded merely as objects for sex and reproduction that we have learned to scrutinize those areas of our culture with particular suspicion. It was Margaret Mead (whose work was held for a period in disrepute by her male contemporaries, but is now being reexamined by younger anthropologists) who first studied how permissive sexual mores in "primitive" cultures informed those societies with unique strength and survival values. Morgan, Lévi-Strauss, Montague, and Benedict have also investigated this theme. Serious anthropologists (as opposed to reactionary popularizers of a pseudo-scientific ethology, like Ardrey, Fox, and Tiger) continue to turn up examples that prove competitive, aggressive cultures are those in which sexual stereotypes are most polarized, while those social structures allowing for an overlap of roles and functions between men and women tend to be more collectivist, cooperative, and peaceful.

*By the early 1990s, this trend showed clearly in U.S. demographics. Women were marrying later (late twenties) and having children later—if at all.

As women, we experience how our past has been taken from us, how our present is confused, our future uncertain. The very semantics of the language reflects our condition. We do not even have our own names, but bear that of the father until we exchange it for that of the husband. We have no word for what we are unless it be an auxiliary term for the opposite: man / wo-man, male / female. No one, including us, knows who we really are.

But we are now pledged to find out, to create new selves if necessary, in a process as revolutionary as giving birth to one's own soul. And that process is inextricably bound up with liberating our brothers, as well, from sick sexual codes and from the enslavement of being the master. It must begin now, this re-creation. No waiting until after the revolution.

Humankind has polluted the air and water and land of our planet; we have all but destroyed ourselves by the twin suicidal weapons of overkill and overbreeding. The famine is upon us, the cities are in flames, our sisters and brothers all over the world are locked in a struggle with the dragon that is imperialism. It is for us in America, the dragon's lair, to put *every* priority of oppression first, to fight on every front for human dignity, to burn our way out of the dragon's gut while our comrades hack away at its scaly exterior, until the beast is dead, and we rise in joy, a woman and a man, phoenix from its ashes.

—Spring 1969

Goodbye to All That

In the late 1960s, Rat *was one of the major "underground" newspapers of the New Left and the so-called alternative culture. Although published in New York and focused partially on local issues,* Rat *(so named because of its identification with the sewer-dwelling, underground creature) had a national circulation and an international list of subscribers. More serious at its inception than most counterculture papers,* Rat *was perhaps best known for having dared to be the first to publish documents stolen by anonymous students from the administrative offices of Columbia University during the Columbia student rebellion. The documents seemed to implicate the university in the U.S. war in Vietnam, and* Rat's *"scoop" in publishing them created a sensation in both the mass and alternate media.*

Yet despite its attempts at genuine muckraking journalism, Rat *had been created and sustained by and for men. As the flower-children style of the middle 1960s coarsened into the confrontational tactics of the late 1960s, male attitudes were solidified in Leftist consciousness, and being tough, "heavy," and "a street-fighter" became prerequisites for being a radical, male or female.* Rat *reflected these changes, and began presenting as well a kind of "cultural nationalism" for young white males: new priorities of rock*

*music coverage, pornographic articles and graphics, and
sex-wanted ads (euphemistically called "Personals") began
to clog the pages.*

In 1968 I had written some articles for Rat *on the emerging "Women's Liberation Front." During the following year
I had been inching my way toward a more feminist position, although my loyalty to Marxism as The Answer per-
sisted. Still, even I could no longer tolerate the blatant
sexism in* Rat, *and by the winter of 1969 I had refused to
write for the paper any longer. I had heard that the women
who worked there (none of them in any positions of power)
were also angry and had been confronting the men about
the paper's sexism and its hierarchy, which employed men
as editors and feature writers, women as secretaries and
bottle-washers who were sometimes permitted to write short
articles. I had even warned one of the* Rat *men that women
might take over the paper if no change was forthcoming.
But I was still unprepared for the phone call I received in
January 1970 from one of the* Rat *women, who informed
me that the women on the paper had decided to seize it
and needed ideas, support, and the physical presence of
Women's Liberationists to accomplish and sustain their
action.*

*We came from groups in all parts of the Women's Move-
ment in New York: from Redstockings and WITCH, from
what remained of New York Radical Women, even from
NOW. There were lesbian women from the Gay Liberation
Front (GLF), Weatherwomen from the not-yet-under-
ground Weather Communes, women from various caucuses in male-Left organizations. Most of us knew precisely
nothing about typesetting, layout, advertising, dealing with
printers, or distribution. But we put out a paper. And the
first "Women's Rat" became a reality.*

A few feminist newspapers were already in existence,
Everywoman, It Ain't Me Babe, *and* Off Our Backs, *among
them. But this was the first time women had seized a male-*

run newspaper, and the action created ripples all over the Left, with women following suit in other cities and taking over their local underground media temporarily or permanently.

"Goodbye to All That" was my contribution to the first issue. Beneath the byline, I identified myself as a member of WITCH—in this case, the flexible acronym stood for "Women Inspired to Commit Herstory." (This was the debut of the word "herstory." I intended it as a consciousness raiser, not as an etymological claim.) Since this women's seizure of a male-run newspaper was the first such action in the Left, it seemed the right moment to express certain thoughts that had been boiling inside me for some time. "Goodbye" apparently articulated the experience of most women in the Left, and became an instant classic. It was read aloud in struggle meetings, quoted, fought about, cried over, excerpted on posters and banners, used (individual lines and phrases) for slogans, and widely reprinted. The Leftist media editorialized rather shockingly while reprinting: the tendency was to cut the critical reference to whatever group was the strongest in the local area. (In Michigan, the denunciation of John Sinclair disappeared; in Boston, ellipses replaced my attack on the Progressive Labor Party; in Berkeley, the Weatherman section was deleted.) This censorship was ultimately overshadowed, however, by the more accurate reprinting of the article in the then-existing feminist media. San Diego women named their newspaper after the article, and in the following months and years, women making their own farewells to various male-dominated groupings (the Gay Liberation Front, the Catholic Church, certain Third World movement groups) would refer to their statements as "daughters" of "Goodbye to All That." Leftist men were furious, and the former Rat *men tried unsuccessfully to re-seize the paper. My article clearly had "gone too far." I received death threats from quite a few revolutionary brothers—a radi-*

calizing experience, that. It seemed I had shut a door behind
me, and when I looked back it had vanished; a solid wall
stood in its place. I was free, then, to go forward, wherever
that direction should lead.

It was not until after that first issue by women that we
realized we weren't about to give the paper back. And our
Rat did continue, with a core collective comprised of those
women who stayed and worked regularly on the publication, and a larger group of women who for various reasons drifted in and out. I remained for a year, as did six
or seven other women of the original collective. During
that time the overall group kept shifting and changing;
this had the salutary effect of refreshing our ideas and
energy; it also negatively expressed our lack of solidity or
real knowledge of each other.

Sometimes I wonder how I could publish my parting
statement to the male Left in the first issue—and then
remain for a full year on such a Leftist newspaper. Yet I
know the answer: in "Goodbye" I was saying farewell to
working with men in the Left. I could not have foreseen
that working with Leftist women on male-Left-defined issues
of importance would be not much different. Besides, I myself
was not that free from a traditional Marxist analysis; my
political priorities were largely defined by guilt for whatever I was not doing at any given moment.

Rat's priorities were never clarified either. We put out a
paper by women, but we didn't want it to be "only" for
women. We wanted to show all those men who thought
we couldn't do it that we could—and so we had to keep
covering subjects interesting to them, to win their approval.
We never openly admitted this last—even among ourselves—but it was pathetically true. And as Leftist women
joined the collective in greater numbers during the ensu-
ing weeks, that tendency became more noticeable. New York
feminists were not without blame, though; many began to
stay away out of a sense of disdainful purism instead of

coming around and helping to turn Rat *into the feminist paper they claimed, accurately, it had not yet become.*

The double guilt suffered by those of us who remained was ulcerating then, if humorous now. We came to be called "the feminist caucus"—a small group of women who dared to be more and more concerned with women, but who still functioned within a larger group of women who were concerned with "the real revolution." We tried frantically to cover all bases. I myself had a six-month-old baby, and I was involved in a union-organizing effort at the publishing house where I had an editorial job. Yet I wrote for and worked at Rat *most evenings. In addition, I took part in a separate weekly consciousness-raising group (with non-*Rat *women of a more feminist stripe); was involved in the founding of the Women's Center (more feminist points on my chart); helped organize two demonstrations in support of the Panthers (Leftist points); carried* Manual of an Urban Guerrilla *or* The Golden Notebook *to different meetings (double points), and actually read both; salivated every time the bell rang that a Weatherperson had been busted, and rushed out to be a rent-a-body at the ritual riot (Leftist points plus a red star); and struggled with my husband (feminist points—although these stung more than being tear-gassed).*

During this same period I was also compiling and editing Sisterhood Is Powerful.* *It was that work, perhaps more than anything else, that gradually drew me to radical feminism. It became harder every day to put other oppressions first when my brain was barraged with objective facts, figures, statistics, and analyses—and subjective anguish—all on and of women. The anthology transformed my own views at least as much as it has those of other women, thousands of whom have told me it wrought drastic shifts*

---

*The first anthology of writings from the Women's Liberation Movement (Random House; Vintage Press paperback, 1970).

in their attitudes and in their daily realities. The statistics came alive vividly in my daily realities, too, when I found myself suddenly unemployed and soon after in jail for having tried to organize a (mostly female) union at the publishing house where I worked, and for leading a sit-in after the employer union-busted.

Meanwhile, back at Rat, *labels like "feminist" or "politico" (incredibly enough implying that feminism wasn't political) were being flung by women against each other. The majority of the collective felt that such issues as rape, abortion, sexuality, child care, and menopause were "insular" and "bourgeois" when compared to those issues that were "universal" and "radical"—like GI rights, or organizing the workers (housewives, of course, were never considered* bona fide *"workers" in the Left). For each token article the feminist caucus was able to push through in an editorial meeting, there were three or four on the NLF, the IRA, the FLN, the BPP, or other acronymed male-led Leftist groups. There was an area of compromise: we ran articles on how well women drove tractors in Cuba, threw grenades in Palestine, carried rifles in Vietnam, and, by implication, obeyed orders with dedicated socialistic consciousness. (We did* not *run articles on how these same women were also cooking, cleaning, washing, birthing, and doing everything else—too bourgeois.) One eight-hour editorial "dialogue" ensued when the feminist caucus insisted on printing a statement critical of Cuba for having held a Miss Havana Beauty Contest.*

There was little space left for me to avoid facing The Awful Truth: that it was the politics of the Left, not solely the men who mouthed them, that were male supremacist. It was the political analysis itself that ignored or patronized more than half the human species. Because of that analysis, which had stopped short at its greatest challenge, the Black Liberation movement as well as the New Left was sexist—and doomed to perpetuate that oppres-

sion. And the student movement. And the GI and war-resister movements. And the emerging Native American move-ment, the Puerto Rican rights movement, the revolution-ary governments of China, Cuba, North Vietnam, Algeria, North Korea—all had sacrificed women in their struggle to attain freedom for "man." It was not merely the prac-tice, but the very politics—created by men—that was the problem. I was terrified of such heretical thoughts.

Then, an unexpected assault on my most cherished "tool for the revolution" delivered me into an unequivocal fem-inist position. My writing, the essence of my existence, was being threatened. We (in the Left, in the Women's Move-ment, in the alternate culture) had all been indulging in an orgy of downward mobility and anti-intellectualism, accompanied, expectably, by a rejection of art. When I look back at such attitudes, they seem to indicate a guilt reflex carried to almost suicidal extremes, combined with con-tempt for "the masses"—for whose sake we were suppos-edly making these sacrifices. (The poor, naturally, were thought of as anti-art dolts.)

Thus, when the Rat *collective decided it was elitist for any member to sign her name to her work, I dutifully dropped my byline (back to Anon.; do not pass Go). When the collective, a few months later, criticized me for writing in a style apparently still identifiable to our readers ("You write too well" was the flattering accusation), I even tried to worsen my writing: I spelled America with* three *k's instead of one, as I had done previously in the Left; I dropped my g's in print; I peppered my articles with phrases like running-dog-of-a-capitalist-swine and other jargon that would have given George Eliot the vapors. But this still was insufficient: it was suggested that I not write for the paper at all—but not quit, either (that would be a "cop-out"). I must stay and work on proofreading, layout, and distribution—but not write. Appallingly enough, I even did that—wearing a fixed Maoist smile to cover my indigna-*

*tion—for about a month. Then something cracked open
inside me, and it was over.*

*I went on a trip around the country to promote the pub-
lication of the anthology; I threw myself into the plans for
The Sisterhood Is Powerful Fund, into which all the roy-
alties from the book were going in order to further wom-
en's projects (this was the first feminist grant-giving
foundation of this wave); I met women in Detroit and Chicago and Oakland and Boston and Atlanta and Dallas
and Baltimore—and they were feminists. They were working on all those "counter-revolutionary, middle-class" issues,
like rape, child care, abortion, and gynecological care (do
only middle-class women have cervixes?). They were not
all white women, either, not all young, not all middle-class-
ashamed-of-their-origins, not all hip or "heavy." They were
quietly going about making genuine change—and liking
one another while doing it.*

*The explosions chain-reacting inside my skull were
indescribable. I felt as if I had discovered a whole new continent: the authentic Women's Movement. When I returned
to New York I told the* Rat *collective that I was leaving
because the paper was not, and at that rate never would
be, a paper for women. The other last few feminist sym-
pathizers were leaving, too, it turned out, and the parting
was tearful but firm. A few months later,* Rat *ceased publication.*

Rat *has become fiction in many recollections—especially
those of women who never were in the core collective but
who since claim to have been (by the hundreds). To me,*
Rat *was a spirited, precedent-setting attempt to seize some
power for women within the Left; to learn and teach each
other the skills involved in putting out a newspaper; to
work committedly together. No more—but no less. Once*
Rat *had been seized, the New Left was never the same.*

*More important, none of us women would ever be the
same. When I think of the* Rat *year, I remember anger,*

excitement, and exhaustion, much laughter, and not a lit-
tle love. I only wish we had done what we had talked of
doing so many times: I only wish we had changed the
paper's name.

Although "Goodbye" has been anthologized repeatedly,
it appears here complete with my own footnotes, clarifi-
cations necessary because (O, triumph of feminism!) most
of the men and male-dominated groups named in the arti-
cle—all of them so revered and notorious at that time—
have oozed ignominiously into oblivion. Women reading
the piece for the first time in anthologies both in the United
States and abroad frequently write to ask me who these
men were. It is a heartening irony that their names seem
relevant mainly as historical curiosities fortunate enough
to have been at one point denounced by a feminist writer.

So, *Rat* has been liberated, for this week, at least. Next
week? If the men return to reinstate the porny photos,
the sexist comic strips, the "nude-chickie" covers (along
with their patronizing rhetoric about being in favor of
women's liberation)—if this happens, our alternatives are
clear. *Rat* must be taken over permanently by women—
or *Rat* must be destroyed.

Why *Rat?* Why not *EVO*[1] or even the obvious new
pornzines (Mafia-distributed alongside the human pornography of prostitution)? First, they'll get theirs—but it
won't be by a takeover, which is reserved for something
at least *worth* taking over. Nor should they be censored.
They should just be helped not to exist—by any means
necessary. But *Rat,* which has always tried to be a really
radical *cum* lifestyle paper, that's another matter. It's the
liberal cooptative masks on the face of sexist hate and

---

[1] *East Village Other,* an "underground" newspaper that celebrated the
so-called hip culture—at the expense of women.

fear, worn by real nice guys we all know and like, right? We have met the enemy and he's our friend. And dangerous. "What the hell, let the chicks do an issue; maybe it'll satisfy 'em for a while, it's a good controversy, and it'll maybe sell papers" runs an unoverheard conversation that I'm sure took place at some point last week.

And that's what I wanted to write about—the friends, brothers, lovers in the counterfeit male-dominated Left. The good guys who think they know what "Women's Lib," as they so chummily call it, is all about—who then proceed to degrade and destroy women by almost everything they say and do: The cover on the last issue of *Rat* (front *and* back). The token "pussy power" or "clit militancy" articles. The snide descriptions of women staffers on the masthead. The little jokes, the personal ads, the smile, the snarl. No more, brothers. No more well-meaning ignorance, no more cooptation, no more assuming that this thing we're all fighting for is the same; one revolution under *man,* with liberty and justice for all. No more.

Let's run it on down. White males are most responsible for the destruction of human life and environment on the planet today. Yet who is controlling the supposed revolution to change all that? White males (yes, yes, even with their pasty fingers back in black and brown pies again). It just could make one a bit uneasy. It seems obvious that a legitimate revolution must be led by, *made* by those who have been most oppressed: black, brown, yellow, red, and white *women*—with men relating to that the best they can. A genuine Left doesn't consider anyone's suffering irrelevant or titillating; nor does it function as a microcosm of capitalist economy, with men competing for power and status at the top, and women doing all the work at the bottom (and functioning as objectified prizes or "coin" as well). Goodbye to all that.

Run it all the way down.

Goodbye to the male-dominated peace movement,

where sweet old Uncle Dave[2] can say with impunity to a woman on the staff of *Liberation* magazine, "The trouble with you is you're an aggressive woman."

Goodbye to the "straight" male-dominated Left: to PL,[3] who will allow that some workers are women, but won't see all women (say, housewives) as workers (blind as the System itself); to all the old Left-over parties who offer their "Women's Liberation caucuses" to us as if that were not a contradiction in terms; to the individual anti-leadership leaders who hand-pick certain women to be leaders and then relate only to them, either in the male Left *or* in Women's Liberation—bringing their hang-ups about power dominance and manipulation to everything they touch.

Goodbye to the Weather Vain,[4] with the Stanley Kowalski image and theory of free sexuality but practice of sex on demand for males. "Left Out!"—not Right On!— to the Weather Sisters who (and they know better—*they know*) reject their own radical feminism for that last desperate grab at male approval that we all know so well, for claiming that the machismo style and the gratuitous violence is their own style by "free choice," and for believing that this is the way for a woman to make her revolution . . . all the while, oh my sister, not meeting my eyes because Weather*men* chose Charles Manson[5] as their—and your—hero. (Honest, at least, since Manson is only the logical extreme of the normal American male's fantasy, whether he is Dick Nixon[6] or Mark Rudd[7]: mas-

[2] David Dellinger, a leader in the male-run peace movement, subsequently divorced by Betty Peterson, his wife of many years.

[3] Progressive Labor (Party).

[4] Weathermen, or the Weather Bureau—militant New Left group named after a Bob Dylan song lyric. A reference to the group's attitudes before their years of underground fugitivity, attitudes as sexist as their later ones.

[5] Convicted mass murderer and self-styled harem-keeper of "slaves."

[6] Then president of the United States; "not," in his own words, "a crook," but someone who did invite comparison with a used-car salesman.

[7] Used-revolution salesman; Weatherman leader.

ter of a harem, women to do all the shitwork, from raising babies and cooking and hustling to killing people on
command.) Goodbye to all that shit that sets women apart
from women; shit that covers the face of any Weatherwoman which is the face of any Manson Slave which is
the face of Sharon Tate[8] which is the face of Mary Jo
Kopechne[9] which is the face of Beulah Saunders[10] which
is the face of me which is the face of Pat Nixon[11] which
is the face of Pat Swinton.[12] *In the dark we are all the
same*—and you better believe it: we're in the dark, baby.
(Remember the old joke: Know what they call a black
man with a Ph.D.? A nigger. Variations: Know what they
call a Weatherwoman? A heavy cunt. Know what they call
a hip revolutionary woman? A groovy cunt. Know what
they call a radical militant feminist? A crazy cunt. Amer-
ika is a land of free choice—take your pick of titles.) Left
Out, my sister—don't you see? Goodbye to the illusion of
strength when you run hand in hand with your oppressors; goodbye to the dream that being in the leadership
collective will get you anything but gonorrhea.

Goodbye to RYM II, as well, and all the other RYMs[13]—
not that the sisters there didn't pull a cool number by
seizing control, but because they let the men back in after
only a day or so of self-criticism on "male chauvinism."
(And goodbye to the inaccurate blanket use of that phrase,
for that matter: male chauvinism is an *attitude*—male
supremacy is the objective *reality,* the *fact.*) Goodbye to
the Conspiracy,[14] who, when lunching with fellow sexist

[8]Victim (murdered) of Manson "family."
[9]Victim (dead) of Senator Edward Kennedy in the "accident" at Chap-
paquidick, Massachusetts.
[10]Victim of the welfare system; organizer in welfare rights.
[11]Victim of alleged used-car salesman.
[12]Victim of male Leftist loyalties that led to her indictment in a bombing
conspiracy.
[13]Revolutionary Youth Movements (I, II, and III), spin off groups from
Students for Democratic Society (SDS).
[14]The Conspiracy Seven or the Chicago Seven. Male activists who were

bastards[15] Norman Mailer[16] and Terry Southern[17] in a Bunny-type club in Chicago found Judge Hoffman[18] at the neighboring table—no surprise: *in the light they are all the same.*

Goodbye to Hip Culture and the so-called Sexual Revolution, which has functioned toward women's freedom as did the Reconstruction toward former slaves—reinstituting oppression by another name. Goodbye to the assumption that Hugh Romney[19] is safe in his "cultural revolution," safe enough to refer to "our women, who make all our clothes" without somebody not forgiving that. Goodbye to the arrogance of power indeed that lets Czar Stan Freeman of the Electric Circus[20] sleep without fear at night, or permits Tomi Ungerer[21] to walk unafraid in the street after executing the drawings for the Circus advertising campaign against women. Goodbye to the idea that Hugh Hefner[22] is groovy 'cause he lets Conspirators come to parties at the Playboy Mansion—goodbye to Hefner's dream of a ripe old age. Goodbye to Tuli and the Fugs[23] and all the boys in the front room—who always knew they hated the women they loved. Goodbye to the notion that good ol' Abbie[24] is any different from any other

on trial for conspiracy in organizing demonstrations against the 1968 Democratic Party Convention.

[15] An example (along with the phrase "son-of-bitch") of male-supremacist linguistics that can transform a word into a pejorative term in order to place the blame for sins of the son upon—who else?—his mother. This had not been borne in upon me yet, in 1970.

[16] and [17] Two hack writers.

[18] The extremely conservative judge who presided over the trial of the Conspiracy Seven; supposedly their adversary.

[19] A counterculture "leader," dictator of the traveling commune so delicately named the Hog Farm.

[20] A New York discotheque of the period that capitalized on sexism.

[21] A misogynist cartoonist.

[22] Founder and owner of *Playboy* magazine. Enough said.

[23] A vulgar rock band of the period specializing in sexist lyrics.

[24] Abbie Hoffman, a "nonleader" leader of hip culture and the "Yippie movement." Later, a fugitive from the FBI (after being charged with selling

up-and-coming movie star who ditches the first wife and kids, good enough for the old days but awkward once you're Making It. Goodbye to his hypocritical double standard that reeks through the tattered charm. Goodbye to lovely "pro-Women's Liberationist" Paul Krassner,[25] with all his astonished anger that women have lost their sense of humor "on this issue" and don't laugh any more at little funnies that degrade and hurt them: farewell to the memory of his "Instant Pussy" aerosol-can poster, to his column for the woman-hating men's magazine *Cavalier,* to his dream of a Rape-In against legislators' wives, to his Scapegoats and Realist Nuns and cute anecdotes about the little daughter he sees as often as any properly divorced Scarsdale middle-aged father; goodbye forever to the notion that a man is my brother who, like Paul, buys a prostitute for the night as a birthday gift for a male friend, or who, like Paul, reels off the names in alphabetical order of people in the women's movement he has fucked, reels off names in the best locker-room tradition—as proof that *he's* no sexist oppressor.

Let it all hang out. Let it seem bitchy, catty, dykey, frustrated, crazy, nutty, frigid, ridiculous, bitter, embarrassing, man-hating, libelous, pure, unfair, envious, intuitive, low-down, stupid, petty, liberating. *We are the women that men have warned us about.*

And let's put one lie to rest for all time: the lie that men are oppressed, too, by sexism—the lie that there can be such a thing as "men's liberation groups." Oppression is something that one group of people commits against another group specifically because of a "threatening" characteristic shared by the latter group—skin color or sex or age, etc. The oppressors are indeed *fucked up* by being masters (racism hurts whites, sexual stereotypes

hard drugs), and a self-proclaimed bigamist of wives No. 2 and No. 3; eventually a suicide in 1989.

[25] Editor of *The Realist* (a sexist paper of satire); also the former son-in-law of Norman Mailer, cited earlier.

are harmful to men) but those masters are not *oppressed*. Any master has the alternative of divesting himself of sexism or racism; the oppressed have no alternative—for they have no power—but to fight. In the long run, Women's Liberation will of course free men—but in the short run it's going to *cost* men a lot of privilege, which no one gives up willingly or easily. Sexism is *not* the fault of women—kill your fathers, not your mothers.

Run it down. Goodbye to a beautiful new ecology movement that could fight to save us all if it would stop tripping off women as earthmother types or frontier chicks, if it would *right now* cede leadership to those who have *not* polluted the planet because that action implies power and women haven't *had* any power in about 5,000 years,[26] cede leadership to those whose brains are as tough and clear as any man's but whose bodies are also unavoidably aware of the locked-in relationship between humans and their biosphere—the earth, the tides, the atmosphere, the moon. Ecology is no big shtick if you're a woman—it's always been there.

Goodbye to the complicity inherent in the *Berkeley Tribe*smen[27] being part publishers of *Trashman* Comics[28]; goodbye, for that matter, to the reasoning that finds whoremaster Trashman a fitting model, however comic-strip far-out, for a revolutionary man—somehow related to the same Super-male reasoning that permits the first statement on Women's Liberation and male chauvinism that came out of the Black Panther Party to be made *by a man,* talking a whole lot about how the sisters should speak up for themselves. Such ignorance and arrogance ill-befits a revolutionary.

[26] I had not yet learned that it has actually been ten to twelve thousand years since the rise of patriarchy.

[27] Male publishing collective of counterculture newspaper *The Berkeley Tribe.*

[28] Particularly offensive comic books promulgating violent pornography.

We know how racism is worked deep into the unconscious by the System—the same way sexism is, as it appears in the very name of The Young Lords.[29] What are you if you're a "macho woman"—a female Lord? Or, god forbid, a Young Lady? *Change* it, change it to the Young Gentry if you must, or never assume that the name itself is innocent of pain, of oppression.

Theory and practice—and the light-years between them. "Do it!" says Jerry Rubin[30] in *Rat's* last issue—but he doesn't or every *Rat* reader would have known the pictured face next to his article as well as they know his own much-photographed face: it was Nancy Kurshan, "his woman," the power behind the clown.

Goodbye to the New Nation and Earth People's Park[31] for that matter, conceived by men, announced by men, led by men—doomed before birth by the rotting seeds of male supremacy transplanted into fresh soil. Was it my brother who listed human beings among the *objects* that would be easily available after the Revolution: "Free grass, free food, *free women,* free acid, free clothes, etc."? Was it my brother who wrote "Fuck your women till they can't stand up" and said that groupies were liberated chicks 'cause they dug a tit-shake instead of a handshake? The epitome of male exclusionism—"men will make the Revolution—*and* make their chicks." Not my brother. No. Not my revolution. Not one breath of my support for the new counterculture Christ—John Sinclair.[32] Just one less to worry about for ten years. I do not choose my enemy for my brother.

Goodbye, goodbye. To hell with the simplistic notion

[29] Puerto Rican radical group of the period.

[30] Still another "nonleader" leader of the hip Left. Later into "bio-karma," and still later into the stock market.

[31] New Nation and Earth People's Park: both of them so-called radical organizing projects that dissolved.

[32] Then leader of the "White Panther Party" (a pale male imitation of the Black Panther Party), given a ten-year jail sentence on a drug charge—but soon after released.

that automatic freedom for women—or nonwhite peoples—will come about *zap!* with the advent of a socialist revolution. Bullshit. Two evils pre-date capitalism and clearly have been able to survive and post-date socialism: sexism and racism. Women were the first property when the Primary Contradiction occurred: when one-half of the human species decided to subjugate the other half, because it was "different," alien, the Other. From there it was an easy enough step to extend the concept of Other to someone of different skin shade, different height or weight or language—or strength to resist. Goodbye to those simple-minded optimistic dreams of socialist equality all our good socialist brothers want us to believe. How merely liberal a politics that is! How much further we will have to go to create those profound changes that would give birth to a genderless society. *Profound,* Sister. Beyond what is male or female. Beyond standards we all adhere to now without daring to examine them as male-created, male-dominated, male-fucked-up, and in male self-interest. *Beyond all known standards,* especially those easily articulated revolutionary ones we all rhetorically invoke. Beyond—to a species with a new name, that would not dare define itself as Man.

I once said, "I'm a revolutionary, not just a woman," and knew my own lie even as I said the words. The pity of that statement's eagerness to be acceptable to those whose revolutionary zeal no one would question, i.e., any male supremacist in the counterleft. But to become a true revolutionary one must first become one of the oppressed (not organize or educate or manipulate them, but *become one of them*)—or realize that you *are* one already. No woman wants that. Because that realization is humiliating, it hurts. It hurts to understand that at Woodstock[33] or Altamont[34] a woman could be declared uptight or a

---

[33] and [34] Rock festivals attended by masses of people, where all women, and black men, were vulnerable to rape and murder.

poor sport if she didn't want to be raped. It hurts to learn
that the sisters still in male-Left captivity are putting down
"the crazy feminists" to make themselves look unthrea-
tening to our mutual oppressors. It hurts to be pawns in
those games. It hurts to try and *change each day of your
life right now*—not in talk, not "in your head," and not
only conveniently "out there" in the Third World (half of
which are women) or the black and brown communities
(half of which are women) but in your own home, kitchen,
bed. No getting away, no matter how else you are
oppressed, from the primary oppression of being female
in a patriarchal world. It hurts to hear that the sisters in
the Gay Liberation Front, too, have to struggle continually against the male chauvinism of their gay brothers.[35] It hurts that Jane Alpert[36] was cheered when rapping
about imperialism, racism, the Third World, and All Those
Safe Topics but hissed and booed by a movement crowd
of men who wanted none of it when she began to talk
about Women's Liberation. The backlash is upon us.

They tell us the alternative is to hang in there and
"struggle," to confront male domination in the counterleft, to fight beside or behind or beneath our brothers—
to show 'em we're just as tough, just as revolushunerry,
just as whatever-image-they-now-want-of-us-as-once-
they-wanted-us-to-be-feminine-and-keep-the-home-fire-
burning. They will bestow titular leadership on our
grateful shoulders, whether it's being a token woman on
the Movement Speakers Bureau Advisory Board, or being
a Conspiracy groupie or one of the "respectable" chain-
swinging Motor City Nine.[37] Sisters all, with only one real

[35] This, of course, was before most lesbian activists abandoned mixed
gay groups for the Feminist Movement.

[36] A leading Leftist revolutionary woman, later a fugitive who, in an open
letter from the underground ("Mother-Right—A New Feminist Theory," *Ms.*,
August 1973), denounced male-style politics and embraced feminism.

[37] A male-approved, "toughie" group of Detroit-based Leftist women who
expressed contempt for feminism.

alternative: to seize our own power into our own hands, all women, separate and together, and make the Revolution the way it must be made—no priorities this time, *no suffering group told to wait until after.*

It is the job of revolutionary feminists to build an ever stronger independent Women's Liberation Movement, so that the sisters in counterleft captivity will have somewhere to turn, to use their power and rage and beauty and coolness in their own behalf for once, on their own terms, on their own issues, in their own style—whatever that may be. Not for us in Women's Liberation to hassle them and confront them the way their men do, nor to blame them—or ourselves—for what any of us are: an oppressed people, but a people raising our consciousness toward something that is the other side of anger, something bright and smooth and cool, like action unlike anything yet contemplated or carried out. It is for us to survive (something the white male radical has the luxury of never really worrying about, what with all his options), to talk, to plan, to be patient, to welcome new fugitives from the counterfeit Left with no arrogance but only humility and delight, to push—to strike.

There is something every woman wears around her neck on a thin chain of fear—an amulet of madness. For each of us, there exists somewhere a moment of insult so intense that she will reach up and rip the amulet off, even if the chain tears the flesh of her neck. And the last protection from seeing the truth will be gone. Do you think, tugging furtively every day at the chain and going nicely insane as I am, that I can be concerned with the puerile squabbles of a counterfeit Left that laughs at my pain? Do you think such a concern is noticeable when set alongside the suffering of more than half the human species for the past 5,000 years—due to a whim of the other half? No, no, no, goodbye to all that.

Women are Something Else. This time, we're going to kick out all the jams, and the boys will just have to hustle to keep up, or else drop out and openly join the power structure of which they are already the illegitimate sons. Any man who claims he is serious about wanting to divest himself of cock privilege should trip on this: all male leadership out of the Left is the only way; and it's going to happen, whether through men stepping down or through women seizing the helm. It's up to the "brothers"—after all, sexism is their concern, not ours; we're too busy getting ourselves together to have to deal with their bigotry. So they'll have to make up their own minds as to whether they will be divested of just cock privilege or—what the hell, why not say it, *say* it!—divested of cocks. How deep the fear of that loss must be, that it can be suppressed only by the building of empires and the waging of genocidal wars!

Goodbye, goodbye forever, counterfeit Left, counterleft, male-dominated cracked-glass-mirror reflection of the Amerikan Nightmare. Women are the real Left. We are rising, powerful in our unclean bodies; bright glowing mad in our inferior brains; wild hair flying, wild eyes staring, wild voices keening; undaunted by blood we who hemorrhage every twenty-eight days; laughing at our own beauty we who have lost our sense of humor; mourning for all each precious one of us might have been in this one living time-place had she not been born a woman; stuffing fingers into our mouths to stop the screams of fear and hate and pity for men we have loved and love still; tears in our eyes and bitterness in our mouths for children we couldn't have, or couldn't *not* have, or didn't want, or didn't want *yet,* or wanted and had in this place and this time of horror. We are rising with a fury older and potentially greater than any force in history, and this time we will be free or no one will survive. *Power to all the people or to none.* All the way down, this time.

Free Kathleen Cleaver!   Free Kim Agnew!
Free Anita Hoffman!   Free Holly Krassner!
Free Bernardine Dohrn!   Free Lois Hart!
Free Donna Malone!   Free Alice Embree!
Free Ruth Ann Miller!   Free Nancy Kurshan!
Free Leni Sinclair!   Free Lynn Phillips!
Free Jane Alpert!   Free Dinky Forman!
Free Gumbo!   Free Sharon Krebs!
Free Bonnie Cohen!   Free Iris Luciano!
Free Judy Lampe!   Free Robin Morgan!

Free Valerie Solanas!

Free our sisters!   *Free ourselves!*[38]

—January 1970

---

[38] All of the women on this list were at that time literal or figurative captives of a male-supremacist Leftist man and/or of patriarchal Leftist political beliefs—with two exceptions: Kim Agnew, the publicly rebellious daughter of then Vice-President Spiro Agnew (used-cash salesman), and Valerie Solanas, then serving time on a conviction of shooting Andy Warhol (used-decadence salesman).

A New Fable of the Burning Time

As the 1960s ceded to the 1970s and the Vietnam War ended, what had been called the New Left in the United States was directionless and dying—and those who remained in it frequently blamed the demise on the Feminist Movement. How ironic that the humanistic vision originally expressed so stirringly in the early SDS "Port Huron Statement" should have degenerated into jargon, and the one-upman(sic)ship of a central-committee mentality. How tragic that the unique U.S. character-mixture of impatience, pride, ahistoricity, and violence should have put its indelible mark on a movement supposedly antipathetic to it. The failure was due to "the patriarchy within," not to the rise of feminism. It is decidedly true, though, that as women in the Left (and Right and Center, for that matter) began to see a similarity in all those groups—patriarchal structure and content—and began to move out on our own and create a stronger, more independent, and more universal movement of our own, those "divorced" groups were left high and dry without their basic labor force of secretaries, cooks, speechwriters, Panther-Breakfast-program fixers (at 4:00 A.M.), and mimeograph-machine churners. The New Left, like the Old, ran on womanpower. And womanpower was now beginning to be recycled toward women.

But the New Left's vision died hard and bitterly, and blame was fixed unfairly wherever it could be smeared. In reality, FBI harassment of radicals and the scandals unraveling from Watergate made the most fantastic paranoia seem perfectly rational. Suspicion, accusation, and counter-accusation seemed to feed like birds of prey on the carrion of the sixties. Panic, that most contagious of superficial emotions, seized many good women as well as many men in its grasp.

This article was an attempt to comment on that panic, to shake women into a better mood about one another, and to remind us, possibly, of the concrete and continuing danger we claimed we were fighting (instead of each other).

Humor can be a weapon of extraordinary power. For years we feminists have been accused of having lost our sense of humor because we no longer chuckled good-naturedly at dumb-blonde stories, farmer's-daughter jokes, and other examples of boyish wit. More recently, though, our own style has been surfacing, and it has all the marks of classic "oppressed" humor; it is sharp, rich, acrid, sourly perceptive, and sometimes self-deprecating, like the humor of the African-American street-rap or the Yiddish curse. Much great humor is born of pain; not surprisingly does one speak of "laughing till we cried." For those who would use that pain to probe their way to freedom, another skill must be learned—that of crying till we laugh.

Once upon a time, there lived a witch. Her closest friend in all the village was a peasant woman who, alone among the others, knew she was a witch. They had good times together, and they helped each other out.

But it was quite important that no one else around discern their friendship, in case, you see, the witch should

be discovered and her friend, by their association, impli-
cated. They both were very careful. But then, the witch
was also lonely, for although it wasn't known she was a
witch, it was suspected. She wasn't ... "popular." Now
and then, when the townsfolk paid her any mind, she
found she talked with pride about her friend.

Horrified later, she would blurt out her error to the
peasant woman, and together they would try to estimate
the danger. Never in this talking of betrayal did they speak
except in jest of how the peasant woman held within her
hands a possible betrayal of the witch greater than any
error the latter could commit.

Nor did this strike them as peculiar.

One day, the townsfolk noticed that the peasant woman
had a cat who always followed her. They gossiped that
she kept strange hours—and she could read and write!
They came and took her, for to burn her as a witch.

Someone remembered that the other woman (the real
witch) once had claimed to be this witch's friend—but
they dismissed the notion that the other crazy ever could
have *had* a friend, even a witch, and let her go.

One version of this story ends that when the priest came
in the morning to fetch the prisoner to the stake, he found
both women—their stone-stiff hands clutching their ribs,
and pools of salt tears gathered in the creases of their
rigor-mortis grins.

"Dead," he gasped, "of laughter! They have eluded us,"
he droned.

The people marveled.

The other version goes that they both disappeared on
one or the other's broom, and still circle the moon on
dark nights, like two amused figure skaters coasting the
sky.

There are three morals to this story—fragments of a
conversation overheard one night by village idiots who
could comprehend no meaning in these words:

Whisper One:

> *All your betrayals of me, my dear*
> *are somehow payments against what we both fear*
> *and never speak of: mine.*

Whisper Two:

> *Friendship is mutual blackmail*
> *elevated to the level of love.*

Whisper Three:

> *We may as well trust each other.*
> *They're going to try to burn us, anyway.*

—1974

On Women as a
Colonized People

This short essay was written at the request of Colorado women, to be the introduction to a self-help health handbook, "Circle One," being published by the women's health movement. Although the piece was written in 1974, I had been making the analogy between women and colonized peoples for a number of years in speeches, as it was borne in upon me that the oppression of women was more pervasive than I had imagined. One could compare sexism with class and race and even caste, and still be left with an alienation more fundamental.

Such comparisons are invidious in terms of human suffering—no scale dare weigh that, and no analysis, political or otherwise, had better "compare and contrast" that—although such more-oppressed-than-thou approaches are attempted all the time. I was searching for a means of articulating sexism—a way of translating into generally understood and accepted terms of political philosophy "what it was we women wanted." Hence the analogies—which are always dangerous, since the terms themselves have been formed and even reformed by and in the interests of patriarchy. We resort to them because any conditions of oppression that women share with men (racism, homophobia, discrimination due to class, age, physical disability, etc.) are always taken more seriously—simply because the oppression affects male human beings, too. For precisely this reason, the colonial analogy itself is insufficient to describe women's predicament: we are not only colonized as women per se but also as members of mixed-gender populations who have been colonized in the traditional sense. Not surprisingly, the latter condition is still taken more seriously than the former.

The search continues. We not only define and redefine but create entirely new terms to interpret—and change—our condition as women. When I first proposed that we view women as a colonized people, the suggestion was met with incredulity, even from other feminists. But what was "going too far" yesterday becomes something assumed, even taken for granted, today. So has the theory of women's colonization been assimilated into feminist thought.

For myself, this essay now stands as an artifact, a brave if superficial first hazarding on the subject—one I would later take on in greater depth in The Demon Lover.* *For one thing, I underestimated the extent to which the colonized, for survival, adopt the colonizer's attitudes and ingest his psychology, until it becomes extremely difficult to locate where the self (even the rebellious self) begins. For another, there is the problem of how to go about de-colonization when you have no borders men ever recognized in the first place. Then, too, there is neo-colonization, that subtler economic cooptation that follows all the so-called independence ceremonies. As it turns out, this analogy was only a beginning . . .*

Frantz Fanon and Albert Memmi, as sexist as other men but considerable authorities on the process of coloniza-

---

The Demon Lover: On the Sexuality of Terrorism (New York: W. W. Norton, 1989).

tion and its effects, wrote of certain basic characteristics by which that process could always be identified. Primary among these were: The oppressed are robbed of their culture, history, pride, and roots—all most concretely expressed in the conquest of their *land itself.* They are forced (by a system of punishment and reward) to adopt the oppressor's standards, values, and identification. In due course, they become alienated from their own values, their own land—which is of course being mined by the oppressor for its natural resources. They are permitted (forced) to work the land, but since they do not benefit from or have power over what it produces, they come to feel oppressed by *it.* Thus, the alienation from their own territory serves to mystify that territory, and the enforced identification with their colonizing masters provokes eventual contempt both for themselves and their land. It follows, of course, that the first goal of a colonized people is to *reclaim their own land.*

Women are a colonized people. Our history, values, and (cross-cultural) culture have been taken from us—a gynocidal attempt manifest most arrestingly in the patriarchy's seizure of our basic and precious "land": our own bodies.

Our bodies have been taken from us, mined for their natural resources (sex and children), and deliberately mystified. Five centuries of Judeo-Christian-Islamic tradition, virulent in its misogyny, have helped enforce the attitude that women are "unclean." Androcentric medical science, like other professional industries in the service of the colonizer, has researched better and more efficient means of mining our natural resources, with (literally) bloody little concern for the true health, comfort, nurturance, or even survival of those resources. This should hardly surprise us; our ignorance about our own primary terrain—our bodies—is in the self-interest of the patriarchy.

We must begin, as women, to reclaim our land, and the most concrete place to begin is with our own flesh. Self-and-sister-education is a first step, since all that fostered ignorance and self-contempt dissolve before the intellectual and emotional knowledge that our female bodies are constructed with beauty, craft, cleanliness, yes, holiness. Identification with the colonizer's standards melts before the revelations dawning on a woman who clasps a speculum in one hand and a mirror in the other. She is demystifying her own body for herself, and she will never again be quite so alienated from it.

From education we gain higher expectations, and from there we move through anger and into the will for self-determination, to seizing power over our own lives, to reclaiming the "products" of our labor (our own sexual definitions; our own children), and ultimately, to transforming the quality of life itself in society as a whole— into something new, compassionate, sane.

This is why, as radical feminists, we believe that a women's revolution is potentially the most sensible hope for change in history. And this is why the speculum may well be mightier than the sword.

—1974

Theory and Practice: Pornography and Rape

*Few issues so clearly show both the progress and the stag-
nation of anti-sexist consciousness over the past twenty
years as the interlocking subjects of rape and pornography.*

*In 1974, when the following essay was written, the two
issues were largely regarded as being totally separate—
and each was controversial in its own way. Today, in North
America, rape, at least, is generally considered not an act
of sex but a crime of violence, and one for which the victim
is not to be blamed. In the United States, as of this writing,
the still-pending Violence Against Women Act of 1990 (S.
2754), introduced by Senator Joseph Biden (Democrat–
Delaware), would make such gender-motivated crimes as
rape categorizable as bias or "hate crimes" and civil rights
violations. (The 1990 Hate Crimes Statistics Act, signed by
President Bush into law, directs the Department of Justice
to collect data on crimes motivated by the victim's race,
religion, ethnicity, or sexual orientation—but purposefully
ignores gender-based crimes.) Many states have enacted
marital-rape laws and legislation that makes the victim's
sexual history inadmissable in court proceedings against
the accused rapist. New terms—"date rape" and "acquaintance rape"—have entered the general vocabulary. Because*

of pressure from local rape crisis centers and women's groups, many urban police forces now have special units, staffed by policewomen, to deal more sensitively with rape survivors.

On the other hand, rape statistics continue to escalate— both because women have been reporting such attacks more frequently and because they are happening more.

As of 1991, in the United States, a woman is raped every six minutes; one out of seven married women is the victim of marital rape. An estimated two to three percent of all men who rape outside of marriage go to prison for their crimes—and 52 percent of men convicted of rape will be arrested again within three years (20 percent of all rapes by a single offender are committed by men under the age of twenty-one; in 62 percent of assaults involving multiple offenders, the rapists are under age twenty-one). Campus rape, too, is on the rise: 25 percent of college women in one survey had experienced rape or attempted rape (of these, 84 percent knew their attackers); a 1989 study at the University of Illinois, Urbana-Champagne, found that fraternity men perpetrated 63 percent of student sexual assault on campus; 15 percent of college men in another study admitted they had forced a woman to have sex, and 51 percent of college men in a third survey said they would rape if they were certain they could get away with it.*

In this essay, I was naive in thinking that no rapist's defense would dare claim that small children or old women had "incited" the attack; both defenses have since been made repeatedly—and successfully. I was also understating the enormity of the problem by putting it solely in a U.S. context and calling it "corn-fed"; I meant to describe it as "normal" in terms of my own culture—but the hideous truth

*Statistics cited from *Ms.*, special issue on violence against women (September / October 1990), and Dr. Peggy Reeves Sanday, *Fraternity Gang Rape: Sex, Brotherhood, and Privilege on Campus* (New York: New York University Press, 1990).

*is that it is "normal" on a worldwide scale of patriarchal
culture (see* Sisterhood Is Global**), a reality I came to grips
with fully only in doing research for* The Demon Lover
*(1989). Indeed, some languages have no word for "rape"
at all, since female human beings are assumed to be the
sexual property of men.*

*As for pornography, it has gone mainstream: one out of
every eight Hollywood movies depicts a violent rape theme;
by age eighteen, the average youth has watched 250,000
such acts of violence on television. Continuing feminist
efforts to exercise our First Amendment rights of free speech
and thus educate about pornography as propaganda have
been made even more difficult, on two major fronts: consistent attacks from the left-liberal establishment, which
keeps misreading such efforts as "censorship," and unwel-
come support from right-wing conservatives and religious
fundamentalists who* do *want censorship, and who regard
sex education in the schools and public education campaigns about HIV/AIDS as forms of pornography.*

*On the plus side, studies done during the 1970s and 1980s
(including those by Dr. Edward Donnerstein at the University of Wisconsin-Madison, and Drs. Neil M. Malamuth
and James V. Check at the University of Manitoba, Win-
nepeg, Canada), legitimized what women had been saying: causal links did exist between pornography and acts
of violence in general—and against women in particular.
Studies on serial killers have confirmed that such men were
addicted from an early age to high consumption of violent
pornography. As recently as the Persian Gulf War in early
1991, a furor was created by the U.S. government's initial
denial and later admission that bomber pilots on aircraft
carriers in the Gulf were deliberately shown films of violent pornography before taking off on missions over civilian areas in Iraq.*

*Robin Morgan, ed. *Sisterhood Is Global: The International Women's
Movement Anthology* (New York: Doubleday / Anchor, 1984).

Yet feminists persist, not *in censorship campaigns but in grass-roots actions against pornographic dealers, in efforts to educate as to the real effects of this propaganda, in trying to clarify the definitions themselves. (Etymology is, as always, enlightening: "pornography" comes from the Greek root words* porné *and* graphos; *the former meant female slave and the latter meant writing or depicting. "Erotica," however, comes from the Greek root* eros—*sensual desire and love. In other words, the message of the former is power and dominance, the message of the latter is mutuality and equality. That should help us differentiate.) Possibly the most creative strategy was the civil-rights ordinance* devised in the 1980s by writer Andrea Dworkin and attorney Catharine A. MacKinnon; it defined pornography as a form of sex discrimination and therefore a violation of civil rights; this allows anyone injured by pornography to file a civil lawsuit against pornographers.***

Since pornography is now estimated as being a $10 billion industry in the United States alone, and a multinational one as well (it constituted the first and largest influx of Western media into Eastern Europe after the political shifts of 1989), it remains a formidable adversary.

I still wonder how those who would silence women's voices on this subject can fly the banners of "free speech" and the precious Bill of Rights from a double standard.

*The ordinance in its various forms—and its struggle for adoption by various city councils around the country—is a story in itself. See Andrea Dworkin and Catharine A. MacKinnon, *Pornography and Civil Rights: A New Day for Women's Equality* (Minneapolis, MN: Organizing Against Pornography Resource Center for Education and Action, 1989); also see separate books by Dworkin and by MacKinnon on the subject.

**In February 1992, the Supreme Court of Canada unanimously ruled, in a landmark decision, that it was legitimate to outlaw pornography that was harmful to women, a related analysis (albeit a different approach) to that of MacKinnon and Dworkin. Canada thus becomes the first country to note that *what is obscene is what harms women, not what "offends values."* The decision noted that pornography harms women personally, exploits them, negatively affects their right to be equal, affects their security, and influences attitudes toward them so as to make them more subject to violence.

There is perhaps no subject so deliberately distorted as that of rape. This is because rape is the perfected act of male sexuality in a patriarchal culture—it is the ultimate metaphor for domination, violence, subjugation, and possession. But the most insidious aspect of rape is the psychological fiction that accompanies it—with which all women are beseiged until, for survival's sake, we even pretend to believe that what we *know* is a lie. The fiction has many versions. A few representative examples:

There is the Pity the Poor Rapist approach. This version tells us that we must be sorry for our attacker. He is sick, he needs help. He decidely does need help (if he can be apprehended), but his victim needs it more—and first. She is not even supposed to defend herself, for fear of being unwomanly. A woman who notices her child being molested by a dirty old (or young) man on the playground and who shampoos the man with a brick is considered a proper mother, "the tigress defending her cubs." Yet should the same man molest *her,* she ought to, in society's view, welcome him and admit that she relishes being pawed or, if she must, plead winningly with him to stop. It is acceptable to defend one's child but not oneself, because it is considered the epitome of selfishness for a woman to place her own concerns first. We are supposed to wipe the noses of all humanity before we dare think about ourselves. But we must learn to mother those selves, and defend them, at least as valiantly as we do our children.

The Spontaneity Lie is an offshoot of Pity the Poor Rapist. It assures us that he was just an average guy walking along the street, who was helplessly seized with the urge to attack a woman. He couldn't stop himself: sudden lust. But it's important to remember that more than half of all rapes occur in breaking-and-entering situations—which certainly require a modicum of premeditation.

There is always the basic Every Woman Loves a Rapist / All Women Want to Be Raped / Good Girls Never Get

Raped / It's Always the Woman's Fault cliché. Thus, if she wears slacks, that's obviously meant as a challenge; if a skirt, it's an incitement. If she glowers as she strides down the street, it's meant as an attention-getter; if she looks pleasant, it's a come-on. And besides, what was she doing, anyway, out walking all alone by herself—in broad daylight? Doesn't she know her place?

Knowing our place is the message of rape—as it was the message of lynchings for black men. *Neither act of violence is an act of spontaneity or sexuality—they are both acts of political terrorism,* designed consciously *and* unconsciously to keep an entire people in its place by continual reminders. For that matter, the attitudes of racism and sexism are twined together in the knot of rape in such a way as to constitute the symbolic expression of the worst in our culture. These "reminders" are perpetrated on victims selected sometimes at random, sometimes with particular reason. So we have rape murders of children and of eighty-year-old women—neither of whom anyone can claim were salaciously enticing the rapist—and we also have the deliberate "lesson-rapes" to which feminist students have been prey on their campuses—acts based on the theory that all these frustrated feminists need is a good rape to show 'em the light.

Thus the woman is rarely unknown to her attacker, nor need the rapist be a stranger to his victim—although goddess help her deal with the more-than-usual scorn of the police if she reports date rape, or rape by a former jealous boyfriend, or an ex-husband, or her faculty advisor or boss, clergyman, or psychiatrist. Many policemen already delight in asking the victim such sadistic, illegal questions as, Did you enjoy it? Consequently, any admission on her part, whether elicited or volunteered, that the rapist was actually an acquaintance seems to invite open season on *her* morals.*

---

*The Blame (or Disbelieve) the Victim syndrome was still in full force in the early 1990s, with the U.S. Senate confirmation hearings on the

But radical feminists see the issue of rape as even more pervasive than these examples. For instance, *I would claim that rape exists any time sexual intercourse occurs when it has not been initiated by the woman, out of her own genuine affection and desire.* This last qualifier is important, because we are now familiar with the cigarette-commercial image of the "liberated woman," she who is the product of the so-called sexual revolution: a Madison Avenue–spawned male fantasy of what the liberated woman should be—a glamorous lady slavering with lust for his paunchy body. We also know that many women, in responding to this new pressure to be "liberated initiators" have done so *not* out of their own desire but for the same old reasons—fear of losing the guy, fear of being thought a prude, fear of hurting his fragile feelings, *fear.* So it is vital to emphasize that when we say she would need to be the inititiator (in tone if not in actuality) we mean because *she* wants to be. Anything short of that is, in a radical feminist definition, rape. Because *the pressure is there.* It might not be a knife-blade against the throat; it can be in his body language, his threat of sulking, his clenched or trembling hands, his angry put-down or silent self-pity at being rejected. How many millions of times have women had sex "willingly" with men they didn't wish to have sex with? Even men they loved? How many times have women wanted just to sleep instead, or read, or watch the Late Show? It must be clear that, under this definition, most of the decent marital bedrooms across the U.S.A. are settings for nightly rape.

This normal, corn-fed kind of rape is less shocking if it can be realized and admitted that the act of rape is merely the expression of the standard, "healthy," even

Supreme Court nomination of Clarence Thomas and the accusations against him by Professor Anita Hill, the William Kennedy Smith rape trial in Florida, and the rape trial of celebrity boxing champion Mike Tyson. But what had changed was women's conscious—and articulated—rage, now expressed in a "mainstream" fashion.

encouraged male fantasy in patriarchal culture—that of aggressive sex. And the articulation of that fantasy into a billion-dollar industry is pornography.

Civil libertarians recoil from linking the issues of rape and pornography, dredging up yellowing statistics from the Scandinavian countries that appear to show acts of rape decline where pornography is more easily pro-cured. (This actually ought to prove the connection.) I am not suggesting that censorship should rule the day here—I abhor censorship in any form (although there was a time when I felt it was a justifiable means to an end—which is always the devil's argument behind thought control, isn't it?). I'm aware that a phallocentric culture is more likely to begin its censorship purges with books on pelvic self examination for women or books contain-ing lyrical paeans to lesbianism than with *See Him Tear and Kill Her* or similar Mickey-Spillanesque titles. Nor do I place much trust in a male-run judiciary, and I am less than reassured by the character of those who would pre-tend to judge what is fit for the public to read or view. On the contrary, I feel that censorship often boils down to some male judges getting to read a lot of dirty books—with one hand.

Some feminists have suggested that a cabinet-level woman in charge of Women's Affairs (in itself a contro-versial idea) might take pornography regulation in her portfolio. Others hearken back to the idea of community control. Both approaches give me unease, the first because of the unlikeliness that a cabinet-level woman appointee these days would have a genuine feminist consciousness or, if she did, have the power and autonomy from the administration to act upon it; the second because com-munities can be as ignorant and totalitarian in censor-ship as individual tyrants. A lot of education would have to precede community regulation to win my paranoid support for that proposal.

But women seem to be moving on the issue with a different strategy, one that circumvents censorship and instead is aimed at hurting the purveyors themselves, at making the business less lucrative by making the clients less comfortable. In one southern town, women planned their action with considerable wit; they took up positions on their local porn strip and politely photographed each man as he entered or left the bookstores and movie houses. They used a very obvious camera—the large newspaper-photographer type—sometimes chasing the man for a block as he fled in chagrin. One group of women who used this tactic deliberately worked with cameras that had no film—scaring and embarrassing the men was their aim. Another group, however, did use film, and developed the shots. They then made up Wanted posters of the men, which they plastered all over town, to the acute humiliation of the porn-purchasers—some of whom turned out to be influential, upstanding citizens of the community. In Seattle, women's antipornography squads have stink-bombed smut bookstores—and the local papers were filled with approving letters to the editors. In New York, three porn movie houses have been fire-bombed.

The massive porn industry grinds on, of course. In a replay of the liberated-woman shill, we are now being sold so-called female-oriented pornography, as if our sexuality were as imitative of patriarchal man's as *Playgirl* (read more by gay men—for its male centerfold—than by women) is of *Playboy*. It must be frustrating to the pushers of such tacky trash to realize that for most women *Wuthering Heights* is still a real turn-on. Yet pornography today is becoming chic—serious movie houses that usually run art films are now cashing in on so-called art-porn. The Mick Jagger / sadism fad, the popularity of transvestite entertainers, and the resurgence of "camp" all seem part of a backlash against what feminists have been saying. It is no coincidence that FBI statistics indicate the incidence of rape increased 93 percent in the

1960s. When people refuse to stay in their place, the message must be repeated in a louder tone.*

And what is this doing to us? We are somewhat more educated now as to the effects of rape on women, but we know less about the effects of pornography. Some obvious trends can be noted: the market for go-go girls, nude models, and pornofilm "actresses," which in turn affects women's employment (why be a waitress when you can make more money taking off your clothes?); the overlapping boundaries of the porn and prostitution industries; the erosion of the virgin / whore stereotypes to a new "all women are really whores" attitude, thus erasing the last vestige of (even corrupted) respect for women as human beings; the promotion of infidelity as a "swinging" alternative to committed relationships. But how to chart the pressure sensed by women from their boyfriends or husbands to perform sexually in ever more objectified and objectifying fashion, as urged by porn movies and magazines? How to connect the rise of articles in journals aimed at educated, liberal audiences—articles extolling the virtues of anal intercourse, "fist-fucking," and other "kinky freedoms"?

And how far-reaching is the effect, how individual, how universal? Individual in terms of the specific humiliation felt by the woman whose husband hides *Penthouse* or some harder-core version of it in the bathroom and then forces himself on her at night—or on other women when she

---

*The *New York Post* of October 1, 1975, carried a story about a nationwide investigation into "snuff films" or "slashers"—pornographic movies that culminate in the actual murder and dismemberment of the actress. These movies, shot for the most part in South America, circulate, according to the *Post* story, on the "pornography-connoisseur circuit" where the select clientele can afford fifteen hundred dollars for a collection of eight reels. Four months after the *Post* story, a porn movie called *Snuff* opened at a first-run movie theater on New York's Broadway. Advertised as "the bloodiest thing ever filmed," *this* print was priced to make it available to Everyman.

fends him off—and then blames her for her frigidity and his inconstancy? Individual and universal enough to explain the recent horrifying rise in the rate of marital violence? Universal enough to have influenced twentieth-century theology? Yet this has happened, through the work of that intellectual giant, the Christian theologian Paul Tillich—he who is revealed to us with such compassionate but uncompromising honesty by his widow Hannah Tillich in her brilliant, controversial book *From Time to Time.** After his death, Hannah Tillich tells us, she "unlocked the drawers." There was the pornographic letter hidden under his blotter; the revelation of his favorite fantasy of naked women, *crucified,* being whipped; the discovery of all the photos, the affairs, the mistresses, the sexual secretaries, the one-night stands, the abuse of the worshipful female students who had sat at his feet, his "houris . . . tinkling their chains." She writes: "I was tempted to place between the sacred pages of his highly esteemed lifework these obscene signs of the real life that he had transformed into the gold of abstraction— King Midas of the spirit." Instead, Hannah Tillich dared write a book about herself, alchemizing her own integrity out of "the piece of bleeding, tortured womanhood" she says she had become.

So we must admit that pornography is sexist propaganda, no more and no less. *Pornography is the theory, and rape the practice.* And what a practice. The violation of an individual woman is the metaphor for man's forcing himself on whole nations (rape as the crux of war), on nonhuman creatures (rape as the lust behind hunting and related carnage), and on the planet itself (reflected even in our language—carving up "virgin territory," with strip mining often referred to as a "rape of the land"). Elaine Morgan, in her book *The Descent of Woman*** pos-

* (Chelsea, MI: Scarborough House, 1973).
** (New York: Stein and Day, 1972; rev. ed., Chelsea, MI: Scarborough House, 1986).

its that rape was the initial crime, not murder, as the Bible would have it. She builds an interesting scientific argument for her theory. In *The Mothers,** Robert Briffault puts forward much the same hypothesis for an evolutionary "fall" from the comparable grace of the animal realm; his evidence is anthropological and mytho-historic. In more than one book, Claude Levi-Strauss has pursued his complex theory of how men use women as the verbs by which they communicate with one another (men themselves are the nouns, of course), raping being the means for communicating defeat to the men of a conquered tribe, so overpowered that they cannot even defend "their" women from the victors. That theory, too, seems relevant. The woman may serve as a vehicle for the rapist expressing his rage against a world that gives him pain—because he is poor, or oppressed, or mad, or simply human. Then what of her? We have waded in the swamp of compassion for him long enough. It is past time we stopped him.

The conflict is escalating now, because we won't cast our glances down any more to avoid seeing the degrading signs and marquees. We won't shuffle past the vulgarity of the sidewalk verbal hassler, who is *not* harmless because he is broadcasting the rapist's theory and is backed up by the *threat of capacity to carry out the practice* itself. We will no longer be guilty about being victims of ghastly violations against our spirits and bodies merely because we are female. Whatever its age and origin, the propaganda and act that transform the most intimate, vulnerable, and tender of physical exchanges into one of conquest and humiliation is surely the worst example patriarchy has to offer women of the way it truly regards us.

—1974

*(1927; Grosset and Dunlap Universal Library Edition, 1963).

The International Crime of Genital Mutilation

By Robin Morgan and Gloria Steinem*

When this article was written, in 1979, (and published in Ms. *in March of that year), we used the most conservative estimate of 30 million women who were suffering the results of genital mutilation. Since then, official estimates made by the World Health Organization (WHO) have increased the number to more than 75 million.*

The United Nations International Children's Fund (UNICEF) was the first UN agency to make the elimination of these practices a goal of its program, and then only as a part of its larger concern with children's health. For the first time, UNICEF's executive board meeting in May 1980 raised "female circumcision" among the issues in a special report on women and the overall development and economic well-being of their countries. WHO has also now taken up this concern as a formal part of its program. Furthermore, the four recommendations listed in the article, the results of the first WHO conference on the subject in 1979, were approved by the World Conference for the UN Decade for Women that met in July 1980, in Copenhagen.

Some governments had already taken a stand. The

---

*Although this article was coauthored, we have each chosen to publish it as part of our respective work because of the subject's importance.

*Sudan outlawed infibulation in 1946, Egypt passed legis-
lation against clitoridectomy in the 1970s. In 1982, President Daniel T. arap Moi of Kenya banned clitoridectomy
and Kenyan medical authorities forbade it—after fourteen
excised girls had died. Norway, Denmark, and Sweden
have banned excision procedures by law (some African and
Middle Eastern families residing there had made this
practice an issue by requesting that it be done in hospitals). It is not yet banned in France or England, although
it has now become a public issue, since there are many
reports of local surgeons who perform the operation for
substantial fees. In 1982, the father of a family from Mali
residing in France was arrested for removing his three-
month-old daughter's clitoris with a pocketknife. In 1991,
a case hit the French courts regarding Aminata Diop, a
young woman from Mali seeking political asylum in France
on the grounds that she had fled mutilation in her own
country. (She won the right to remain in France, but not
as a "precedent." Since women are not covered by the
Geneva Conventions, this case may in time be the grounds
for an international test case for female human rights.)
There have been unconfirmed reports that a few women
in the United States who have converted to Islam have had
this operation as a tribute to cultural nationalism.*

*The most hopeful sign is that women themselves in the
countries most affected are at last being heard—since it is
they who have for decades been taking the leadership in
the controversial campaign to eliminate genital mutilation. Such courageous women as Nawal El Saadawi, Marie
Angélique Savané, Edna Adan Ismail, Marie Bassili Assad,
Evelyne Accad, Esther Ogunmodede, Fawzia Assad, Awa
Thiam, and others have for years been doing studies on
the disastrous effects of this custom, and have been pres-
suring governments and international agencies to oppose
the practice. Many nongovernmental organizations
(including the Association of African Women in Research*

and Development, the International Commission for the Abolition of Sexual Mutilations, and the Coalition of African, Arab, and Western women who formed the Women's Action Group on Female Excision and Infibulation), and the United Nations agencies already mentioned have organized conferences to develop creative educational and / or legislative strategies that would effectively combat the practice.

In 1990, the U.N. commission monitoring CEDAW (the U.N. Convention to Eliminate All Forms of Discrimination Against Women) unanimously passed a recommendation condemning the practice as being deleterious to women; this was a first.

It's also hopeful that such patriarchal practices are beginning to be understood as a universal problem in varying degrees—not the fault of only one culture or religion.

The following article has been distributed by UNICEF.

Warning: These words are painful to read. They describe facts of life as far away as our most fearful imagination and as close as any denial of women's sexual freedom.

As you read this, an estimated thirty million women in the world are suffering the results of genital mutilation. The main varieties of this extensive custom are:

1. Sunna "circumcision," or removal of the prepuce and / or tip of the clitoris.
2. Clitoridectomy, or the excision of the entire clitoris (both prepuce and glans), plus the adjacent part of the labia minora.
3. Infibulation (from the Latin *fibula*, or "clasp"), that is, the removal of the entire clitoris, the labia minora, and labia majora—plus the joining of the scraped sides of the vulva across the vagina, where they are secured with thorns or sewn with catgut or thread. A small opening is preserved by inserting a sliver of wood (commonly a matchstick) into the

wound during the healing process, thus allowing passage of urine and menstrual blood. An infibulated woman must be cut open to permit intercourse, and cut further to permit childbirth. Often, she is closed up again after delivery, and thus may be subject to such procedures repeatedly during her reproductive life.

The age at which these ritual sexual mutilations are performed varies with type of procedure and local tradition. A female may undergo some such rite as early as the eighth day after birth, or at puberty, or after she herself has borne children. In most areas, however, the ritual is carried out when the child is between the ages of three and eight, as she may be considered unclean, improper, or unmarriageable if it is not done.

To readers for whom such customs come as horrifying news, it is vital that we immediately recognize the connection between these patriarchal practices and our own. They are different in scope and degree, but not in kind. Not only have North American and European women experienced the psychic clitoridectomy that was legitimized by Freud,* but Western nineteenth-century medical texts also proclaim genital mutilation as an accepted treatment for "nymphomania," "hysteria," masturbation, "deviance," and other nonconforming behavior. Indeed, there are women living in North America and Europe today who have suffered this form (as well as other, more familiar forms) of gynophobic, medically unnecessary, mutilating surgery.

As a general practice and precondition of marriage, however, some researchers cite recent evidence for genital mutilation in areas as diverse as Australia, Brazil, Malaysia, Pakistan, and among the Skoptsi Christian sect

---

*"The elimination of clitoral sexuality is a necessary precondition for the development of femininity." Sigmund Freud, *Sexuality and the Psychology of Love* (New York: Macmillan, 1963).

in the Soviet Union. In El Salvador, it is still not uncommon for a mother to carve the sign of the cross with a razor blade on the clitoris of her little girl for reasons such as to "make her a better worker and keep her from getting ideas." But international health authorities find the most extensive evidence of such customs on the African continent and the Arabian peninsula. The majority of mutilations take place without anesthetic at home (in the city or the village), but many are now performed in hospitals as approved procedures. Nor are these rites limited to one religion; they are practiced by some Islamic peoples, some Coptic Christians, members of various indigenous tribal religions, some Catholics and Protestants, and some Fellasha, an ancient Jewish sect living in the Ethiopian highlands.

The form most common on the African continent is clitoridectomy, which is practiced in more than twenty-six countries from the Horn of Africa and the Red Sea across to the Atlantic coast, and from Egypt in the north to Mozambique in the south, also including Botswana and Lesotho. According to Awa Thiam, the Senegalese writer, clitoridectomy—in the form of either complete excision or the more "moderate" Sunna variant—also can be found in the two Yemens, Saudi Arabia, Iraq, Jordan, Syria, and southern Algeria. Infibulation appears to be fairly standard in the whole of the Horn—Somalia, most of Ethiopia, the Sudan (despite legislation prohibiting it in 1946), Kenya, Nigeria, Mali, Upper Volta, and parts of Ivory Coast. Many ethnic groups have local versions: some cauterize the clitoris with fire or rub a special kind of nettle across the organs in order to destroy nerve endings; some stanch the flow of blood with compounds made of herbs, milk, honey, and sometimes ashes or animal droppings.

The health consequences of such practices include primary fatalities due to shock, hemorrhage, or septicemia (blood poisoning), and such later complications as genital malformation, delayed menarche, dyspareunia (pain suffered during intercourse), chronic pelvic complications, incontinence, calcification deposits in the vaginal walls, recto-vaginal fistulas, vulval cysts and abscesses, recurrent urinary retention and infection, scarring and keloid formation, infertility, and an entire array of obstetric complications. There is also increased probability of injury to the fetus (by infection) during pregnancy and to the infant during birth. Psychological responses among women range from temporary trauma and permanent frigidity to psychoses. A high rate of mortality is suspected by health officials, although there are few fatality records available, because of the informality or secrecy surrounding the custom in many areas.

Although such practices are frequently described as "female circumcision," the degree of damage is not comparable to the far more minor circumcision of males. Certainly, the two procedures are related: both are widely practiced without medical necessity and are extreme proofs of subservience to patriarchal authority—whether tribal, religious, or cultural—over all sexual and reproductive functions. But there the parallel stops. Clitoridectomy is more analogous to penisectomy than to circumcision: the clitoris has as many nerve endings as the penis. On the other hand, male circumcision involves cutting the tip of the protective "hood" of skin that covers the penis—an area whose number of nerve endings are analogous to those in the earlobe—but does not damage the penis. This procedure does not destroy its victim's capacity for sexual pleasure; indeed, some justify the practice as increasing it by exposing more of the sensitive area. The misnomer "female circumcision" seems to stem from conscious or unconscious political motives: to make it appear that women are merely experiencing something men undergo—no more, no less.

Politics are also evident in the attribution of this custom. The Sudanese name for infibulation credits it to Egypt ("Pharaonic circumcision"), while the Egyptians call the same operation "Sudanese circumcision." The more moderate "Sunna circumcision" was supposedly recommended by the Prophet Muhammed, who is said to have counseled, "Reduce, but don't destroy," thus reforming, but legitimizing, the ritual. That version was termed "Sunna," or traditional, perhaps in an attempt to placate strict traditionalists, although such rituals are mentioned nowhere in the Koran, a fact Islamic women who oppose this mutilation cite in their arguments.

The overt justifications for genital mutilation are as contradictory as are theories about its origins. Explanations include custom, religion, family honor, cleanliness, protection against spells, initiation, insurance of virginity at marriage, and prevention of female promiscuity by physically reducing, or terrorizing women out of, sexual desire, this last especially in polygynous cultures. On the other hand, the fact that some women in the Middle East who work as prostitutes also have been clitoridectomized is cited as proof that it *doesn't* reduce pleasure, as if women become prostitutes out of desire.

A superstition is a practice or belief justified by simultaneous and utterly opposing sets of arguments. (For instance, male circumcision is not only said to increase desire but to decrease it through toughening of the exposed skin or removing the friction-causing "hood.") Thus, a frequently given reason for sexual mutilation is that it makes a woman more fertile, yet in 1978 Dr. R.T. Ravenholt, then director of the United States Agency for International Development's Population Bureau, failed to oppose it on the ground that it was a *contraceptive* method, claiming that "because it aimed at reducing female sex desire, [clitoridectomy / infibulation] undoubtedly has fertility control as part of its motivation." In fact, some women's behavior indicates the reverse. The pain of

intercourse often leads mutilated women to seek pregnancy as a temporary relief from sexual demands.

In some cultures, the justification is even less obscure.
Myths of the Mossi of Upper Volta, and the Dogon and
Bambaras of Mali, clearly express the fear of an initially
hermaphroditic human nature and of women's sexuality:
the clitoris is considered a dangerous organ, fatal to a
man if brought into contact with his penis.

Similarly, in nineteenth-century London, Dr. Isaac
Baker Brown justified scissoring off the clitoris of some
of his own English patients as a cure for such various ills
as insomnia, sterility, and "unhappy marriages." In 1859,
Dr. Charles Meigs recommended application of a nitrate
of silver solution to the clitoris of female children who
masturbated. Until 1925 in the United States, a medical
association called the Orificial Surgery Society offered
surgical training in clitoridectomy and infibulation
"because of the vast amount of sickness and suffering
which could be saved the gentler sex. ...." Such opera-
tions (and justifications) occurred as recently as the 1940s
and 1950s in the United States. For instance, in New York,
the daughter of a well-to-do-family was clitoridectomized as a "treatment" for masturbation recommended by
a family physician. Some prostitutes were encouraged by
well-meaning church social workers to have this procedure as a form of "rehabilitation."

During the 1970s, clitoral "relocation"—termed "Love
Surgery"—entered some medical practice. As late as 1979,
the feminist news service Hersay carried the story of Dr.
James Burt, an Ohio gynecologist who offered a fifteen-
hundred-dollar "Mark Two" operation, which involved
vaginal reconstruction in order to "make the clitoris more
accessible to direct penile stimulation."

Whatever the supposed justifications for these efforts
to make women's bodies conform to societal expectations, we can explore the real reasons for them only within

the context of patriarchy. It must control women's bodies as the means of reproduction, and thus repress the independent power of women's sexuality. Both motives are enforced by socioeconomic rewards and punishments.

If marriage is the primary means of economic survival for a woman, then whatever will make her more marriageable becomes desirable. If a bride who lacks virginity literally risks death or renunciation on her wedding night, then a chastity belt forged of her own flesh is a gesture of parental concern. If the tribal role of clitoridectomist or midwife who performs such mutilations is the sole position of honor, power, or even independent livelihood available to women, then the "token women" who perform such rites will fight to preserve them. If those who organize the ceremonies of excision (sometimes whole families by inherited prerogative) have the right, as they do in some cultures, to "adopt" the excised children to work in their fields for two or three years, then such families have a considerable economic motive for perpetuating the custom. If Western male gynecologists also believed women's independent sexuality to be dangerous and unnatural, then surgery was justified to remove its cause. If a modern gynecologist still presumes that men may not be willing to learn how to find or stimulate the clitoris for female pleasure, then he will think it natural to move the clitoris closer to the customary site of penile pleasure.

Illogical responses can be carried to new depths by bureaucrats. The White House and its concern for "human rights," the various desks of the U.S. State Department, and such agencies as the United Nations International Children's Fund and the World Health Organization all have expressed reluctance to interfere with "social and cultural attitudes" regarding female genital mutilation. This sensitivity has been markedly absent on other issues, for example, campaigns to distribute vaccines or vitamins despite resistance from local traditionalists.

Clearly, "culture" is that which affects women while "politics" affects men. Even human rights and other admirable political statements do not include those of special importance to the female majority of humanity. (This is true not only for genital mutilation and other areas of reproductive freedom. Many women of the Middle East cannot leave their countries without a male family member's written permission, yet this is not classed with, for instance, Jews who are forbidden to leave the Soviet Union, or other travel restrictions that affect men as well.) Some international agencies take a reformist position— that clitoridectomy and / or infibulation should be done in hospitals under hygienic conditions and proper medical supervision. Feminist groups and such respected organizations as Terre des Hommes, the (ironically named) Swiss-based international agency dedicated to the protection of children, repeatedly have urged a strengthening of this position to one condemning the practice outright.

The situation is further complicated by the understandable suspicion on the part of many African and Arab governments and individuals that Western interest in the matter is motivated not by humanitarian concerns but by a racist or neocolonialist desire to eradicate indigenous culture. In fact, as Jomo Kenyatta, Kenya's first president, noted in his book, *Facing Mount Kenya,* the key mobilization of many forces for Kenyan independence from the British was in direct response to attempts by Church of Scotland missionaries in 1929 to suppress clitoridectomy. Patriarchal authorities, whether tribal or imperial, have always considered as central to their freedom and power the right to define what is done with "their" women. But past campaigns against female mutilation, conducted for whatever ambiguous or even deplorable reasons, need not preclude new approaches that might be more effective because they would be sensitive to the cultures involved and, most important, supportive of the *women* affected, and in response to *their* leadership.

Precisely such an initiative began in February 1979, at a historic meeting in Khartoum, Sudan, attended by delegates (including physicians, midwives, and health officials) from ten African and Arab nations and supported by many who could not attend. Initiated by the WHO Regional Office for the Eastern Mediterranean with the assistance of the Sudanese government, this meeting was cautiously called a seminar on "Traditional Practices Affecting the Health of Women and Children"—such practices as child marriage, and nutritional taboos during pregnancy and lactation, but also including genital mutilation. Four recommendations resulted:

1. Adoption of clear national policies for the abolition of "female circumcision."
2. Establishment of national commissions to coordinate activities, including the enactment of abolition legislation.
3. Intensification of general education on the dangers and undesirability of the practice.
4. Intensification of general education programs for birth attendants, midwives, healers, and other practitioners of traditional medicine, with a view to enlisting their support.

Later in 1979, a United Nations conference held in Lusaka, Zambia—one of the series of regional preparatory meetings for the United Nations' 1980 World Conference for the Decade for Women—also dealt with the subject. Adopting a resolution sponsored by Edna Adan Ismail of Somalia, the meeting condemned female mutilation and called on all women's organizations *in the countries concerned* "to mobilize information and health-education campaigns on the harmful and social consequences of the practices."

It is also true, however, that genital mutilation is not always cited as a priority by women in developing countries: the elimination of famine, general health, agricultural and industrial development may take precedence. Yet the Khartoum and Lusaka meetings showed clearly that many women, and men of conscience, throughout the African and Arab countries have for a long time been actively opposing clitoridectomy and infibulation. Such groups as the Voltaic Women's Federation and the Somali Women's Democratic Organization, and such individuals as Dr. Fatima Abdul Mahmoud, minister of social affairs of the Sudan, Mehani Saleh of the Aden Ministry of Health, Awa Thiam of Senegal, and Esther Ogunmodede, the crusading journalist of Nigeria, have been campaigning in different ways against genital mutilation, with little international support. In fact, according to Fran P. Hosken, a feminist who for years has been trying to mobilize U.S. and international consciousness on the issue, "International and UN agencies, as well as charitable and church groups and family-planning organizations working in Africa, have engaged in a 'conspiracy of silence.' . . . As a result, those Africans who are working for a change in their own countries have been completely isolated or ignored."

Now, victims and witnesses are beginning to be heard as they speak personally about the suffering inflicted, whether in a village hut, a modern apartment, or a sterile operating room, by genital mutilation—suffering that may continue for a lifetime. Their voices are unforgettable. It's long past time that we heard them and understood what is being done—to them, and to all of us. It's time that we began to act—*with* them, the most immediate victims, and in the shared interest of women as a people.

—*1979*

II

From the
1980s

Blood Types:
An Anatomy of Kin

The prose meditation "Slaves of Form," which constitutes the core of the following essay, was written in 1980, and appeared in the Spring 1981 issue of Maenad, *a fine if short-lived feminist journal published in Boston. The rest of the essay grew from that core, as my thoughts on race and racism led to musings on the family. It must be admitted that I was personally somewhat preoccupied with the subject of "family" at this time, as my marriage was in the process of dissolution; it would end in 1983, after twenty years. As always, writing was at once a means of solace, survival, discipline, and revelation. Furthermore, during this particular period it constituted a right-of-passage challenge: this essay was one of the first prose pieces I wrote largely without benefit of a critique by my then-husband, himself a writer who was a considerable influence over my earlier work. Perhaps most importantly, writing relieved the brain from obsession with immediate crises and coaxed the mind into the service of ideas larger than the self. So my thoughts on family led in turn to exploring redefinitions of kinship in a global context. Eventually the entire piece became a chapter in my book* The Anatomy of Freedom: Feminism, Physics, and Global Politics.*

*(New York: Doubleday / Anchor, 1982).

Since that time, racism in the United States has grown—and grown both more subtle and more blatant; bias crimes abound, and performance "hate comics" spew bigotry with unfunny impunity. The back-to-back Reagan and Bush administrations have effectively gutted government regulations and de-enforced legislation on civil rights and affirmative action—and parts of most large U.S. cities have become zones of poverty, rage, violence, and despair.

Similar governmental attitudes toward what is adoringly referred to by the Right Wing as "the family" have proven the hollowness of presidential rhetoric—and have devastated families. The infant mortality rate in Washington, D.C., and in parts of Chicago and Detroit, is now higher than in Honduras. As of 1989, 60 percent of single-parent families headed by women lived under half the median family income—at less than 49 cents to the dollar. Poverty is the number one killer of children in the United States today and, as writer and activist Theresa Funiciello notes, children are poor because their mothers are poor. This is what is meant, very concretely, by "the feminization of poverty."

Domestic violence is the single largest cause of injury to women in the United States; three to four million women are beaten in their homes each year by their husbands, exhusbands, or male lovers; one out of seven married women is the victim of marital rape; 31 percent of all female homicide victims in 1988 were killed by their husbands or boyfriends; 25 percent of abused women are battered during pregnancy; 55 percent of all female victims of domestic sexual abuse are under the age of eleven. Yet the withdrawal of federal funding for most refuges and shelters continues.

On the international front, the United Nations—after ten years of negotiations—has finally adopted a Convention on the Rights of the Child. But because of pressure by the Vatican (which has Observer Status), certain Muslim

countries, and the United States, the convention's lan-
guage is deliberately vague on abortion, child labor, and
the minimum age for military combat.

In the teeth of all this, feminism persists. And the com-
plex, painful confrontations with racism—both without and
within—continue in the Women's Movement, on more
sophisticated levels and with an intensified commitment to
stripping off all the layers of our defensive masks.

It is enraging that in a nation as wealthy as the United
States, women—the poorest of the poor—bear the burden
of helping one another merely to survive. It is outrageous
that feminist aspirations, creativity, and energy are being
spent "running just to stay in place" instead of being able
to move forward in self-challenge as well as in challenge
to the society. And it is appalling that the government of
the United States can think of no more constructive way
to protect and defend children than by protecting and
defending fetal tissue.

How much more blood must run before the men in power
recognize their own mothers—and before all residents of
this nation recognize each other as their own relatives?

The "traditional" nuclear family has undergone fission. It
really never existed to begin with, despite the Right Wing's
rabid defense of it as the basic building block of society.
Yet even liberals can fall into the trap of heated arguments and analyses about how and why the U.S. family is
"suddenly" changing. Actually, the one permanent quality about the family is that it always has been in a state of
perpetual transformation.

What we think of as the traditional nuclear family is a
recent development. The Norman Rockwell depiction of
the small-town unit (breadwinner husband, homemaker
wife, two and a half children statistically, a cocker span-
iel, one or two cars, a picket fence, washing machine,

and television set) is less than a hundred years old—a newfangled experiment masquerading as the Way It Always Has Been. Anthropology and history reveal a vast repertory of family forms that disappear, reappear, coexist, and differ within and across cultures, including blood relationships, kinship systems, language alliances, loyalty groups, households, tribes, networks, clans, communes, the "stem" family, the "conjugal" family, the "pioneer" family, the "extended" family, exogamous and endogamous families, and many more. Even the so-called American Family was always more various than we are led to believe, exuberantly reflecting different racial, ethnic, class, and religious patterns.

The one common denominator of "family" might be said to be a combination of endurance, affection, resilience, and some bond (economic, philosophical, cultural, or chosen) deliberately acknowledged to be larger than the individual elements participating within it. And the notion of family does in fact persist—and even proliferates, diversifies, and strengthens—despite Rightist campaigns to destroy it by narrowly defining it out of existence, and despite their sexual-fundamentalist and religious-fundamentalist attacks on feminism for having energized and supported precisely such growth and variety.

Ironically, in this case feminists are the conservatives in the true sense of the word: *conserving* the family by permitting it to redefine itself.

The Real American Family

The great tribal forms may be vanishing (in Western culture, that is), but new kinship systems flourish all around us: the breadwinner wife / househusband pioneers, the live-in-lovers relationships, the same-sex lovers household, the colleague family that bonds intensely over shared work, the "serial marriage," the single-parent family, the long-term friend-roommate cathexis, and still other vital and evolving forms:

—Only 15.9 percent of all households include a father as the sole wage earner, a mother as a full-time homemaker, and at least one child. (And a 1977 Yankelovich Monitor study found that one-third of full-time housewives planned to enter the salaried work force at some time in their lives.)

—18.5 percent include both the father and the mother as wage earners, plus one or more children at home.

—30.5 percent of households consist of married couples with no children living at home.

—6.2 percent are headed by women who are single parents, with one or more children at home.

—0.6 percent are headed by single-parent males, with one or more children at home.

—2.5 percent consist of unrelated persons living together.

—20.6 percent are single-person households. (Of these, almost a third are women over age sixty-five, more than a third of whom live below the federal poverty level.)

—The remaining 5.3 percent consist of female- or male-headed households that include relatives other than spouses or children.

The statistics are from the *U.S. Statistical Abstract*, 1977.* Children are defined as persons under eighteen years of age. *The government's definition of family does not include*

*As of 1991, these statistics had become even more dramatic: Only 8 percent of all households now include a father as sole wage earner; 26.2 percent now include both mother and father as wage earners; 29.8 percent of households consist of married couples with no children living at home; 20.4 percent are headed by women who are single parents with one or more children at home; 3.6 percent are headed by single-parent males; 4.6 percent consist of unrelated persons living together; 24.6 percent are single-person households (of these, 31.4 percent are women over age sixty-five—42 percent of whom live well below the poverty level); and 6.5 percent (of which 1.9 percent is male and 4.6 is female) consist of households that include relatives other than spouses or children.

single individuals or unrelated individuals living together.
A feminist definition of family does. Therefore, "households" is the basis of the above analysis.

Recent changes in the family have been effected not
only by women's desires to enter the public world, and
by men's desires (not always as openly acknowledged) to
participate more in the raising of children, but also by
automation, a shorter workday or workweek, more lei-
sure time (at least for men), chronic unemployment, the
part-time job as necessity or option, etc.

What the U.S. Right Wing, as a "family fundamentalist"
movement, is trying to protect now exists even less than
ever before. To the extent that their ideal nuclear unit—
as the central cog in the mechanistic machine they view
as society—ever did exist, its very qualities of isolated
defensiveness gave rise to intimate atrocities that were
denied and hidden, or sometimes even hideously affirmed.
In the United States, only in the last decade or so have
true statistics begun to emerge about the almost epidemic frequency of battery, marital rape, child abuse and
sexual molestation, and other scarring emotional "traditions" prevalent in the apple-cheeked normality of the
nuclear family—in all classes, economic groups, and
racial, religious, and ethnic categories.

The proliferation of articles, studies, books, and entire
scholarly journals on the issue of family violence is
uncovering statistics that, although sufficiently horrifying in themselves, still are only prefaces to the full story.
It is estimated that *between 50 and 80 percent of the cases
of family violence still go unreported.*

Have such discoveries helped the family fundamentalists to stop and rethink what it is they are so passionately
defending? Yes and no. They stopped, tried to chafe two
brain cells together to produce a ratiocinative thought,
and came up with more antilogic. Phyllis Schlafly opposes
federal funding of shelters for battered women because

such shelters are merely "resorts for wives running away from their responsibilities"; Christian "crusaders" attack legislation outlawing corporal punishment in the public schools, and also defend "the rod" as parental discipline at home; the Rightist coalition currently influencing the White House "family policy" lobbies against federal backing of refuges for and research on the survivors of child sexual abuse. Clearly, such research and such refuges "invade the privacy of the family" (the subtext reads that such legislation, research, and support networks invade the power of the *patriarch*).

Yet despite all the campaigns in the United States and Europe to preserve family "privacy," or in the Middle East and Latin Catholic countries to preserve family "honor," and in Asia to preserve family "duty"—despite all attempts to tighten familial bonds into ropes of bondage, family forms continue to change and grow, like living organisms: through *interaction* and in *context of the whole*. That "whole" has something to do with human need—for warmth, intimacy, endurance, trust, a shared history.

The Passionate Reflection

Dorothy Dinnerstein* has said that the family is both a teaching structure (to the infant) and a support system, in that it instructs us in the skill of living amicably (or at least cooperatively) with others—an irreplaceably humanizing experience:

> Certain aspects of the need for family are so profound that people invent deities with parental qualities to whom they can be related throughout life.... People can find all sorts of "magic parents" in adult life—in spiritual entities, in friends,

*Psychologist and author of *The Mermaid and the Minotaur: Sexual Arrangements and Human Malaise* (New York: Harper and Row, 1976).

in sex partners, and in themselves . . . [the magic parent being]
a nurturant presence from whom one can learn, and also
giving a sense of another existence in which one's own is
passionately reflected.*

Dinnerstein is dedicated, not coincidentally, to the idea
that *men* must learn how to act as such parents: "The
major thing men can do is child care. This would pro-
foundly alter all gender arrangements." The comparable
big step for women would be to *let* men do this, despite
our sometimes understandable unwillingness to relin-
quish the one little area of power we've been allowed.
The issue is central because in any society where the
person who takes care of the next generation is female
(and seems to have life-and-death power over day-to-day
existence, however little objective power she has), then
the female becomes the scapegoat, in Dinnerstein's words,
leaving "another category of human being (male) who by
contrast burns clean and pure and is just plain human. . . .
When men take an equal part in child care, men will no
longer represent uncontaminated humanity."

"Uncontaminated humanity" is obviously a mechanistic notion—a spotless, dry, everything-in-its-place
universe where some cosmic Mussolini makes the galaxies run on time. But of course the galaxies don't, just
as human beings don't, just as atoms don't. And atoms—
once thought to be *the* building blocks of the universe,
are now known to contain *their* building blocks—electrons, protons, and neutrons—which in turn are subject
to further change into hundreds of various types of
unstable (shocking concept to the Right Wing: "unstable")
particles, which in turn are postulated to contain quarks,
partons, or hadrons, which in turn . . . Just so the family,
whether "nuclear" or extended, "traditional" or sponta-

*"The Changeless Need: A Conversation Between Dorothy Dinnerstein
and Robin Morgan," *Ms.*, August 1978.

neous, is comprised of individual beings, each a universe in her / himself, composed in turn of a billion variables of need, change, environment, growth, desire, curiosity, miracle, *movement.*

As long as "family" is degraded by being used as a means to differentiate an Us from a Them, or to define and constrain the individual capacities of those who constitute it, or to fix itself in a permanent state, location, or attitude—then "family" is doomed to destroy its own components and ultimately itself, because it is in fact *going against what we now know to be "nature":*

> The key features of the quantum theory that challenge mechanism are:
>
> 1. Movement is in general *discontinuous,* in the sense that action is constituted of indivisible quanta (... an electron, for example, can go from one state to another without passing through any states in between).
>
> 2. Entities, such as electrons, can show different properties ... depending on the environmental context within which they exist and are subject to observation.
>
> 3. Two entities, such as electrons, which initially combine to form a molecule and then separate, show a peculiar non-local relationship, which can best be described as a non-casual connection of elements that are far apart.*

A Family Reunion

If politics is to learn from the New Physics—and it would benefit enormously from doing so—then we might realize that just as in the subatomic world *an entity can be both a particle and a wave at the same time,* so "family" can be both an intimate grouping and a universal net-

*David Böhm, *Wholeness and the Implicate Order* (London: Routledge & Kegan Paul, 1980), pp. 174–75.

work at the same time. Abstract and sappy pronouncements about "brotherhood" and "the family of Man" have as much relevance in this context as Billy Graham's definition of god has in the context of NGC4258 (M106)—a galaxy with an "exploding" nucleus (just like the family) in the Canes Venatici I Cloud of galaxies. Plastic "brotherhood" comes to us from the same folks who brought us Auschwitz, Hiroshima, and South Africa, and before that, the Crusades, the "conquest" of the New World, the slave trade.

Naturally, if the brotherly definition of family has an Us *vs.* Them implication then family as a matter of course transfers its isolate loyalties into nationalism. Not for nothing does the word *patriotism* stem from the meaning of loyalty to father authority.

Yet there *are* glimpses of a real universal family, a community already connected and potentially interconnecting via the very persons whose entire existences, for the most part, have been kept within the "family sphere," those defined by stereotypical Man and affirmed by stereotypical Woman as the eternal nurturers, the keepers of the family: women.

Mary Daly's turn-the-concept-inside-out phrase, "The Sisterhood of Man" seems not only a hope but a dynamic actuality—since it's grounded not in abstract notions of cooperation but in survival need, not in static posture but in active gesture, not in vague statements of similarity but in concrete experience shared to an astonishing degree, despite cultural, historical, linguistic, and other barriers. Labor contractions feel the same everywhere. So does rape and battery. I don't necessarily always agree with many feminists that women have access to some mysteriously inherent biological nexus, but I do believe that Elizabeth Cady Stanton was onto something when she signed letters, "Thine in the bonds of *oppressed* womanhood" (italics mine). Let us hope—and act to ensure—that as women break those bonds of oppression, the process of freeing the majority of humanity will so transform human consciousness that women will not use our freedom to be isolatedly individuated as men have done. In the meanwhile, the bonds do exist; let's use them creatively.

Not that the mechanistic universe inhabited by the family of Man takes notice of this quarky interrelationship between the hardly visible subparticles that merely serve to keep Man and his [sic] family alive. No, such particles are unimportant, fantastical, charming perhaps (as quarks or "the fair sex" tend to be). But they are to be taken no more seriously than fairytales.

Yet if Hans Christian Andersen characters so diverse as the Little Mermaid, the Robber Girl, the Snow Queen, and the Little Match Girl had convened a meeting to discuss ways of bettering their condition, one could imagine that the world press would cover that as a big story. When something even more extraordinary, because more real, happened in Andersen's own city for three weeks during July 1980, it barely made the news.

Approximately ten thousand women from all over the planet began arriving in Copenhagen, Denmark, even before the formal opening on July 14 of the United Nations Mid-Decade World Conference for women. The conference was to become a great, sprawling, rollicking, sometimes quarrelsome, highly emotional, unashamedly idealistic, unabashedly pragmatic, visionary family reunion. In 1975, the U.N. had voted to pay some attention to the female more-than-half of the human population for one year—International Women's Year—but extended the time to a decade after the indignant outcry of women who had been living, literally, in the "International Men's Year" for approximately ten millennia of patriarchy. Still, here we were, in the middle of "our" decade, in Copenhagen. We came in saris and caftans, in blue jeans and chadors, in African geles, pants-suits, and dresses. We were women with different priorities, ideologies, political analyses, cultural backgrounds, and styles of communication. The few reports that made it into the U.S. press predictably emphasized those differences, thereby overlooking the big story—that these women forged new and strong connections.

There were two overlapping meetings in Copenhagen. One was the official U.N. conference—which many feminists accurately had prophesied would be more a meeting of governments than of women. Its delegates were chosen by governments of U.N. member states to psittaceously repeat national priorities—as defined by men.

The official conference reflected the government orientation: many delegations were headed by men and many more were led by "safe" women whose governments were certain wouldn't make waves. This is not to say that there weren't some real feminists tucked away even in the formal delegations, trying gallantly to influence their respective bureaucracies toward more human concern with actions that really could better women's lives. But the talents of these sisters "within" were frequently ignored or abused by their own delegations for political reasons.

A case in point was the U.S. delegation, which availed itself greedily of all the brilliant and unique expertise of Koryne Horbal (then U.S. representative to the U.N. Commission on the Status of Women), and of all the groundwork she had done on the conference for the preceding two years—including being the architect of CEDAW, the Convention to Eliminate All Forms of Discrimination Against Women—but denied her press visibility and most simple courtesies because she had been critical of the Carter administration and its official policies on women. But Horbal wasn't the only "feminist within." There were New Zealand's member of parliament, the dynamic twenty-eight-year-old Marilyn Waring, and good-humored Maria de Lourdes Pintasilgo, former prime minister of Portugal, and clever Elizabeth Reid of Australia—all of them feminists skilled in the labyrinthian ways of national and international politics, but with priority commitment to populist means of working for women—who still managed to be effective inside *and* outside the structures of their governments.

The "other" conference, semiofficially under U.N. aegis, was the NGO (Non-Governmental Organizations) Forum. It was to the Forum that "ordinary folks" came, having raised the travel fare via their local women's organizations, feminist alternative media, or women's religious, health, and community groups. Panels, workshops, kaffeeklatsches, cultural events, and informal sessions abounded.

Statements emerged and petitions were eagerly signed: supporting the prostitutes in São Paulo, Brazil, who that very week, in an attempt to organize for their human rights, were being jailed, tortured, and, in one case, "accidently" executed; supporting Arab and African women organizing against the practice of female genital mutilation; supporting U.S. women recently stunned by the 1980 Supreme Court decision permitting federal and state denial of funds for medical aid to poor women who need safe, legal abortions—thus denying the basic human right of reproductive freedom; supporting South African women trying to keep families together under the maniacal system of apartheid; supporting newly exiled feminist writers and activists from the U.S.S.R.; supporting women refugees from Afghanistan, Campuchea, [Cambodia], Palestine, Cuba, and elsewhere.

Protocol aside, the excitement among women at both conference sites was electric. If, for instance, you came from Senegal with a specific concern about rural development, you would focus on workshops about that, and exchange experiences and how-to's with women from Peru, India—and Montana. After one health panel, a Chinese gynecologist continued talking animatedly with her scientific colleague from the Soviet Union—Sino-Soviet saber rattling forgotten or transcended.

Comparisons developed in workshops on banking and credit between European and U.S. economists and the influential market women of Africa. The list of planned meetings about Women's Studies ran to three pages, yet additional workshops on the subject were created spontaneously. Meanwhile, at the International Women's Art Festival, there was a sharing of films, plays, poetry readings, concerts, mime shows, exhibits of painting and sculpture and batik and weaving, the interchanging of art techniques and of survival techniques. Exchange subscriptions were pledged between feminist magazines in New Delhi and Boston and Tokyo, Maryland and Sri Lanka and Australia. And everywhere the conversations and laughter of recognition and newfound friendships spilled over into the sidewalks of Copenhagen, often until dawn.

We ate, snacked, munched—and traded diets—like neighbor women, or family. A well-equipped Argentinian supplied a shy Korean with a tampon in an emergency. A Canadian went into labor a week earlier than she'd expected, and kept laughing hilariously between her contractions, as she was barraged with loving advice on how to breathe, where to rub, how to sit (or stand or squat), and even what to sing—in a chorus of five languages, while waiting for the prompt Danish ambulance. North American women from diverse ethnic ancestries talked intimately with women who still lived in the cities, towns, and villages from which their own grandmothers had emigrated to "the New World." We slept little, stopped caring about washing our hair, sat on the floor, and felt at home with one another.

Certainly, there were problems. Simultaneous-translation facilities, present everywhere at the official conference, were rarely available at the grass-roots forum. This exacerbated certain sore spots, like the much-ballyhooed Palestinian-Israeli conflict, since many Arab women present spoke Arabic or French but not English—the dominant language at the forum. That conflict—played out by male leadership at both the official conference and the forum, using women as pawns in the game—was disheartening, but not as bad as many of us had feared.

The widely reported "walkout" of Arab women during Madame Jihan Sadat's* speech at the conference was actually a group of perhaps twenty women tiptoeing quietly to the exit. This took place in a huge room packed with delegates who—during all the speeches—were sitting, standing, and walking about to lobby loudly as if on the floor of the U.S. Congress (no one actually *listens* to the speeches; they're for the record).

Meanwhile, back at the forum, there was our own invaluable former U.S. congresswoman Bella Abzug (officially unrecognized by the Carter-appointed delegation but recognized and greeted with love by women from all over the world). Bella, working on coalition building, was shuttling between Israelis and Arabs. At that time, Iran was still holding the fifty-two U.S. hostages, but Bella accomplished the major miracle of getting a pledge from the Iranian women that if U.S. mothers would demonstrate in Washington for the shah's ill-gotten millions to be returned to the Iranian people (for the fight against women's illiteracy and children's malnutrition), then the Iranian women would march simultaneously in Teheran for the hostages to be returned home "to their mothers."**

*Wife of then President of Egypt Anwar Sadat—who had recently recognized Israel.

**The women's agreement was successfully sabotaged by their respective patriarchal governments.

Bella's sensitivity and cheerful, persistent nudging on this issue caused one Iranian woman to throw up her hands, shrug, and laugh to me, "What is with this 'Bella honey' person? She's wonderful. She's impossible. She's just like my mother."

The conference, the forum, and the arts festival finally came to an end. Most of the official resolutions were predictably bland by the time they were presented, much less voted on. Most of the governments will act on them sparingly, if at all. Consequently, those women who went naively trusting that the formal U.N. procedures would be drastically altered by such a conference were bitterly disappointed. But those of us who went with no such illusions, and who put not our trust in patriarchs, were elated. Because what did *not* end at the closing sessions is that incredible "networking"—the echoes of all those conversations, the exchanged addresses—and what that will continue to accomplish.

One goal, for example, was to strengthen mechanisms for implementation of the U.N.'s Convention to Eliminate All Forms of Discrimination Against Women (CEDAW). Another was to activate, through programs of political pressure, diplomatic channels, and economic aid, the language Marilyn Waring managed to insert, via the New Zealand delegation, into the official proceedings—language which for the first time in a U.N. document made the feminist analogy of women as a colonized people. By the *end* of the "Women's Decade," we can all look for substantive change within and in response to the "The Family of Women."*

---

*The 1986 World Women's Conference, five years later in Nairobi, Kenya, was an even greater triumph for international feminism. More than 17,000 women attended, in large part from the Third World and the African continent itself. By this time, it was becoming difficult for even the most stubborn male supremacist to claim that "only Western women" were interested in feminism.

Yet we might have to look hard, if our own government and our own free press still are so tediously androcentric that we can't get the word out. Isn't it a big story when an Iraqi refugee tells an American Jewish feminist that her eleven-year-old son has just been sentenced to five years at hard labor by the Saddam Hussein regime, and the American replies, "My God, my son is just that age," and both women weep quietly in each other's embrace? Isn't it a good story when a woman from Zambia trades secrets with another from Iceland and a third from Portugal on how to endure—and be effective without losing your soul—when you are the token woman in your ministry / parliament / government / embassy?

But this was not just a fairytale. It was a family reunion: the trading of old secrets and newfound skills, the latest gossip about other members, the surprised delight in discovering relatives so long lost they had never been encountered, the *recognitions,* dynamism, and grudging love.

And this was only a beginning. "If all actions are in the form of discrete quanta, the interactions between different entities [e.g., electrons] constitute a single structure of indivisible links, so that the entire universe has to be thought of as an unbroken whole." Or a family not only of human beings but of all sentient beings, of all matter, which is really all energy—what David Böhm calls "a totality of movement of enfoldment and unfoldment ... [a] holomovement."*

This requires what I would call a *holopolitics:* a way of looking outward and inward at the same time (as if there really were a difference), of seeing and seeing *through.* Processes of creativity, of art, express this tendency; processes of power oppose it. (Yet art can be "empowering" in an utterly nonoppressive way.)

*Böhm, *op cit,* p. 175 and 178.

If we could learn to apply truly creative processes, as an artist does, to political problems, what might the result be? It isn't as easy as it sounds, since art is—like the electron—both an intensely individualistic and a holistically interconnected activity. But let's try. In fact, let's try to apply the process to a particular political knot that fists itself at the heart of the U.S. experience of "family," however much ignored and denied: the knot of race and sex.

A Skin-Deep Sisterhood?

How do we penetrate the superficiality with which most feminist theory in the United States has so far dealt with racism, even in terms of the largest U.S. "minority," African Americans? This superficiality includes the recent black-white feminist "dialogues" that pop up in print in various places. However important and courageous these attempts, they seem—to many of us, black and white, who first came to political activism years ago in the civil rights movement—familiar, redundant, and shallow. They are still plagued with debilitating rhetoric, and for the most part remain safely mired in the tone of black accusation and rage (however justified) and white breast-beating guilt (however inevitable as a first step). Unless we go beyond these convenient stances, the U.S. Feminist Movement will remain as comfortably racist as the U.S. Left always has been.

Guilt politics per se is a convenient politics: its logical end, if untransformed into hard thinking and action, is paralysis. Paralysis will not stop the double whammy of "dominative" and "aversive" racism, to use Joel Kovel's terms from his book *White Racism: A Psychohistory.** (Kovel analyzes dominative racism as being woven through the

*(New York: Pantheon, 1970).

fabric of society in the U.S. South—an active racism that served as a foundation for the entire social and economic organization of the culture; aversive racism is, Kovel feels, more characteristic of the North—a passive-aggressive sort of racism that gives lip service to equality but keeps black citizens in servitude by exclusion—from jobs, schools, neighborhoods, social congress.) *Within* and in addition to the oppression of race, women of course still suffer the oppression of sex, as searingly demonstrated in a number of major books published in the past decade on the subject.*

As of 1980, almost 60 percent of all rape victims were black women; black women—52 percent of whom work outside the home—have a median income of only $6,611; their cervical cancer rates are increasing, while rates are decreasing among whites; black women also suffer the highest mortality rates from both childbirth and abortion; their children suffer infant mortality rates twice as high as those of whites.

Meanwhile, back at the Women's Movement, the "aversive" form of racism still smiles its ladylike politeness far too often for comfort. It is not enough for white women to say any longer that we "dare" not include the experience, literary influence, and consciousness of black women and other women of color in our work, since we do not "share" that experience. (I never hunted a great whale or fought Napoleon, never worked as a nineteenth-century governess or rafted down the Mississippi River—but that doesn't stop me from identifying with the writings of Melville, Tolstoy, the Brontës, or Mark Twain.) No, this has become a new excuse for excluding black women's experience (for fear of similarities even more than of differences?). Nor is it any longer tolerable for

*See, for example, works by Michele Wallace, Toni Cade, Audre Lorde, Barbara Smith, Toni Morrison, bell hooks, Mary Helen Washington, Alice Walker, Patricia J. Williams, and a host of others.

white feminists to ghettoize black feminists in special panels (as happened, appallingly, at the Second Sex Conference in New York City as late as 1979) under the convenient, patronizing excuse that to invite black women's involvement at every level of the conference, in every panel and at every workshop, would be to divert their energies from black priorities.

I for one, as a white woman and feminist, am sick to death of solemnly pretentious papers, conferences, books, articles, and so-called dialogues that rehash old positions without the risk of fresh thinking, and of self-perpetuating conversations between black and white feminists that end with the pronouncement, "We must open up communication between us"—after which the black women and the white women go their separate ways.

I'm impatient, yes. These Things Take Time, yes. Being stuck in the meaningless pinkish-orange sausage casement that is my skin at a time in history when this is considered meaningful, I realize that it is for black feminists to determine their own priorities and tactics, yes. But it is for white feminists to begin to take some real—not rhetorical—risks, in theory, in commitment, in action. Not for suspiciously Lady Bountiful reasons, but for our own moral salvation.

The following meditation is only a beginning, flawed and certainly insufficient, toward that risk. It was inspired in large part by two books: *Thomas Jefferson: An Intimate History,* by Fawn Brodie,* and *Sally Hemmings,* by Barbara Chase-Riboud.**

Keep in mind, as you read, how quantum theory demonstrates that all motion takes place not smoothly but in a disjointed, discontinuous fashion—jumping with what seems to be no effort from one place to another without

*(New York: Bantam, 1971).
**(New York: Viking Press, 1979, and Avon paperback, 1980).

bothering to travel between the places. Keep in mind, too, the Döppler effect: the phenomenon of light changing color—depending on the perspective and speed of the observer.

Slaves of Form: A Meditation on Race, Sex, Power, and Art

The "shadow family" of Thomas Jefferson is exemplary of the deepest truths about U.S. racism—the horror being not solely what whites did to blacks but *what relatives did to their own families.* Where does this entire vast panoply of interrelationships (complete with a baroque hierarchy of how many crossbreedings were necessary to "clear the blood") fit into a history of the family? Or is a "shadow history" necessary to contain it—this common assumption that a plantation owner had two "families": one slave, one white. The plot thins as the blood thickens.

■

Thomas Jefferson Hemmings, age fourteen, slave son with blue eyes and red hair and freckles, tall and gangling, the image of his father, standing as body servant behind the chair of Thomas Jefferson Randolph, age about the same, same coloring, same characteristics of appearance, grandson legal—looking like a possible set of twins. *What does this do to the mind, the sense of reality,* the reality of Jeffersonian politics, possibly the one trustable democratic tradition in the United States?

■

What does it mean: that Thomas Jefferson could seek the same woman in the features of his white legal wife Martha Wayles (dead at age thirty-four after seven pregnancies) and his illegal whiteblack blackwhite continually recategorized slave wife, mistress, concubine, Sally

Hemmings, *Martha Wayles' half sister?* This was his own sister-in-law—except that she was, fortunately, out-of-law.

■

What does it mean: that Dolley Madison could say in 1837: "The Southern white woman is the chief slave of the master's harem?" And leave it at that. What does it mean: to know and not act, to know and know that action is impossible—and yet not act?

■

Power is after all not a quantity to be taken, shared, divided. Power is a *means:* of defining, categorizing, compartmentalizing—relationships, people, "things"; a means of naming, even more than of accomplishing. It goes to the most basic definition of what something is or is not, by categorizing it through what it *does.* Thus we know a stone from a peculiar cactus that appears identical to a stone because the stone sits there; the cactus grows, changes. The characteristics of something are what it does, how it exists, is, *be's.* What it does and what it is are at the deepest level inseparable, and power, which is literally in the eye of the beholder (the one who can observe) knows this. Power rightly used, then, is that which begins with respecting *what the beheld is as expressed in what it does.* Power abused is that which forces certain behavior from the beheld and then judges its characteristics backward from that doing.

Would power be abusive that witnessed the *is* in the *does,* without judging or forcing anything, then defining backward what the is is? *Is* there a witnessing without defining? Would such a definition be merely stereotypical—or truly fair?

Is the act of defining *in itself* a judgment? Is the act of categorizing in itself ultimately not the abuse? No matter how many "but equal's" accompany the deadly "separate?" If the inert stone is, as we know, composed of atoms and in turn electrons in their dance of energy over / into /

in / *as* matter, then what is so "inert" about the stone, after all? It takes holopolitics to perceive holomovement.

Or is categorizing merely a recognition of life's celebratory variations-in-form of the same basic energy?

> It is a natural tendency for genetically unrelated cells in tissue cultures to come together, ignoring species differences, and fuse to form hybrid cells. Inflammation and immunology must indeed be powerfully designed to keep us apart; without such mechanisms, involving considerable effort, we might have developed as a kind of flowing syncytium over the earth, without the morphogenesis of even a flower.*

Still, even if life itself categorizes and compartmentalizes—thus expressing the most basic defining, the most ongoing power—need we collaborate with this fundamentalism or dare we transcend it? How far could holopolitical vision read? Dare it even see death not as the great equalizer opposed to that compulsive and divisive life, but refuse both and forge some third state, beyond either?

That would be the invention of a new state of consciousness so powerful it would inevitably create a new state of reality—or else recognize, at last, that such a state has never not existed.

■

Sally Hemmings haunts—America, Jefferson, me. And Jefferson was one of the best, perhaps *the* best of the founding "fathers." No Alexander Hamilton he, oh no. Hamilton, rumored to be part black, must express the essentially aristocratic conservative position—to survive, of course. Not Jefferson. No, he staked his life on the belief that the individual soul needs freedom and can tolerate that responsibility, no matter what. [Jefferson fought to insert an antislavery clause into the Declaration, but

*Lewis Thomas, *The Lives of a Cell: Notes of a Biology Watcher* (New York: Bantam, 1975), p. 10.

eventually compromised under pressure and withdrew it.] He staked Sally Hemmings's soul on it, too. But he never asked her permission to do so, first.

Or perhaps he did—and perhaps she said no.

Or perhaps he did—and he forgot what she replied.

Or perhaps it was her idea in the first place, but he didn't note that, being above the petty details of owner-ship.

■

And they dare, they *dare* to speak of the sanctity of the family. They dare claim reverence for blood ties.

O my America, there is blood on your hands—and you don't even recognize it as your own.

You do not exist, white America. The agony you have created for others is real—but has always been to con-vince yourself as well as those in agony that the illusion of your existence was *as* real; that light did not move or change color when it seemed to move. You have never existed, white America. You are a figment of your own brain, which has settled for a petty uncreative imagining. You are a figment of the brains and souls and bodies you *have* lynched and tortured, raped and sold and murdered and denied, starved and whipped—who for sanity's sake had to believe that their torturer was as real as their pain. The blood on your hands, white America, is your own.

■

How easily that realization (that we have disowned ourselves) could be mistaken for expiation. How conve-nient an excuse not to make up for shedding blood that, after all, is "just" our own. What a reassuringly false equation that would be, denying any difference between our experience and the suffering of others caused *by* our experience. No, no, the difference must be seen, recog-nized, understood, expiated, precisely because its most hideous characteristic is to deny and erase as many sweet, hopeful traces of our mutual salvation as possible: life that we hold "in common," however variously we live it.

Camus was correct in calling suicide the only sin. War, murder, all the other -*cides* are cowardly stalling actions that delude the individual, group, society, species, into thinking *he / she / it / them / us / we* are not about the real business of destroying ourself.

But then what will we call Them?

Ah.

The powerless need to imagine Them in order not to identify with *their / our* own destruction of ourself. But then, but then, once there is a Them . . .

■

The reason energy is power is that it *is* the Doing, the movement, the holomovement. For me, "Being"—particularly as an institution—remains a sophomoric expression of the lethal patriarchal philosophical tradition, one especially reactionary where women are concerned, since women have been defined *as* passively existent for rather too long.

■

Does the stone define itself? (Why should it tell us? Why should it tell us especially if we're not listening?)

If activity, existing, defining, are the same at heart, if somatic tissue knows itself different from genetic tissue, if the cactus understands the reasons for its camouflage as a stone but grows nonetheless, then power is not ultimately in the eye of the beholder, *but in the choice of the activity of the beheld.*

Or is it in the beholding of that choice, by either the beheld or the beholder? How can the one exist without the other?

■

Light moves as both particles and wave, but reaches the retina as a discrete, individuated photon.

If individuation is the piston of life, then racism and sexism are no surprise. Because *the deepest fear would be, not as we have thought politically, of the Other, but of the Same.* The terror of the moment when the somatic cell does not know itself as different from the genetic cell, the stone from the cactus. The holoconsciousness. An utterly alien reality. How that terror puts into perspective the mere fears that white and black, male and female, are deeply different!

■■■

Jefferson disowned his slave children not because they were "black"—which by his own racial structure of insanely pedantic blood charts they weren't. He disowned them because he would not cease owning them, that is, because they were slaves. Yet white slaves were unheard of. "If God is God he is not good; if God is good he is not God." If you are white, you are not a slave; if you are a slave, you are not white. Whiteness (or sameness) could not coexist with slavery in the same person. If you are female you are not Man; if you are human, you are not a slave. Yet Dolley Madison knew . . .

Jefferson's slave children, then, were unacknowledged not because they were different but because they were so the same. The terror of this truth (Mark Twain's truth in *Pudd'nhead Wilson*) has been diluted and distorted by the fundamentalist fakeries of brotherhood, kin-under-the-skin, the melting pot, Disneyan Christian all-one-ism. Such pap can be mouthed sentimentally without anyone believing it, because its hypocrisy keeps safe the lived-by truths of continual ceaseless ongoing compartmentalization—the real delights *therein,* the real griefs *therein.* It also keeps safe the even more chthonic dreamed-of (in nightmare) truths: that there are no such things as identity, choice, uniqueness, ego. No inert stone? No "reality"?

■■■

If I am not you, then I must be her or him. If not any of these, then I must be: I. The first thing the infant learns.

■

At least the snowflake is in innocence of its individuation, thereby achieving a kind of negation of it. Yet it *is* unique. (For what purpose, if not realized, though? For the entertainment and illusion of the observer? Yet who has or can observe every snowflake's uniqueness?) There is a negation of individuation, certainly, when the snowflake lands and melts. Is this already in process even in midfall? Why can't we imagine communism as a society not of ants but of snowflakes? Is it because communism did not imagine *itself* in that way? Does the result always bear the imprint of its beginning?

■

Isn't it enough to *be* individuated? Must each individuated thing realize that, too? *Does* each? Or does the cactus but not the stone? Dangerous thinking, that: the white says "I do" but assumes that the black doesn't. The man says "I do" but assumes that women don't. (The quarks and hadrons in each and all just laugh.) Those in power always speak of humanism—and accuse those who have been made powerless and categorized as "Other" of divisiveness. This is done, however, only when the powerless recognize and name their already divided state, and begin to articulate their longing—for union.

The fear is *not* that we are different. The fear is that we are the same.

Civilization has been at once a process of seeking similarities in sentience while creating greater and more elaborate means of differentiation, in wider, more specified, more diverse experiences, variations, forms—all ostensibly in order to better express similarity. Or is that evolution—and has civilization actually opposed it?

■

The lie of the inner and the outer. The lie of kin-beneath-the-skin when we are really saying that we are trying to deny something more fearful: being kin above /

in / at / over / through the skin. Being kin, period. This was Jefferson's lie. His hypocrisy was built on this.

■

Age as category is central here, because if one exists long enough, the mere transition from young to old exposes the lie of differentness in a way we can otherwise more conveniently escape (appearance, or differences of sex or race). We still try: "It's impossible to imagine him ever being young"; "I can't see her as old somehow." Yet as one lives, the lesson is painfully engraved as if by Kafka's harrow on the flesh itself, or rather is painfully sensed in the contradiction between that external garb and the internal cry: *But I'm still the same inside here!* It is our own shadows that precede and follow us—but only when we stand in the light.

■

Existence, or at least "civilized" existence, seems to be a story of sentient life ricocheting between alternate terrors: the fear of being utterly alone, the fear of being totally absorbed. Society, politics, history itself, is nothing but an attempt to reconcile and balance those two fears.

■

If I am not myself, then I must be you. If neither of these, then I must be him. Or her. The first thing the oppressed learn, the basic lesson for enslaving.

■

If I am not you, or myself, or him or her, then I must be nothing. The lesson of the mad.

■

If I am not her, or you, or him, or myself, then I must be each of these in turn, and in fragments. The lesson of the alien.

■

If I am not myself, or you, or her or him, then I must be all of these at once, and whole. The lesson of the saint (or the true revolutionary).

▄

Boundaries, corners, demarcations, grids, maps, endings, zonings, borders. Overflows, spills, run-ons, obliterations, floods, rushes, *the dark,* circles.

Paths delude us into thinking we are not lost.
Art is the map. But remember that "the map is not the territory."*

▄

All art is the tension expressed between the uncontainable and its one perfect inevitable form.

All art is the tension expressed between what is uncontainable and the one structure inevitable for revealing its (un)containability.

The structure, of course, varies with time, place, custom, culture, available tools, and which part(s) of the uncontainable content it is inevitably meant to inexpressibly express. (Which of course makes it harder to recognize.)

▄

Each sentient being: one of life's *objets d'art.* How amusing for the maker, and what hell for the clay. For the slave, the cactus, the man, the master, the stone, the woman, the infant, the mad, the vase, the saint. Unless (as Graham Greene almost hazarded) all of us are evolving to consciousness, Galatea-ing in some collective sense—the snowflake becoming conscious without somehow falling thereby—and will turn and stretch all these somatic cells to face the maker, in so *becoming* the maker, becoming genetic, matter comprehending that it *is* energy, the revolution against a divine dictatorship, seizing not merely power but divinity: the succulent stone, the identical spectrum of rosebrown fleshfolds of every labial surface, the recognition . . .

*Alfred Korzybski, *Science and Sanity* (Lakeville, CT: International Non-Aristotelian Library, 1958).

That would mean Jefferson not separating his one sis-troid wife into two in order to keep his reputation, thereby keeping his power (to use of course for the democratic salvation of his country against the evil men who would destroy the perfection of such ideals—like the fatal flaw of Arthur Dimmesdale in *The Scarlet Letter,* calling one's own acts of cowardice, compromise, and evil "sacrifice to a higher good").

What if, instead, our Jefferson had dared disclose, enfold, embrace, unfold, truly "own" (up to) this, thus refusing to "own" anyone and thus refusing to become precisely one of those evil men he claimed to be fight-ing—thus actually possibly really saving the soul of his country. What if?

Why not? Would it be so much more unamusing for the maker? Is that the flaw the maker has thrown into each of us when we are spinning still on the wheel—the trick that prevents each from *becoming* the maker? The whisper: How do you know you're alive, then? The fear addressed by the Zen kōan "Come in, all that is outside"; the fear addressed by Lao-tzu's "All is in order, let every-thing come; all is in chaos, let everything go"; the fear addressed by Wallace Stevens in his poem "Connoisseur of Chaos": "*A.* A violent order is disorder; and / *B.* A great disorder is an order." The fear of realizing that one is already lost utterly, that one may or may not be: alive, male, master, snowflake or cactus or stone. The lie that illusion and reality are different. The lie that illusion and reality are the same.

How to reconcile all this then with realizing that rac-ism and sexism simply could be speedwritten as: Hate generalizes, love specifies. Or: The movements of hatred are toward generalization; love's movements are toward specification.

The blood on my hands is my own. (Old news to whoever shed it.)

Certainly that's true, on the obvious level: anything as a group—blacks, whites, women, men, succulents, frozen water, slaves, masters, even light—instantly misrepresents what characterizes its component individual elements (the uncontainable content) by an *un*-inevitable structure (bad art, bigotry, indiscriminate discrimination).

It is the individuated uniqueness of one polished pebble, of the story of Sally Hemmings's life, of my own thought-pattern shorthand intimacies with my inner ear, of the blurred outlines of a particular woman's signature, her specific patterns of grief and madness, not her femaleness, or her blackness—these constitute something like love. It is the particular form of one's struggle and love that constitutes one's unique strength, just as it is the general traits, conformities, societal greeds and deceits each of us falls into sharing with others that endanger us. My white racism I hold in common with all whites; only to the degree that I disassociate myself from it can I become more—not less—myself.

I now know, too, that my only hope for fighting my own white racism is, at least at this moment in history, in a context with *women* of other so-called racial groups. This knowledge has been earned slowly and painfully—after years in the civil rights movement and the New Left, years of trying to differentiate between my race guilt and my inculcated deference toward men (of color, in this case): Was I making reparations as a white, or being obsequious as a woman? Were the advantages taken and the power muscles being flexed signs of properly correcting the previously existing *racial* imbalance, or were they reaffirmations of the endemic *male-female* power imbalance, now reinforced by minority men's focus on "manhood"? (In the midst of all this tangle, of course, black women suffered between the sexism of black men and the racism of white women.) Only in an all-woman context, I learned, can I see where my racism *is* racism and not some new wrinkle of sexism. In a mixed-gender context, my recurring rage at the sexism of men of color (who were, in the sycophantic white-radical thinking of the 1960s, supposed to be *better* than white men on this issue) was hopelessly enmeshed with my own racism.

I saw this symptom clearly in a march once, when another white woman marcher, on being sexually harassed by a black male bystander, finally wheeled on him in fury—but instead of exploding at his sexism, screamed racial epithets at him. The problem is also heartbreakingly posed in a passage in *A Rap on Race,** the dialogue between Margaret Mead and James Baldwin. At one point, Mead mentioned that some social scientists in the United States had completed a study in which they asked small white boys which, if they had to be something other than small white boys, would they rather be: little white girls or little black boys? She asked if Baldwin could guess what they answered; he couldn't. Mead said, "They would rather be small black boys," to which Baldwin—whose complex and passionate consciousness about oppression I had admired for years—responded, "How encouraging! It show that they still have some sense left."

Not only was maleness more important than race (to both the little boys and to Baldwin), but the choice of being *little black girls* was never even raised as an option.

Yet on the philosophical stage, as opposed to the political, is it reversed? Is it hate that specifies and love that generalizes?

Perhaps not, if, *in the doing,* the powering (the one

*(New York: Lippincott, 1971, and Dell paperback, 1972).

encompassing, inseparable, energizing, *making*, uncontainable content) can express its one-quality, its identicality and universality, only by flashing glimpses of it through the inevitable breakable forms of ourselves? The danger being only that we will come to believe in our containing merely ourselves' lone ego (hence, need to differentiate it further, hence hate, maps, the illusion of paths, etc.), rather than understand continuously that our *very uniqueness, variety, diversity, exists in order to reveal, humorously and celebratorily, the truth of its opposite reality?*

Then the maxim proves renewed: to generalize without going first through the valley of the shadow of specificity *is* to abstractify—to characterize without the care of an artist, with no maker's precision but with mere sloppy assumptions: racism, grouping, sexism, ageism. Hate.

Love specifies because it would, through the precise, reach what is unspecifiable (although, regrettably, capable of abstraction), and thus vibrate to a state so free-form but integrated it cannot be generalized. And love must be synthesis, since it makes separateness into new entities by merging their disparate yearnings.

■

In such a state all things—the *dis*-atrophy of a cactus after long drought, the overlap of crystal (stone) pattern and snowflake pattern—*are possible.* In such a state, it is possible even for Sally Hemmings to love Jefferson without that being a slave's forced "love," and for him to love her without that being a master's hypocrisy. In such a state, the holopolitical revolution is both everywhere and nowhere at the same instant on its orbit of holomovement. In such a state, freedom is free to exist.

Surely this was the joke that Mozart and Bach knew, the joke dreamed in Lady Murasaki's stories and whispered in Xuan An's poems. Surely this was the joke that George Eliot knew when, in *Middlemarch,* she described how a

pier-glass or extensive surface of polished steel made to
be rubbed by a housemaid [*a housemaid, ah* ...], will be
minutely and multitudinously scratched in all directions; but
place now against it a lighted candle as a centre of illumi-
nation, and lo! the scratches will seem to arrange themselves in a fine series of concentric circles around that little
sun.

And if (as Eliot smiled) the scratches are going everywhere impartially, so that it is only the candle producing
the flattering illusion of an arrangement; and if the
scratches are events and the candle the egoism of the
interpreter (the little sun of a reflected face circled by
scars in the two-way pier glass)—then is it not even more
of a joke that the shifting universe will deign to arrange
its arbitrary shapes into a pattern haloing the bright wick
of love? Surely this was the joke known by Kathleen Raine
when she wrote "The center of the mandala is everywhere," the family joke told on cold winter nights over
fires down in the cabins, passed on generation to generation with laughter floating out into the night like smoke.
The old joke, told by those of us who are the slaves of
form.

—Spring 1981

The New Physics of
Meta-Politics

I have chosen to include the following essay—parts of which appeared as a chapter in The Anatomy of Freedom *(1982)—in this collection for three reasons.*

First, in our rapidly advancing technological context, it is crucial for women to break through our "physics anxiety," and this work attempts to demystify physics precisely in order to help speed that break-through; thus it bears repeating.

Second, I still have found no more apt metaphor for the deep societal transformations feminist consciousness is capable of inducing than theoretical physics, which is provoking the same kind of profound changes in visionary concepts about reality itself, in the scientific community.

Last, I like this essay. In a world where the politically engaged writer finds herself so often facing the grimmest of daily truths, and tries to report on and analyze them as honestly as possible without flinching, it is a matter of some pleasure to rediscover and pass along stories and facts—however humbly perceived—about the awesome wit and craft of the universe. It gives us hope, even joy. It gives us a rather impressive role model. And it sure as hell gives us perspective.

> In the context of cosmic values only the fantas-
> tic has a chance of being true.
>   —Pierre Teilhard de Chardin
>
> The world is quite right. It does not have to be
> consistent.
>   —Charlotte Perkins Gilman

It has been said that three developments, more than any others in history, have shaken Man's sense of himself. *Copernican astronomy* changed Man's cosmocentric vision of himself as being at the center of the universe. Darwin's *On the Origin of Species by Natural Selection* changed Man's biocentric vision of himself as being at the center of life forms. The birth of the science of *anthropology* changed Man's ethnocentric vision of himself as being at the center of one and only one possible, foreordained culture.

These three developments may well have been the most crucial ones in unsettling what has been called "Man," at least in the past. But the list is incomplete if we would have it include the present and reach toward the future. In that case, we would have to add two more developments, in their immediate and especially their potential effects equal to if not greater than the shifts in consciousness listed above: *feminism,* which challenges Man's androcentric vision of himself as being at the center of humanity—and *modern physics,* which challenges Man's vision of reality itself.

For almost two decades, I've written about, lectured on, and organized for the ideas and politics of *feminism for the sake of women,* with the emphasis on women's right to freedom, access, self-determination, and empowerment—as a matter of simple justice. If, in fact, these were the sole reasons for the goals of the movement and consciousness we call feminism, they would be sufficient unto themselves as such. It might not even be necessary to try to envision, much less articulate, what the ripple effects might be from that single dropped pebble releasing the creative energy of more than half the human species after so long. Nor is it necessary to apologize for feminism's concerning itself "merely" with women, or to justify feminism on the "Please, may I" grounds that it's good for men too, and therefore-won't-you-let-us-have-it? In the long run, it *will* be good for men, but even were it permanently to prove as discomfiting for men as it seems to be in the short run, that wouldn't make women's needs and demands any the less just.

So the fact that I place feminism in the "larger context" is neither an apology nor a justification. It is simply to show that feminism *is* the larger context.

The potential of feminism lies not only in those aspects of its vision expressed now and in the past, individually and collectively by women, but even more in the chain reaction set off by its most minute accomplishments. This chain reaction can't yet be predicted by those of us still groping toward that vision through the pain and confusion of the present. We can only begin to imagine the results, and the results of the results; only begin to glimpse or intuit them, like optical illusions of an as-yet-undreamed-of celebratory reality, like revolucinations unsullied by one jot of embarrassment, like the petals of a desert cactus flower opening and opening before our eyes as if in time-lapse photography.

What we imagine, glimpse, intuit, is that feminism is not only about women (which would, remember, be sufficient cause for it), or even about women and men, or even about women and men and political / emotional / spiritual / economic / social / sexual / racial / intellectual / ecological revolution, or even about all the above plus a revolution in sentience on this planet. All that. And more.

Feminism is, at this moment and on this planet, the DNA /

*RNA call for survival and for the next step in evolution—
and even beyond that, feminism is, in its metaphysical and
meta-feminist dynamic, the helix of hope that we humans
have for communication with whatever lies before us in
the vast, witty mystery of the universe.*

I base my premise—that feminism is the key to our
survival and transformation—not on rhetoric but on facts:

· The "Otherizing" of women is the oldest oppression
known to our species, and it's the model, the template,
for all other oppressions. Until and unless this division is
healed, we continue putting band-aids on our most mor-
tal wound.

· Women comprise the majority of humanity. This
means that a variety of strategic options are open to us
that are not available to an oppressed minority group,
which, because of its relative size, often must resort to
desperate or violent tactics even to be noticed.

· The suffering of women *is* the suffering of the human
species, and vice versa. Numerically and geographically,
it is women who are the world's poor, the world's starving, the world's refugees, the world's illiterates.

· Women share this suffering (in the category of Other)
across the barriers of age, race, class, nationality, culture, sexual preference, and ethnic background: a Hong
Kong prostitute and a Grosse Pointe matron are battered
because both are women; a sixty-year-old nun in England
is raped and a seven-year-old girl in Yemen is sold in
marriage because both are female; an Indonesian peasant dies in childbirth and a Brazilian socialite dies of a
butchered illegal abortion because both are women; a
Kenyan adolescent is physically clitoridectomized and a
Swiss nurse is psychologically clitoridectomized because
both are female human beings. The tactical potential for
unification across such Man-made barriers as race, class,
and nationality is limited only by the extent to which all
women are willing to recognize the similarity of our con-

dition, develop acute sensitivity to a diversity of priorities, and commit ourselves to exposing and unmaking those very barriers.

· The physiological reality experienced by every woman is one of continual change: change at menarche, thereafter approximately every twenty-eight days for an average of forty years, then menopause—and, in between, the possibilities of pregnancy, childbirth, postpartum, and lactation. This experienced reality lends to most women an inescapably less rigid psychological attitude toward physical existence in all of its forms, including the political and strategic.

· Women in all cultures have been assigned (stereotypically, as "Woman") the positive values of pacifism, nurturance, ecoconsciousness, and a practical reverence for life. While these values have been (1) regarded by Man as amusingly irrelevant and (2) understood by women not to be inherently "womanly," nonetheless they *are* objectively positive values. Women are perforce more familiar with them than are men; this in itself affects our strategical approach to change and could give us, at least for a while, a certain moral imperative that could be useful.

· Women in all cultures and times seem to have developed a "spiritual dimension" to our lives—whether as a code for secular rebellion, an escape from temporal suffering, or an ongoing strand of connection to cosmic mystery. This tendency has shown itself repeatedly in women's political movements, including the present feminist wave. At its most superficial level, such a tendency can lead to superstition and political evasion. But at its most sophisticated level, it can lead to political change as deep as those religious and cultural revolutions that affected not only political and economic aspects of society but, in a longer-lasting manner, consciousness itself.

· Last: *it will happen because it is happening.*

Nor is it any longer women alone who are seeing feminism as central to survival, evolution, and transformation on this planet. Among the most recent male converts are some of the hard-core scientists themselves, who are accustomed to seeing the handwriting on the wall—and analyzing it.

The physicist Fritjof Capra sees three imminent transitions that will shake the very foundations of our lives: "the reluctant but inevitable decline of patriarchy," the decline of the fossil-fuel age, and a "paradigm shift" in our basic way of perception. Of these three, he feels that the end of patriarchy is the first and perhaps the most profound transition, because patriarchy "has influenced our most basic ideas about human nature and about our relation to the universe. . . . It is the one system . . . whose doctrines were so universally accepted that they seemed to be the laws of nature." Consequently, he concludes that "the feminist movement is one of the strongest cultural currents of our time and will have a profound effect on our further evolution." Capra further understands the value of science not only for itself but in this political context:

> Physicists can provide the scientific background to the changes in attitudes and values that our society so urgently needs. In a culture dominated by science, it will be much easier to convince our social institutions . . . if we can give our arguments a scientific basis. This is what physicists can now provide. *Modern physics can show the other sciences that* scientific thinking does not necessarily have to be reductionist and mechanistic, that *holistic and ecological views are also scientifically sound . . . that such a framework is not only scientific but in agreement with the most advanced scientific theories of physical reality.** (Italics mine.)

*Fritjof Capra, *The Turning Point: Science, Society, and the Rising Culture* (New York: Simon & Schuster, 1982), pp. 29–30, 48–49.

I am not a physicist. I am a poet, a writer, a political theorist, and a feminist activist. Being a poet, I understand the lifesaving value of audacious and serious play. Being a theorist and activist, I understand the urgency of communicating this message in ever newer, more connective, and far-reaching ways. Being a writer, I understand the power of words, their independent life and energy, the way *logos* can use a writer as a vehicle for its blessing even when one thinks one is using *it* as a tool. What, then, if we were to combine the supportive framework some of the new physicists are offering humanity, with this politics, these living words? What then?

The Physics of Feminism

First, we need to know more about the framework, the background in terms of physics itself—even a few basics. This overview will of necessity be encapsulated and superficial, will contain material familiar to some readers and surprising to others, but restricted as I am by space considerations and my own nonphysicist's knowledge of the subject, I'll do the best I can with a brief summary.

Until the beginning of the twentieth century, "Western" science mostly had followed the train of thought implicit in Aristotle's "why" rather than Galileo's "how." In the wake of Newton's then-radical discovery of gravity (which in itself laid the basis for relativity theory), post-Newtonian science became mired in a mechanistic view, seeing the universe as a great clock with some central godlike Watchmaker constructing and perpetuating each cog and wheel for a specific purpose and in a specific place. The mechanical explanation (the "why") saw the cosmos as a series of parts of building blocks that might be *combined* in a wide variety of ways but that surely had to be ultimately *reducible* to some block or cog—the atom, for instance. Since the atom is about one hundred times smaller than the head of a pin, this seemed the ultimate building block. Aptly enough, at the start of this century, in 1900, Max Planck put forth the Quantum Theory—showing by mathematical abstraction an equation that explained how the amount of radiant energy emitted by heated bodies varies with wavelength and temperature. The remarkable feature of this equation was that Planck was driven to assume that radiant energy is emitted *not in a continuous flow* but in *dis*continuous bitlets Planck termed *quanta.*

In 1905, at the age of twenty-six, Albert Einstein took Quantum Theory beyond the confines of the equations of radiation: Einstein proposed that *all forms of radiant energy,* including heat, x-rays and light itself, were comprised of and *traveled in space as separate and discontinuous quanta.* This new perception of electromagnetic radiation was to become basic to quantum theory, the theory of atomic phenomena. Furthermore, he took the Michelson-Morley finding (that light's velocity is a constant, unaffected by Earth's motion), and he took the Galilean Relativity Principle (that all uniformly moving systems are governed by the same mechanical laws) a giant step further: the laws governing light and other electromagnetic phenomena—in fact, *all* the phenomena of nature and all its laws—are the same for all systems that move uniformly *relative* to one another. (Even "simultaneity" is relative. As Einstein said, "Every reference body ... has its own particular time; unless we're told the reference body to which the statement of time refers, there is no meaning in the statement of the time of an event." In an oft-cited example, if you're in an airplane and the flight attendant takes two minutes to walk from the galley to your seat, that two minutes is two minutes to you and to him. *But,* let's say that the plane is flying at the rate of four hundred miles an hour; in that case, if someone on the ground looking up at the plane could see that flight attendant move inside it, the two-minute walk would blitz by in a much faster blur.)

This meant that the concept of absolute time was discarded along with the concept of absolute space. Since motion can be detected only as a change in position *relative* to another body, and since motion takes place in space and through time—then both space and time are one, and relative to everything else. If one could ride on a beam of light, for example, there would be no sense of motion whatsoever, and time itself would stand still. One would not age, since light is the fastest thing known in the universe. (The tachyon, however, is a postulated particle that can move faster than light. I have a special affection for this hypothetical bitlet of mattery.) Einstein had in effect constructed a common framework for electrodynamics and mechanics, in what was to be his lifelong search for a unified foundation of physics.

The most stunning aspect of this framework resulted from Einstein's having reasoned that since a moving body's mass increased with its motion, and since motion itself is a form of energy (kinetic energy), then the increased mass in that moving body is derived from its increased energy—that is, *energy has mass.* This realization of the relation between energy and mass—that even an object at rest is merely stored energy, that when the object is destroyed (as in burning a log or in nuclear reaction), energy is released, that mass *is* simply a form of energy—was expressed in the now-famous equation $E = mc^2$, or energy equals mass times the square of the velocity of light in centimeters per second. *Space and time were discovered to be the same thing. Matter and energy were discovered to be the same thing.*

This framework, which Einstein offered in 1905, was his Special Theory of Relativity. Science is still staggering under its latest implications. In 1915, Einstein expanded this theory, and endorsed Ernst Mach's principle of inertia: "Mach's Principle" (that the properties of inertia in terrestrial matter are determined relative to the total universal mass surrounding them / it). Einstein, going further, proposed the General Theory of Relativity, extending the framework to include gravity: the mutual attraction of all massed bodies and the effect this has, in turn, on bending or curving time and space (the way an object displaces water).* *This did away with the notion of absolute motion and of absolute space.* The world in which we three-dimensionally live is actually a four-dimensional space continuum.

Quantum physics shattered the two basic assumptions of classical science—causality and determinism—and opened up the internal, microcosmic universe. Relativity theory shattered all previous assumptions of space, time, movement, and gravitation, and exposed the external, macroscopic universe. Nothing now would ever be the same.

In 1925, the concept that particles sometimes acted like waves and vice versa—through the work of de Broglie, Schrödinger, Börn and Jordan, and Heisenberg and Bohr—culminated in the discovery that a particle could be a wave, and the reverse (in the same way that a subway passenger at rush hour is both an individual with her own destination and, when the doors open to discharge her with a crowd, a wave).

In 1927, Werner Heisenberg conceived what is now his famous statement of physical law, the Principle of Uncer-

---

*The latest of many challenges to Einstein's General Theory of Relativity was recently raised by solar physicist Henry A. Hill of the University of Arizona, based on a study of how various calculated characteristics of the sun affect the orbit of Mercury in ways not foreseen by Einstein. Whether proven right or wrong, this latest controversy is likely to provide the stimulus for new thinking about Einstein's theories, and a potential for developing them even further.

tainty—that it is impossible to determine both the position and the velocity of an electron at the same time; the more accurately one can determine its velocity, the more indefinite its position becomes, and the reverse. The Principle of Uncertainty was following the thread of two Einstein statements that are lovely aphorisms: "One may say the eternal mystery of the world is its comprehensibility," and "It is the theory which decides what we can observe." Strict determinism went out the door along with absolute space, time, movement, gravity, and all the other "constants."

This in turn gave rise to Niels Bohr's new philosophy of "Complementarity," which went something like this: Even if it is impossible to determine both the velocity and the position of an electron at the same time, nonetheless each (separately) is needed to gain a full picture of the atomic reality—just as both the "particle picture" and the "wave picture" are two complementary portrayals of the same reality, even if *they* can't be charted at the same time. In other words, despite one's *methods* being limited to either / or, one's *conception* can embrace both, and glimpse the whole.* From this philosophy an entirely new holistic direction in physics was born.

*Ironically, Einstein rejected Heisenberg's Uncertainty Principle (saying "God does not play dice with the world") and also Bohr's philosophy of Complementarity; until his death, Einstein continued to seek a deterministic cause that would unify all the contradictions he himself had exposed. An extraordinary series of debates ensued between Einstein and Bohr. Although these debates took place in 1927 in Belgium, they became known as the Copenhagen Debates because Bohr was Danish, and his viewpoint seemed to prevail. One might epitomize the two positions with Bohr saying: The quality of my observation changes—or even creates—reality, and Einstein saying: Reality is reality and follows its own laws, even if, so far, those laws are concealed from our understanding. As physicist Fred Alan Wolf has put it, "It was as if the left half and the right half of the cosmic brain were in dialogue." (*Taking the Quantum Leap,* New York: Harper and Row, 1981.) For the last sixty years, the so-called Copenhagen School of thought has been the dominant one in modern physics, the Aristotelian /

Various other developments followed rapidly. I'll arbitrarily skip about in time, since (1) time is relative, (2) if a particle can, who am I not to? and (3) I'm always a pushover for form mirroring content.

John A. Wheeler of Princeton (who says delightful things like "There is no law except the law that there is no law") coined the term Black Holes for energy-dense pockmarks in distant space—possibly burned-out stars that have collapsed internally because of their enormous gravity, and that suck space / time and light into themselves. Wheeler posited that a Black Hole in this universe might emerge as a White Hole exploding energy into another universe, and that the birth of a star in this universe might be happening through the looking-glass of some other universe's Black Hole. Wheeler also proposed that the stage on which (the space of) the universe moves is itself a larger stage—a *superspace*.

Then there was R.P. Feynman, whose diagrams showed that particles can be made to move backward in time—if only for a moment. There was the philosophy / physics paradox of Erwin Schrödinger (the paradox of "Schrödinger's cat") which posited perception as All; it showed that a (hypothetical) cat in a (theoretical) box can be "proven" to be alive and dead concurrently, until the moment one looks into the box and perceives the situation. (This experiment always disconcerts me. Being a cat lover, I wish Schrödinger had postulated it with, say, a leech.) There was J.S. Bell, who formulated Bell's Theorem: when two particles interact and then fly off in different directions, further interference with one affects the other, no matter how distant they are, as if there were a telepathy between them, or a "quantum interconnect-

late Einsteinian world view—of a mechanistic, deterministic, causal universe—being considered anachronistic. But with new nonsystematic systems, including Chaos Theory, being developed, the debate is clearly an ongoing one.

edness of distant systems." And there was Wolfgang Pauli, who developed the so-called Pauli Exclusion Principle: that no two electrons in an atom can be identical: the presence of one with a particular set of properties or "quantum numbers" excludes another with the same set, a mathematical precision that shows the universe certainly has an eye for detail. (Pauli also collaborated with Jung on the famous paper "Synchronicity: An Acausal Connecting Principle" in which Jung coined the term *synchronicity*.)

Recent theoretical developments include David Böhm's idea that there is an "implicate order" in the universe, a cosmic web of relations at a "nonmanifest" level that demonstrate an "unbroken wholeness." There is also Geoffrey Chew's S-matrix theory, sometimes known as the "bootstrap approach" (bootstrap because all particles are seen as having properties and interactions derived solely from their own self-consistent requirements); the S-matrix theory radically posits that *there are no fundamentals whatsoever in the universe*—no fundamental laws, principles, building blocks, equations, constants. Rather, the universe is seen as a network or web of events continuously and dynamically relating. No one property of this web is fundamental; each follows from the properties of every other part, and it is the overall consistent interrelation that defines and describes the web's structure: "Each particle helps to generate other particles, which in turn generate it." This is quite stunning, if you dwell on it, especially because, as Chew puts it, "Carried to its logical extreme, the bootstrap conjecture implies that *the existence of consciousness,* along with other aspects of nature, *is necessary for self-consistency of the whole.*" (Italics mine.) Physicist Eugene Wigner also states that "It was not possible to formulate the laws [of Quantum Theory] in a fully consistent way without reference to consciousness." And Capra has added, "the explicit inclusion of human consciousness may be an essential aspect of future theories of matter."

If your head is spinning with excitement, not to worry. So is mine; so are the physicists', and so is each electron, planet, solar system, galaxy, and, probably, universe. Yet the above cursory tourist trip through the expanding landscape of the New Physics is not half so brain-boggling as a longer visit there, made possible through the proliferation of books on the subject written in a style accessible to the lay reader. A number of conclusions, always tentative, begin to emerge: physics has found the border with metaphysics a permeable one; just as yesterday's magic is today's medicine, so yesterday's philosophy is today's science. Or in the phrase of Sir James Jeans, "The universe begins to look more like a great thought than like a great machine."

That everything is energy, that everything moves, that everything is somehow discrete or separate yet interrelated or interconnected—these are scientific facts that politics would do well to examine. Furthermore, as Arthur Koestler wrote, "The nineteenth-century model of the universe as a mechanical clockwork is a shambles and since the concept of matter itself has been dematerialized, *materialism can no longer claim to be a scientific philosophy.*"

Nor, I might add, can materialism any longer claim to be a political philosophy.

Both quantum physics and feminism are "second generation" critiques of the old order, going even further than those "first generation" revolutions that acted against the dominant theory of determinism.

But how far *can* we go? We can risk plying the tool of metaphor to anatomize freedom. So, using as our metaphor first classical physics and then quantum physics (less in a strict chronological progression than in a revelatory unfolding), we might take a quantum leap and look at political evolution.

THE PAST

Mechanical (Classical) Physics
"Building blocks" comprise the stuff of the universe.

The "ultimate" building block is the atom.

Building blocks can assemble in variable ways, but are also reducible.

Material and matter are seen as real.

Mechanical (Traditional) Politics
"Building blocks" are the stuff of society: sexes, races, classes, the family, clans, tribes, nations, etc.

The "ultimate" unit is the individual.

Comparable variables are social systems: the rule of chiefs, the warrior class, institutional monarchy, feudalism, the rise of the bourgeoisie.

Materialism—and dialectical materialism—are seen as realistic systems of analysis, especially after the Industrial "Revolution."

THE PRESENT

Quantum Mechanics

Energy seems fluid but is composed of discontinuity.

The Beginning of Quantum Politics
The idea of progress breaks down; the "building blocks" disturb the system's fluidity (socialist and anticolonial revolutions); discontinuity in "norms" begins (family structures shift, sexual options are openly articulated).

Special Theory of Relativity
Mass / energy is seen as one; space / time also is seen as one, and as relative. This is the end of the notion of "matter." The theory is limited in not yet including movement.

Special Theory of Feminism
The majority of humanity (female) is seen as sharing one condition, relative to the (male) minority of humanity. This is the beginning of the end of materialism. The theory is so far limited to intrafeminist movement impact,

not yet including its full constituency.

The Concept of Particles Being Waves and Waves Being Particles

The Feminist Emphasis on "Process"

Means are affirmed as being more vital than goals or ends. Freedom is intuited as being both a state and a dynamic.

The Principle of Uncertainty

One can see a "wavicle" either as a wave or particle, but not both at once; one can chart its position or velocity, but not both at the same time.

The Principle of Polarity

Either / Or thinking emerges in (fundamentalist) feminist theory; radical *or* reformist, activist *or* thinker, lesbian *or* heterosexual, economic analy- sis *or* cultural / spiritual approach, race *or* sex priority, work within the system *or* out- side it, etc. *ad nauseam.*

The Theory of Complemen- tarity

One doesn't need to see wave and particle at once; one can imagine the whole from its fragments or assume their complementarity. The possi- bility of interpenetration and permeability of particles is explored. It is no longer nec- essary to impose a system of coherence in order to work with and study disparate parts.

Pragmatic but Fragile Coali- tions

Alliances emerge among women despite mutual mis- trust and cynicism: women of color and white women in dia- logue, growth of international networks, connections sought with activists on environmen- tal, academic, economic, age, cultural, and other "fronts"; a lessening of alienation between lesbian and hetero- sexual women and the emer- gence of bisexual affirmation; a skittish attempt on the part of some feminists to under- stand and reach out even to women in the grip of the Right Wing and other fundamental- isms.

Fission: Splitting the Atom

The end of the "ultimate building block" notion. The study of subatomic particles and *sub*-subatomic particles begins.

Fragmentation of the Individual

Feminists *and* nonfeminists, women *and* men feel this: chronic anxiety, doomsday political tactics and increased terrorism, psychological reductionism combined with a desperate search for "self," burn-out.

Fusion: Thermonuclear Fusing of the Atom Is Risked

The hydrogen bomb is created, with the possibility of nuclear energy through forced fusion, even with its incomprehensibly great dangers.

Fusion of the Old Order Is Risked

An alliance is forced between the "workers" and state capitalism (contemporary "communism"); an alliance is forced between the "consumer" and the megamerchant corporations (contemporary "capitalism"); various attempts are made to pass off old ways as new ones, ignoring the incomprehensibly great dangers this presents.

THE FUTURE

General Theory of Relativity

Discovery that gravitational attraction between massive bodies is also relative.

General Theory of Feminism

Theory begins to reach out beyond the loose confines of what has been considered the Women's Movement; the feminist vision begins to make an impact on all human beings, and *relative to their own situations,* they make an impact, in turn, on feminism. The discovery is made that feminism is inherent in Third World freedom struggles; that feminism is central to solving crises in population growth, hunger,

war, illiteracy, disease, "development," nationalism, environmental destruction, etc.;
that feminism affects all per-
ceptions of sexuality, age,
socioeconomic, cultural / spiritual, and scientific / aesthetic
issues. Nationalism and other
traditional political systems–
communist *and* capitalist–
begin to fragment and col-
lapse in the enormous gravitational pull among and
between individuals and
groups within them who are
making these connections.

Concept of the Participatory Observer

The experiment changes what
is being observed by the very
observing of it; all things
interact.

The End of "the Exception"

The global beginning of "I'm
no feminist, *but* . . . ," that is,
the inescapable (admitted)
recognition among women
and the inescapable (not yet
admitted) recognition among
men of their participation in
the situation identified by feminism, and their (admitted *and*
nonadmitted) longing for the
changes feminism addresses.

Quantum Field Theory

The theory attempts to merge
quantum mechanics and relativity, posits that particles are
actually interactions between
fields "instantaneously and
locally": the concept that
space itself isn't empty at all.

Metafeminist Synchronicities

Metafeminism attempts to
synthesize the breakdown of
global systems with the
energy of feminist vision as a
relevant solution toward
change; the realization dawns
that this synthesis is precisely
what has been intuited, longed
for, and feared by the species
for millennia.

Ongoing Attempts at a Unified Field Theory

These approaches include the diverse concepts of the "hidden variables" and the "concealed order"; the Yang-Mills gauge field theory of symmetrical but unstable interactions; Böhm's "implicate universe"– a cosmic web of interrelations; Chew's S-matrix theory and "bootstrapping"–particles "involving" one another in patters of "self-consistency." The possibility is explored that there are no fundamental constituents of matter, no fundamental principles or laws except, possibly, those of consciousness.

Ongoing Discovery of Sub-subatomic Particles

These discoveries amount so far to almost three hundred, including protons (and their possible decay), leptons, gluons, baryons, mesons, and hadrons–and then hadron "particles" postulated as quarks (a quark is sized at 10 million times smaller than the atom), or charmed quarks (because they seem to obey only their own erraticism), or red, white, and blue quarks, or "psi-particles," or particles referred to merely as "resonances" which have "a tendency to exist"–postulatable, but traceable only by the trails of light their nonmoving movement leaves when monitored in bubble chambers.

Metafeminism as the Bridge to Metapolitics

All fundamental laws, categories and categorizing, and "norms" of behavior are discovered to be illusory. *Fundamentalism vanishes along with fundamentals.* Consciousness is reinvented anew. A balance emerges between the individual and the collective / species / sentient life / universal movement; uniqueness and commonality are seen as *un*contradictory; differences and similarities are held in a celebrated balance, each self-consistent and mutually involved.

Micro- and Macrocosmic Revo- and Evolution in a Vertical Curve

All facets of consciousness flower, new forms of intelligence develop and create still newer forms in turn. Eccentric and eclectic agnostic acrostic solutions to old problems fall into place via quarky ingenious strategies. Freedom actually is *traceable* now as well as *postulatable;* freedom, which has a "tendency to exist" and which, through the rapidity and energy of its movement, can be known to have existed only by the trail of light it leaves behind.

Meanwhile, Back at "The Personal Is Political". . .

Well, you say. This is all very impressive and cosmic— but I'm not sure how glimpsing the implicate order or the tendencies of certain resonances "to exist" is going to help me get Herman to pick up his socks, stop Mr. Smithjones from pinching my behind at work, make me less nervous when alone on the street at night, get me a decent salary, babysit for me, get rid of the military-industrial complex, or, or, or . . . make a goddamed plain old feminist revolution.

I agree. But we've just begun to comprehend the vast implications of our own politics, and even though these implications seem most startling when they lead forward into infinity, they also pertain directly to the present. (Time / space is the same, and relative to the observer, remember?)

For one thing, a full awareness in each of us of the centrality of feminist vision will have a monumental effect on the way each of us carries her / himself, the way we each conduct our personal lives and construct our political strategies:

No more begging for "rights": the future of intelligence itself is at stake. *No more single-issue politics* (sacrifice reproductive-freedom rights for fear of endangering the Equal Rights Amendment, sacrifice the ERA for fear it isn't radical enough, drop everything and work on economic analyses or on violence-against-women issues or on international networking): since when does the electron not touch everything in its orbit at once? *No more victimization* (permitting the grief and pain of our situation as women to paralyze us into hopelessness, cynicism, depression, burn-out, or sell-out): just because you can see the picture only as wave or particle at any given time doesn't mean it isn't both at all times, and dynamic in its movement. *No more correct-line politics:* just because one of us is focusing on velocity and the other on position doesn't mean that we don't need each other to put together the whole picture (Principle of Uncertainty), and that the very diversity of our conditions doesn't make for a stronger ultimate unity (Theory of Complementarity).

When we fully comprehend the meaning of what it is we are fighting for, that in itself will inspire the strategies, and give us the endurance necessary to win.

Carry yourself as one who will save the world. Because you will.

On an even simpler level, it's possible to apply our framework of the Physics of Feminism to what is laughingly called daily life. Three areas, especially, may be most crucial to our immediate survival. One is the problem of leashed powers of emotion. A second is involved with ways and means for conducting personal relationships—which are necessary to anyone but a solipsist if she / he is going to survive long enough to wave her / his particle self along the field of magnetic change. A third is the contradiction inherent in the human lack of and longing for connectedness—with all the perils that implies. Let's call our framework the F-matrix Theory, equated as $F = et^2$ or: Feminism equals equality / empowerment / evolution times the squared velocity of transformations. And let's apply $F = et^2$ to these three daily-life areas.

1. *The leashed powers of emotion.* Nothing so simple as "repression" here. I'm referring to stereotypical Man's refusal to acknowledge the hidden variable in men (love), and stereotypical Woman's refusal to acknowledge the hidden variable in women (rage). (These are, in fact, inversions of violence and romance.) What any good consciousness-raising group does, among other things, is give a woman permission to rage. It's what any good friend

or good therapist does too, for that matter. It's what the Women's Movement did up until about 1976—when we got worried about "alienating" and tried to be accommodating (to whom?), tried to dilute the intensity of our own message. That many women subsequently became slightly bored by the Women's Movement and that many feminists turned apoplectic from bottling up our rage all over again ought not to come as a surprise. And it oughtn't to be much of a surprise, either, that (some) men tried to "practice loving" very, very awkwardly at first, met head on with our smilingly suppressed rage, got confused and— rather lazily in many cases—gave up. (They had concrete privileges to lose by this "experiment," remember, and the enlightened self-interest we tried to foster in them would only click on its light some decades—or millennia—hence.) Now, all over again, and definitively, we must split the atom of our Man-and-Woman-made emotions, releasing the vast energy of rage and love into action. I ask again: if women don't give themselves and each other permission to rage, to be audacious, who will? Men have it easier: If men don't give themselves and each other permission to love—women will. But the emotions of real women and real men must be fissioned from the shells of "Man" and "Woman"—and this time that fission must continue.

2. *Ways and means for conducting relationships.* Complex, this. But relativity theory may be helpful in suggesting a relative approach (this is *not* recommended among strangers, but *is* operable within relationships, among partners, lovers, friends, colleagues, etc.): What if you treat a woman as you would a man—and the reverse? Before I expire under the weight of "feminist fundamentalist" bricks thrown at me for such heresy, let me explain. For example, let's say you (a woman) live with another woman—a lover or simply a roommate. Let's say that she at times puts her muddy boots up on the furniture, spills cigarette ashes all over the table, is congenitally late for

appointments, or leaves a ring around the tub. (Women, being human, have been rumored to do such things. And I'm deliberately picking the small aggravations.) Think, for a moment, how you would regard such behavior if she were a man. Instantly a knee-jerk feminist analysis comes into play: that sloppy, inconsiderate, male-supremacist deliberately exercising his power over you! You probably wouldn't take this behavior from a man (I *hope* you wouldn't), yet many women do accept it from other women. And that's nonsensical twaddle, I think (having been guilty of it frequently). Why lower our standards of civility for women?

If, on the other hand, one is putting up with attitudes or actions from a *man* that one wouldn't take from another woman . . . aha. The only way to overcome *that* very real power-tremble is to leap quantumly out of *that* nonsensical twaddle, I say (having trembled therein many a time), and point out that such behavior would strike you as intolerable in a woman and is no more tolerable in a man. What if, in other words, we dare begin to express a postrevolutionary consciousness even in this prerevolutionary time—at least in personal relationships? Elsewhere, out in the big world, such a tactic is highly questionable: toughing it out by insisting on going for a walk alone at 3 A.M. may be putting on a postrevolutionary façade but unfortunately it's likely to wind one up in a prerevolutionary hospital. Still, it *is* possible to begin to leave victimization behind us, at least in personal relationships—not by changing the other person, but by changing *oneself.* Oneself is the only person over whom one has the real power to affect change, ultimately. But those changes within the self *are* possible, and can have, like the gravitational interpenetration of fields, an astounding influence on the others one cannot change directly. *It is your life*—and the only one you're certain of. In sum, if you develop the velocity of your own light-of-self as a constant, then you can choose (and choose how) to beam it on those with whom you interrelate in a way that sees them as relative to you, you as relative to them, and them as relative to one another. This returns you to yourself, and accomplishes two rather nice bonus rewards: first, it gives you balance, perspective, and a modicum of power—and second, it's *fair.*

3. *The human lack of and longing for connection*—and all the attendant dangers, sufferings, and evasions that implies. In this case, $F = {}^2$ suggests a reassuring course, one that rejects the notion of fusion in relationships and points instead to a more balanced "model": *symbiosis.* I am not using the term in the Freudian sense (as a pejorative description of overly dependent tendencies within a human relationship) but rather in its original, value-free sense as commonly used in biology. This is the at-first-vigilant, then carefully developed, interdependence, the give-and-take many life forms practice for their survival. The yucca plant would not exist without the one particular insect who pollinates it—and that insect would not survive without the yucca for food, and for shelter of its eggs. A particular crab and a particular anemone know by each other's markings that each means survival to the other. Lewis Thomas's memorable example of the Medusa jellyfish and its symbiote, the snail—who even switch roles in virtuoso fashion in their symbiosis—is an especially heartening model.* "Love is more complex than theory," I wrote once in a poem, long before I had the sense to know I knew that. Douglas Hofstadter might have had something similar in mind when he paraphrased the mathematician Gödel: "The fact that truth transcends theoremhood, in any given formal system, is called the incompleteness of that system."** Why do any of us permit the socially constructed stereotypes of Man or Woman

*Lewis Thomas, *The Medusa and the Snail: More Notes of a Biology Watcher* (New York: Bantam Books, 1980).

**Douglas R. Hofstadter, *Gödel, Escher, and Bach: An Eternal Golden Braid* (New York: Basic Books, 1979), p. 86.

to distort the life-giving process of symbiosis into the subsummation of fusion? Why, in reaction to that distortion, do any of us permit fundamentalist politics to tell us that we have no right at least to try to love, connect, interconnect, and interdepend where we choose, so long as that makes us feel good, stronger, more empowered— and so long as no one is demeaned or robbed of her / his empowerment in the process? As the Wicceans say, "Do what thou wilt, *an it harm none.*"

The old audacity of this wave of feminism was that women dared to name our pain. Today we need a new audacity—one that leaves the familiarity of our victimization behind us (while we remain keenly aware of the surrounding danger). That new audacity would dare to affirm the ultimate radical politics reflected in and reflective of the universe itself: radical integration. Integration of the self with the self (literally: integrity), and integration with each other and our vision and all of life. It would involve daring to act out of that postrevolutionary integrity even in a prerevolutionary context—but without false consciousness.

The courage required decades ago for feminists to name the already existing division between men and women, the separation, the anguish—and to relate that division to all the other separations based on race, age, nationality, and so forth—that courage would need to be squared (the velocity of transformation) in order to accomplish *this* naming of the already existing "implicate" *integration* that connects, surrounds, and embraces us all. It would have to be a courage equal to the task. It would have to refuse to sacrifice the integrity of self or the integrity of feminism for some illusory "second stage," as Betty Friedan has suggested; a "second stage" that leaves sexual politics behind (and still unsolved) sounds alarmingly like forced fusion all over again. No, *this* approach— of radical integration—sacrifices nothing except false categories and burned-out strategies. It has the potential to turn (embittering) hatred into (energizing) rage, and to connect the energy of that rage to the even greater energy of love. *This* approach suggests that the power is already there for the touching by audacious hands. And this approach suggests a way for those hands, once having touched that power, to have the grace to use it well.

The Lucy-Dolphin Alliance

It certainly is understandable that we "new" women at times regard mercy, compassion, and altruism with suspicion—since those are "Woman's" attributes that have been foisted on us for eons. Yet they're excellent attributes in themselves: it would be nice if men acquired them and if women practiced them more on each *other* instead of always casting them like proverbial pearls before men.

After all, a particle can combine with other particles and then reconstitute itself whole, losing none of its integrity. Each individual spider's web is as distinctive as a fingerprint. Elephants are said to mourn their dead, and to bury them. Dolphins midwife one another, care for their ill and dying, and have been known to tend other dolphins caught in tuna nets, even though butchery for all may result. Whales, traveling in pods of three or four, sing to one another not only for sounding location but, it appears, to keep each other's spirits up; when a sick whale beaches itself, a healthy whale has been known to do the same—possibly an altruistic gesture of companionship, albeit a suicidal one. Surely humanity, surely women, surely *feminists* at least, could approximate the individuality and altruism of a particle, a spider, a dolphin?

The cliché "It's always darkest before the dawn" was put far more elegantly by Kafka when he wrote that grace, transcendence, salvation come "not at the last, but at the very last." This moment in history is a—perhaps the—hinge moment. The panic such pressure creates is like the panic in a burning room full of people who fear they don't know the way out. Feminists are no exception. We fear that we lack "order" and "leadership" and "chains of command"—forgetting that this seeming "disorder" has always been our strength. It's a natural disorder, like erosion. *It's the "implicit disorder" of the universe itself— and the way change happens.* As Ellen DuBois described the beginnings of the nineteenth-century women's movement, women's energy was "unexamined, *implicit,* and above all, disorganized."* (Italics mine).

I'm not suggesting that we stop examining our political and personal vision, or that we lie back and assume it's implicit, or that we intentionally expand our lack of organization wherever it exists. I *am* saying that we might look a little positively on the underlying force that fuels all our examination and all our organization, call it what you will: DNA's thirst toward perfecting things, or $F = et^2$.

I suggest that, in moments of despair, we let ourselves be comforted by the calm urgency of our great fore-mother Elizabeth Cady Stanton: "If I were to draw up a set of rules for the guidance of reformers . . . I should put at the head of the list, 'Do all you can, no matter what, to get people to think about your reform, and then, if the reform is good, it will come about in due season.' "

So why don't we denounce the patriarchal notion of "inside" and "outside" the system partitioning? It's really as restricting as the idiocy of national boundaries. If matter doesn't really exist, who are we to quibble over "within the system" or "outside the system"? We need to be lob-bying *and* marching, striking by night *and* going on strike

---

Feminism and Suffrage: The Emergence of an Independent Women's Movement in America, 1848–1869 (Ithaca, NY: Cornell University Press, 1978).

by day, writing letters *and* literature, wielding the spray-paint can *and* the artist's brush.

The New Right has focused on the Feminist Movement because they know—even when we forget—how profound a force for social change feminism is. We can no longer afford to forget.

We can no longer afford to be so pure, or so afraid, or so despairing, that we don't avail ourselves of whatever we can: scientific knowledge, self-defense arts, networking, humor, computers, art, the wisdom of our own dreams and the drive of our own curiosity and desire, the hologrammatic depths of our chosen committed relationships, the true kinship blood types we need no longer deny, the vitality of play, the lost child in each of us, the ripening old woman or man in each of us, our own individual deaths, each other, the world.

It's tiring, you say? Then rest for a while. We—who have only this urgent minisecond—have eternity. *Bend time to yourself.* We—who have only this tiny fragment of space in which to maneuver—have space itself, in all its dense-packed energy. *Bend space to yourself.* We—each of whom huddles in the "solitude of self" fearing that no other ever can really understand—are unique integrities nonetheless permeable, interchangeable, combinable, and many; we are part of the field itself. *Bend that consciousness to yourself,* wrap yourself in its warmth.

Me, I like to think about Lucy. You may have heard about Lucy; she's the oldest known ancestor of our species. She lived in what is now the Afar region of Ethiopia. She was in her late twenties when she died, and she was just under four feet tall. She might have had a touch of spinal arthritis, but she seems to have died a peaceful death, by the banks of what today is the Awash River—where her bones lay undisturbed for almost three and a half million years, until their discovery in 1974 by Donald Johanson of the Cleveland Museum of Natural History.

Not just a few bones, either. She turned out to be, in Johanson's words, "the oldest, most complete, best-preserved skeleton of any erect-walking human ancestor that has ever been found." They catalogued Lucy as No. AL 288-1 and eventually labeled her *Australopithecus afarensis.* Some called her "the missing link." In time, the team found more of Lucy's people—about thirteen individuals they nicknamed "the First Family." The discovery of Lucy pushed estimates of the existence of human precursors on earth further back—by about a million years.

I like to think about Lucy. She had a rather small skull but quite "modern" legs and hands, and she must have roamed around making a few tools here and there, gathering and foraging but able to carry her baby in her arms as her human descendants would do later. She must have communicated in some way with her people. I'll wager they had their means of making rhythms if not "music," of moving with joy if not "dancing," of grieving when one of their own fell prey to a wild animal, or wandered off, or simply died. I imagine her lying there, on the banks of that river-which-was-yet-to-be, lying there in her desert or veldt under the wide horizon-to-horizon curve of black night sky alive with the two hundred billion stars in the Milky Way, which is merely one galaxy in a galactic cluster, which in turn is only one of the galactic clusters in our Local Group . . . I imagine Lucy lying back and resting her small neat skull on her arms and gazing up at all that glory. And trying to think it through. Trying to think. Trying.

And space / time curls back on itself, displaced by the sudden rush of my love for her, this tiny wobbly animal on her way to becoming not "Woman" by women; this creature settling herself somehow toward the task of intelligence, this indomitable unique absurd being, and the impossibly hopeless unthinkable task she set herself: becoming human. $F = et^2$. If she could do it, I can.

Both / And (Dedicated to Regina Olsen—and with Respectful Apologies to Kierkegaard)

"We violate probability, by our nature," wrote Lewis Thomas. "To do this, systematically, and in such wild varieties of form . . . to have sustained the effort successfully for the several billion years of our existence, without drifting back into randomness, was nearly a mathematical impossibility."*

Thomas, the biologist and medical doctor, sees the earth as a single cell.

James Lovelock, the British chemical biophysicist, and Lynn Margulis, the U.S. microbiologist, see the earth as a single organism, an entity they call Gaia (after the Greek goddess of Earth)—a homeostatic system of "feedback loops" with the (possibly conscious) capacity to make and keep the planet fit for life. They too point out how much we violate probability: Earth has "too much" ammonia, "too much" hydrogen, nitrogen, nitrous oxide, carbon monoxide. Computer models of the atmosphere of Earth in the absence of life suggest that its composition should be somewhere between those of our nearest neighbors, Mars and Venus. Yet it is conveniently out of kilter chemically and thermodynamically—convenient, that is, to supporting life. Lovelock posits that the presence of life itself managed to drive the atmosphere into this convenient disequilibrium—and then to maintain it.

David Böhm sees this entire universe as one possible wavelet spontaneously pulsed up in a sea of cosmic energy.

Arthur Koestler, a political and literary figure with a friendly obsession about science as both fact and metaphor, saw not the cell or the Gaian organism, but the

*Lewis Thomas, *The Lives of a Cell: Notes of a Biology Watcher* (Bantam Books, 1975).

"holarch," and beyond that—beyond the dual tendency for living beings to behave as individual wholes and at the same time as parts in the hierarchies of existence— he saw the "holon," a Janus mask of separateness, oneness, and integration. One of the nicest things about relativity theory is that it proves how different people from different perspectives can all be telling different truths about the same truth at different (or the same) times, rather like a subtle slant-rhyme scheme in a sonnet. A "relativity consciousness" also precludes ethnocentricity, egocentricity, and pretty much every other kind of -centricity. It is, to say the least, a different perspective from fundamentalism, from Either / Or thinking.

Of course, the really good Either / Or thinkers like Kierkegaard haven't been fundamentalists at all, and were in fact drawn to the dialectic only because of the electromagnetic promise of some sort of synthesis on the other end, a synthesis that in turn becomes a new thesis that in turn gives rise to a new antithesis that necessitates the search for yet a newer synthesis. There's a comfortingly unsettling quality to this process, since it gives one the seeming reassurance of "categories"—that is, a grid or system of interpreting a diffuse reality—but the categories, far from being fixed, are in dynamic movement. That quality of inherent relativity lends the dialectical process a verisimilitude—in much the same way that one is more easily prone to trust a person with a sense of irony than someone apparently lacking that capacity.

The irony of Søren Kierkegaard's *Either / Or* is, to be sure, everywhere and nowhere at once, both where he intended it to be and where he didn't. (Irony's whole point, after all, is to pop up where least expected.)

A cell. A Gaian organism. A holon. Both / And—and then some. How devoutly we've all—women and men—hoped that we could scuttle through life avoiding the whole impact of freedom's "tendency to exist," wishing "to be merely observers." Now, even scientists are faced with being participators and not observers—the retina of the experimenter's eye affecting the photon that lands upon it as much as the photon affects the retina. Metaphysics has joined physics; objective data impinge on consciousness. The neurologist and biochemist Candace Pert has said that where she used to see the brain in Newtonian terms—all locks and keys—she now sees it in terms of quantum mechanics—an energy field constantly vibrating and oscillating. The firm earth on which we stand is only a skin of solidity stretched undulating over the restless movement of its tectonic plates, themselves jostled by a greater energy at the center, the whole bright bead strung spinning in the net of a living field.

And all this while, in terror, we've walked only a single strand of that web—a tightrope held on one end by the hand of "Man," and on the other by the hand of "Woman," each of us keeping the public secret that what we walked on wasn't ever solid, fundamental ground, each of us believing that to one side lay only Either, to the other side only Or:

> In morals, as in everything, there are two opposite tendencies. The first is to say: "Everything matters infinitely." The second is to say: "No doubt that is true. But mere sanity demands that we should not treat everything as mattering all that much. Distinction is necessary; more-and-less is necessary; indifference is necessary." The contention is always sharp. The Rigorous view is vital to sanctity; the Relaxed view is vital to sanity. Their union is not impossible, but it is difficult; for whichever is in power begins, after the first five minutes, to maintain itself from bad and unworthy motives. Harshness, pride, resentment encourage the one; indulgence, falsity, detestable good-fellowship the other.

So wrote Charles Williams in *The Descent of the Dove.** He might as well have been speaking about "radical" and

*(1939; rpt. Grand Rapids, MI: William B. Eerdman's Publishing Co., 1974).

"liberal" feminists. Ah well, it is the theory that decides what we observe. Yet the universe around—and in—us has maintained that union of rigor and relaxation for five-minute eternities, Both / And providing the very tension of energy that made everything else possible.

The Roman Catholic Church—ever as psychologically shrewd as it has been politically sadistic—has in its theology the concept of "actual grace." This grace is distinct from "sanctifying grace" (achieved purposefully through those copyrighted sacraments) in that it seems to come unasked for, a gift, a gratuitous perk to the spirit. It comes and goes, and it's up to the recipient how to use it or whether to invite it in for a longer visit. (Poets are untrustworthy addicts of metaphor, you see; I will go anywhere, shamelessly, in pursuit of a good one, once I've caught a glimpse of it—follow it into quantum physics, even follow it into Catholic theology. After all, it was feminism as the most apt metaphor for a metapolitical vision that got me into the Women's Movement in the first place. You never can be sure where these metaphors will lead you. You can only follow them lovingly, intuiting their path by the resonances of energy they trail behind them.)

Actual grace is an amiable metaphor, you must admit. It seems so *grounded.* Lightning forks, leaf veins, river tributaries, and the blood vessels of a human lung all express the same branching pattern. The spiral winds around and beyond itself in the smallest virus, the uplifting of a fiddlehead fern, the dance of water down a kitchen-sink drain, the twirl of the largest galaxy.

To look through the surface of things—*to develop microcosmic vision*—would be to pass through the two-way mirror and encounter the idea of freedom. How early on the shade or shape of one's skin would become irrelevant; we can hardly see or remember back that far, it's so long ago. Was it really possible that we permitted one another to die of hunger or thirst, of wounds or anger or loneliness? Did we actually feel revenge or jealousy, hatred or fear? Can it be that we ever suppressed curiosity and desire, experienced lack and longing, ignored intelligence in any form, denied or distorted the existence of love?

To feel through the density of space / time—*to develop macrocosmic sensibility*—would be to encounter the futility of trying to anatomize freedom, would be to discover not its anatomy but its living physiology, to study as a participant rather than an observer its shifting shapes, never still long enough for any dissection. How early on the form of form would become irrelevant, except insofar as it was a metaphor for the insouciance of formlessness, its cosmic joke; we can barely recall the time we didn't realize this, it's so long ago. Did we ever really confine one another—our own relatives—in walled prisons, in disease-infested slums, in asylums, concentration and detention and refugee camps, old-age institutions? Can we really have been afraid of people with similarly shaped genitals laughing together in love and pleasure? Is it possible that we erased forever from all space / time the form of the Tennessee coneflower—its now-extinct commonweed wild lilaceous petals exclaiming their thermodynamic explosion from an amethyst center? Could it have been possible, such a nightmare?

Microcosmic vision and macrocosmic sensibility are waiting to be used, patient in the genetic holograph of our DNA. To begin to use them and dream a better reality might mean that we, and the universe itself, were coming to consciousness—and showing distinct signs of a tendency to exist. And that would metamorphose the metaphor of our $F = et^2$ equation into: *Freedom* equals Energy times the square of the velocity of Transformation.

—1982

The World Without
de Beauvoir

There are people who seem to take more than their own individual lives with them when they die—as if their passing lessens the sum of humanity's parts by more than a single existence. Such persons can be private or public losses, or both; they can be famous or little known outside of a small circle. The quality of loss I refer to is one that rends the frayed fabric of hope—the assumption that somewhere out there this particular unique intelligence is alive, contributing in intangible ways to the evolution of humanity.

For me, in recent years, Martha Graham's death was such a loss, as was that of Jacqueline du Pré, Georgia O'Keeffe, Graham Greene. (I have mourned certain political figures, yes, but it's no coincidence that I find myself citing artists; even with all their faults, they're generally more trustworthy.)

The death of Simone de Beauvoir—who was at once an artist, a philosopher, a political figure, and an activist—struck such a chord of mourning, amplified in my case because she lived for me not only in her books and public actions, but also in a private correspondence over a number of years. She had been to me—as to many women of my generation—an intellectual mother, generous with the severity of her love.

I wrote the following piece—part eulogy, part obituary—for Ms. *magazine where, only two years earlier, I had reviewed her book,* Adieu: A Farewell to Sartre,* *after his death. With her characteristic refusal to sentimentalize— unflinching existentialist to the end—she had written in that book: "His death does separate us. My death will not bring us together again. That is how things are. It is in itself a splendor that we were able to live our lives in harmony for so long."*

Six years after her death, I miss her distant presence still, at times with an intensity she herself would doubtless have chided me for, shrugging simply, "That is how things are." But were I then to point out that her entire life was that of a woman never content to leave things "as they are," she would have smiled, raised her wine glass and her eyebrows and, without ego, ceded the point.

One figure, more than any other, has inspired twentieth-century feminism: Simone de Beauvoir. For myself, as for millions of women worldwide, it is not possible to analyze where we've been or to estimate where we're going without acknowledging de Beauvoir's influence. On April 14, 1986, we lost her. She died at age 78, in Paris.

As philosopher, artist, and political activist, de Beauvoir burned through almost eight decades with fierce intelligence and energy. She was a founder of French existentialism. Her writing embraced philosophical works, memoirs, political tracts, a play, and fiction. Even a cursory list includes many modern classics,** among them

---

*(New York: Pantheon, 1984).

**The Mandarins* (1954; New York: Norton, 1991), *Memoirs of a Dutiful Daughter* (1958; New York: Harper & Row, 1974), *The Prime of Life* (1960; New York: Paragon House, 1992), *Djmila Boupacha* (1962), *A Very Easy Death* (1964; New York: Pantheon, 1985), *The Woman Destroyed* (1968; New York: Pantheon, 1981), *The Coming of Age* (1970), *All Said and Done* (1972).

*The Ethics of Ambiguity** and *The Second Sex.*** She was a founder of the intellectual journal *Les Temps Modernes* in 1945, and worked actively against the Vichy collaborationist government in World War II and against the French and U.S. involvements in Vietnam in the 1950s and 1960s.

Despite the sonorous governmental eulogies after her death, during her life de Beauvoir was constantly in trouble with officialdom—always the mark of a principled citizen's existence. Even at age 62, she was still being arrested, this time for publicly selling a banned Maoist newspaper (a protest against the ban, since she also denounced the paper's politics). Ten years earlier, she herself had been banned from French television appearances because of her support for the Algerian independence struggle—yet her books were later put on the boycott list of an Algerian newspaper because she also supported the existence of Israel. She defied the law repeatedly, as when she openly permitted the use of her home in the late 1960s and early 1970s as a site for then-illegal pregnancy termination procedures. She founded Choisir (To Choose)—the group devoted to women's reproductive freedom, which sponsored demonstrations and the first famous abortion-rights petition (in which she and other well-known women signatories proclaimed that they had had abortions).

Of all her causes, female human rights were central. She founded or cofounded numerous French and international feminist organizations and institutions, including the League for Rights of Women (1974), the newspaper *Nouvelles Féministes* (which published from 1974 to 1976), the journal *Questions Féministes* (1979), and the Sisterhood Is Global Institute (1984). But public activism was

* (Secaucus, NJ: Citadel Press, 1962).
** (New York: Random, 1989).

ly one expression of her commitment to and impact on contemporary feminism.

Her private life could be said to be an example of "the personal is political." She acknowledged John-Paul Sartre as her lifelong companion but refused to marry him (at age 19 she had written, "I don't want my life to obey any other will but mine"). She had relationships with other men. In her mid-sixties she criticized her own inability to expand her deep friendships with other women to include an erotic component, forthrightly analyzing this in herself as a matter of upbringing, a fault of logic, and a failure of nerve.

She continually reexamined her writing with the same critical eye; in the mid-1970s she noted that she hadn't gone far enough with her feminism in *The Second Sex*, that the intervening years had taught her the insufficiency of all male political ideologies of the Right or the Left in obtaining freedom for women.

In *Force of Circumstance** she had written, "I prefer to fathom rather than flatter myself"—and she lived by her words. Insistently and consistently she made the connections: the political with the philosophical with the economic with the sexual with the aesthetic. Her vision was unflinching, holistic, and relentlessly in motion. She never stopped noticing. She never stopped growing. She dared to speak and act for herself. In so doing, she spoke and acted for all of us.

I too can ultimately speak only for myself. I learned of her death on the day the United States bombed Libya, killing and maiming farmers and children "by accident" in a "surgical strike" supposedly to stop terrorism from killing and maiming civilians. She would have been at her typewriter about it—and on the streets, protesting, as well. At the time of this writing, news breaks of the Cher-

*(New York: Harper & Row, 1977).

nobyl nuclear "accident" in the Soviet Union, the deaths, the fallout, the radioactive cloud of long-term catastrophe. She would have spoken, acted, moved. I can no longer tell which of my tears are for which of these mournings; our despair has now become as integrated as our vision for saving the world.

I only know that she, the "mother" of existentialism as well as of contemporary feminism, lived daily with despair and daily transcended it. She found the status quo unacceptable; in turn, the status quo never accepted her.

Of all her letters to me over the years (always hand-scribbled on simple graph-pad paper), the one that shocked me most was her humble thanks for the "generosity" of my review of her book, *Adieux: A Farewell to Sarte* (in *Ms.* magazine, May 1984); apparently the book had been savaged elsewhere. To the end, she was attacked—for her radical feminism, for her refusal to separate thought from action, for her art (too subtle), for her politics (too blatant), for her style (too cold—since this was one woman they couldn't condemn as "too emotional"). The love and reverence many women felt for her seemed an ever-renewing surprise to her, most welcome but disproportionate to her deserts and her own severe self-standard of excellence.

We have few titans. Simone de Beauvoir was one, and she is gone. More than any legacy of tactics or theory, she leaves us her life: a challenge toward audacity, clarity, movement, and—in both senses of the word—integrity. Our last communication, only a few months before her death, was about my trepidation in finishing my first novel and my unease about stealing time from being at the barricades in order to "indulge" myself in a work of art. Her reply was swift and firm: "For now," she wrote, "forget politics and write the novel. For you, they will be the same thing, in any event. It will demand an act of courage. *Bon voyage.*"

I took her advice. I will feel the absence of that advice in years to come as a constant ache. It's a lonelier, colder, more endangered little planet without her.

"But," she would say, as she did a few years ago, "the changes women are struggling for, I am certain in the long run women will win."

I wish I could reply to her, "Yes. It's up to us now, each of us, to locate in herself her own greatness, because to see the world as it is and transform it will take our collective greatness. Your loss impoverishes us, but it is in itself a splendor that you were with us for so long. *Bon voyage.*"

—*Spring 1986*

A Paler Shade of Racism

*A characteristic of feminist consciousness I've come to trust
(sometimes grudgingly) is relentlessness. Once welcomed
into the brain and heart, this consciousness is there to stay—
and grow—at once dybbuk and shadow, conscience, curse,
and blessing. There's no convenient getting rid of it. Deny
it, and it will outwait you. Defy it, and it will trip you up
embarrassingly. Flee it, and it will follow. It is protean in
its form. I sometimes think of it as a humble but pungent
onion—with endless translucent layers.*

*The more I travel, the more I learn and re-learn basic
lessons I thought by now thoroughly ingested. The further
away I go from my own country, the more I discover its
interior landscapes, especially those internal, determining
ones—the shifting tectonic plates of sex and race.*

*This article was written as a plea to citizens of another
country, a plea that they not repeat a particularly scarring
moment in U.S. history. But more, it was written as a discovery—of yet another layer of racism in myself. Central
to it is the deceptively simple realization that styles of racism and sexism differ, though the content remains the same.
The essay was published in the New Zealand weekly magazine,* The Listener, *and provoked quite a few letters—
some even sympathetic to the audacity of a foreigner dar-*

ing to try and counsel across nationalities, hopefully without preaching.

Meanwhile, to this day, wherever I go, the layers of the onion skin that is consciousness keep relentlessly peeling away . . .

It began days after I arrived in New Zealand—a country I love—on this, my second visit. I found I was wrestling with a new and unexpected form of racism—in myself.

Three decades of political activism in my own country had not prepared me for this, although they had at least trained me to be alert to subtle symptoms of bigotry in my own reactions or those of others. As a European American involved since the early 1960s in the civil-rights movement, the anti-war and environmental movements, and the birth of the current wave of feminism, I'd been working for years with people of color in the United States—a multi-ethnic country with its own history of virulent racism, and one enriched by the presence of Native Americans, African Americans, Latino Americans, and Asian Americans. And work with other feminist activists, women of color in the United States and internationally, had deepened my consciousness about the integral links between sexism and racism, and had intensified my commitment to fighting both. What a shock, then, to find myself feeling an impatience bordering perilously on contempt—towards the Maori, Samoan, and other Pacific peoples of Aotearoa.* I would come away from conversations with Maori women friends feeling bewildered and vaguely irritated by such gentleness, such seeming patience in the face of Pakeha** racism. I knew enough to recognize that the problem was mine, as the outsider-

*Aotearoa ("Land of the Long Shining Cloud") is the original Maori name for New Zealand.

**Pakeha is the Maori term for New Zealanders of European ancestry.

observer, not theirs. I knew that I must be misreading as passivity or resignation something I did not understand. But for the moment I could push my comprehension no further. It wasn't until I discovered the other side of the coin—the particular characteristics of Pakeha racism—that the origins of my own reactions became clearer.

One after another, white New Zealanders—average, good people—would express a (to me, less than deserved) great affection for the United States. Then, on learning that I lived in New York City, they would suddenly shift into conversational alarm. Now, New Yorkers are accustomed to this, even elsewhere in the U.S.A. With plucky smiles masking a sense of *déjà vu,* we gamely point out that New York is actually eleventh on the crime-rate list of cities in the United States, and that one should hardly trust Hollywood movies as accurate social indicators. I can add that, despite having lived in New York all my life, I have never been robbed, burgled, mugged, or held up. Nor have I ever been raped—that is, by a stranger. Nor had any of these offenses been visited on the white New Zealanders with whom I spoke. What, then, was the cause of their fear?

There were all these *black* people, you see, really *dark-skinned* black people, wandering around the streets of Manhattan. Some, even many, spoke Spanish, or English with "odd" accents—of Caribbean origin, or the lilting dialects of the U.S. South. But whatever their accent, they *spoke* to you in it! They came right up to you on the street, in a restaurant, in the subway; they came right up and said things! And some of the men were *tall.*

What incendiary remarks did these African Americans make? Oh, it turned out that one "black" was merely asking for the correct time; another noticed that the visitors seemed lost, and wanted to offer directions. Did this then disprove the stereotype? No. To these otherwise sensible and sensitive New Zealanders, New York still equalled violence—and violence still equalled tall, dark-skinned, strange-talking blacks.

I began to understand the connection between Pakeha racism and my own. It was a matter of style.

The style with which I had become familiar in decades of North American political activism was an insurgent, urban, African-American style. It had originated in street-rapping (the trading of greetings or news in a hard-edged, metaphor-rich, affectionately adversarial manner) and had been honed to a fine art by years of confrontation with a white power system. It ranged from the friendly josh-ing—"Mess with me and you get hit up 'side yo' haid, man"—to the politicized "Move on over or we'll move on over you." It had been adopted by other peoples of color in North America, including those in rural settings, and by white male radicals, and by women activists. It encompassed a classic bittersweet ghetto humor, and it was / is nothing if not direct and vivid. This style obviously alarmed Pakeha New Zealanders and evoked a blatant racism on their part. It was precisely the lack of this style— or, rather, the articulation of an altogether different style— on the part of Pacific women that awakened my own rac-ism. Where, I wondered, was their energy, their anger? Then a further revelation thudded into my brain. I was accustomed not only to a North American version of a Third World style, but to a *male* North American version. What I was encountering in Aotearoa was literally a *pacific* style. More, it was and is a female style.

It is neither placid nor resigned, but it does not enjoy confrontation for its own sake and it does not lust after gratuitous violence. It is a style redolent of dignity, rit-ual, and wit. (For example, the Maori community adopts the tactic of courteously challenging the Pakeha state regarding land rights, on that state's own terms—the Treaty of Waitangi; white men's law, white men's sys-tem.) It is the subtlety that asks the Pakeha, Do you intend to abide by your own justice? And, at the same time, that style puts its energy into organizing its own community, feeding the body with *kai* (food), the brain with *Maoritanga* (lore), and the soul with ancient *wairua* (spiritual wisdom), and gently but insistently prodding the men of that community to understand that Maori women, too, need a place to stand, as *women.*

New Zealand newspapers, radio, and television inform us that Maori "militancy" is growing; they give more coverage to the gangs and the so-called radical men than to the ongoing work of, for example, the Maori Women's Welfare League. Meanwhile, many otherwise good-hearted Pakeha confide a quiet panic over the court challenges on the Treaty, all the while expressing that morbid fascination with, and fear of, those violent New Yorkers. It makes me wonder. And it makes me sad.

To me, white New Zealanders should be dancing in the streets with gratitude that the peoples of color in this land choose to move toward their human rights (which happily include the rights of the environment itself) so intelligently, humanely, generously. Yet many Pakeha seem bent on a self-fulfilling prophecy of fear: that violence is the only way in which power is gained or shared. Male prophecy, male style.

So this turns out to be an appeal, especially to my Pakeha sisters, but also to Pakeha men of conscience who are willing to listen. You have the chance to do something different. You need not repeat our northern hemisphere mistakes, need not resist constructive change by a preoccupation with violence, until your very resistance provokes and demands that violence. New Zealand gave the world many firsts: women's suffrage, national superannuation (social security), and the recent shining example of standing up to a superpower to remain nuclear free.

I remember a time when there was that chance in my

own country. It was in the 1960s, in Alabama, during the voter registration and school integration campaigns. A particular southern police chief, a proud member of the Ku Klux Klan, had been brutal to all of us who were civil rights workers, but especially so, of course, to those who were black. He went into the hospital with a case of ulcers. Black women, the spine and soul of the civil rights struggle, brought their children and stood for hours outside his hospital, holding candles, singing gospels, praying for his recovery. He did recover—and went after them with high-pressure fire hoses and electric cattle prods. But that moment—those scrubbed-faced, starched-pinafored children trying to sing him into health—glows in my memory as a high moment of the human spirit, of hope and possibility.

The women and children were not listened to. The marches, the singing, the prayers, the pleading, the legal approaches, the community organizing, the voting, were not respected. Such tactics were considered too effete, too "feminine," not manly enough. So Uncle Sam got his longed-for nightmare: the Black Panthers, the SLA,* the shoot-outs—John Wayne stand-offs at the OK Corral, just like in the movies. Now, years later, after much blood has been spilled, it is again the women who are picking up the pieces and organizing anew, whether in their own communities, in the feminist movement, or in the gleaming words of Toni Morrison and Alice Walker.

It *can* happen in New Zealand—the worst, all over again. Or, of all places, it can be different. But only if the Pakeha blessed by living in Aotearoa listen carefully to the style of energized hope, to the *wahine toa* (strong women), and dare to do so with *aroha* (love) in their hearts.

—1987

*Symbionese Liberation Army, a paramilitary group of the period.

The Politics
of Silence

These notes constitute a further attempt to develop work I started on the politics of silence in Going Too Far *(1977) and* The Anatomy of Freedom *(1982), and to expand the germinal explorations begun by other feminist writers on the subject. I am especially indebted to the following work: Tillie Olsen's* Silences *(Delacorte Press, 1978), Adrienne Rich's* On Lies, Secrets, and Silence *(Norton, 1979) and in particular her essay "Women and Honor: Some Notes on Lying" (1975), Michelle Cliff's "Notes on Speechlessness," and Catherine Nicholson's writing on the "power of deafness," (both in* Sinister Wisdom *no. 5), and Nelle Morton's concept of "hearing each other into speech" ("Beloved Image," paper delivered at the National Conference of the American Academy of Religion, San Francisco, December 1977). Many women, myself included, have written on the silencing committed by the patriarchal structures of sexism and racism, by patriarchal history, culture, language, even modes of perception and definition; some of us have also written on the silences among and between groups of women. The following meditation focuses instead on the politics of silence between two individual women, in particular between two women in a relationship, as close friends.*

This essay has never been published in full before.

> Comprehensive talkers are apt to be tiresome
> when we are not athirst for information, but, to
> be quite fair, we must admit that superior reti-
> cence is a good deal due to the lack of matter.
> Speech is often barren, but silence also does
> not necessarily brood over a full nest.
>   —George Eliot, *Felix Holt*

Among the Padaung tribes in Burma's Kayah State, there persists a custom of pressing down a girl's collarbones with brass rings; the ritual of "beautification" begins when the female child is five years old, with one ring at a time added during intervals until, as an adult, she may be wearing as many as twenty rings in a tight necklace. Tourists have called the wearers "giraffe women" because of the effect of grossly elongated necks. In fact, the neck muscles tend to atrophy; removal of the rings (said to be a punishment for adultery) can cause suffocation. Padaung men take pride in the thin "inherently feminine" voices of "soft-spoken" Padaung women.

In London, Paris, or New York, such a practice would be considered barbaric. In London, Paris, or New York, the short necklace now coming back into style for the sophisticated woman is referred to as a collar or choker.

Wherever she waits, and only rarely dares whisper, the silent woman is not to blame. Blame, in addition to being counterproductive and boring, is not the point.

Let us say there are two women. Each is keenly aware of the politics of silence between women and men; each is publicly articulate about the effect (: erasure) of such silencing on women. In private, one is talkative, accus-tomed to trying to express—on the page or in conversa-tion—thoughts and emotions, as well as their psychological and political valences. In private, the other woman tends toward silence about such matters, calling herself (as she has heard others do for years) "a silent person," "a private person," or even "shy." These two styles persist and inform the friendship between the two women.

Sometimes the silent one feels under assault by the other's speech. Sometimes the talkative one feels assaulted by the other's silence. (These descriptive terms are themselves only semi-articulations: the talkative one can be taciturn, the silent one can be loquacious.)

There is a politics at work here. It is a politics qualitatively different (albeit related, given the context of patriarchy) from that between a man and a woman. In an androcentric world, male power is power *over*, enactable by a man via whatever mode he chooses: we recognize how the dominant conversationalist male acts from a position of power over women ("Women make such good listeners!"), but so does "the strong silent type" (*"Talk* to me, Arnold, *please?"*). Traditionally and cross-culturally, men are accustomed to / expected to pronounce themselves endlessly on matters of "public concern"—for which read the power of running the world—while retreating into inarticulate mumblings in the "womanly" realm of private affairs: emotion.

Between two women, however, another politics is alive, in the engagement of two different kinds of power—power *over* and power *to*—made more complex by the dexterity with which each can be manipulated to masquerade as the other.

For example, the talkative woman has power not only *to* express herself but also power *over* her friend regarding the other's difficulty in / choice in not doing so. Indeed, the common perception (and what perception in patriarchy is common but a patriarchal perception?) is that talkers have privilege and power over non-talkers. This is one truth.

Another truth—the underside to the truth above—is that

she who expresses reveals, intentionally or even unintentionally, her thirst to communicate, her vulnerabilities, her willingness to be known, her very self; and longs to inspire a comparable process of revelation, either by response or by the other's initiative, in the silent partner. She spends her power in this place of powerlessness.

■

Lesbian silence battering at the unhearing ear of heterosexual assumptions.

The silencing of the subjective voice by the myth of objectivity.

Very well, then. Let us say that these two women are not merely friends, but lovers.

~~Very well, then. Let us say "you" and "I."~~

■

Silence creates silence, proselytizing and propagating its message: I fear my talking monopolizes the conversational oxygen between us; I hope fewer words from me will give you the space in which to speak; waiting, I fall silent; my silence comes to have a life of its own.

Or: Communication creates communication: expression as a form of contagion. The contagion can be one of disease, if language is used as a vehicle for lying, control, manipulation, or hypocritical compensation for the absence of other forms of communication (touch, hearing, alternative enriched forms of silence such as an exchange of "knowing" glances). Such an abuse of language is commonplace, truly "sound and fury, signifying nothing," a barrage of words as defense against authentic communication. But if language is valued as a means of understanding, of bridging difference, and of hazarding truth(s), then the contagion is one of health.

As a feminist activist, for instance, I could define myself as an agent of contagion—an instrument for naming, for spreading hitherto unspeakable truths about and between women—in a political attempt to foster an epidemic of human health.

As a lover, it is both simpler and more complicated.

Simpler because every cell of my being aches to talk with, and to hear, the beloved.

More complicated because I fear invading your privacy, bullying your silence. More complicated because you can claim (not without some justification) your own respect for words is so great that you use them sparingly. More complicated because your exactitude of speech—when you do speak—is so finely honed it was one of the reasons I first loved you, which means that I must, to be fair, credit your silence as a quality that drew me to you in the first place. More complicated because I fear your anger (often the initial and most accessible means by which your silence overflows into speech) if I prod too much. More complicated because I do not wish to seem probing into your rights to yourself, in an emotional imperialism. More complicated because I fear attributing to you, in a one-sided analysis, objectifying motives projected out of my own enforced solipsism, motives that bear no relation to whatever you really are thinking and feeling.

Both simpler *and* more complicated because you tend to discover what you think and feel in a process of silence and only then, if at all, to share it. Whereas I tend to discover what I have previously only intuited as my thoughts and feelings while in the act of verbalizing or writing them: the word made flesh. This frequently means that I grope aloud, risking the ungainly posture of self-discovery with a witness present, however embarrassing.

So I, ostensibly from a position of (expressive) power, feel actually naked, vulnerable—powerless, as if I used my power in order to set it aside. So you, from a position of ostensible (silent) powerlessness, actually operate with power: power *to* define what is said and not said, heard and not heard (because failing a response from you how can I know that my soundings were heard, much less misunderstood?), power *over* the entire process of communication between us. You alone know what both of us are thinking.

▪

Knowledge is power. Information is power. The secreting or hoarding of knowledge or information may be an act of tyranny camouflaged as humility.

But: honesty can be a bludgeon disguised as a gift.

Silence accrues slowly, like the minuscule skeletons of a coral reef; it can wear as many colors, take on as many formations; it is just as sharp, but can cut more deeply. Silence can also rise suddenly, at the speed of darkness.

Silence may defend itself by calling its methods "discretion" or "tact." In an erotic context, silence may be defended as a means of preserving mystery, a supposed aphrodisiac (which in itself precludes such glad possibilities as "The more I know you, the more I love you.") It was Colette who wrote "I do not necessarily respect what I do not understand."

Colette also wrote of the silence between two women intimates as one in which the participants can be utterly at peace in the certainty that out of that quiet fullness anything can be spoken, yet nothing need be. This presumes that the silence is one chosen mutually by both participants. Such a silence vibrates with an equal power *to*. You have introduced me to the speechless pleasures of such a silence, it is true.

A rediscovered clue: the Biblical phrase (in the King James version—translated so brilliantly by seventeenth-century English metaphysical poets): *and they knew one another.* To know, to "ken" something, has the same etymological root as the old English word "cunt." Etymology is political code.

Logos as a concept meant not only the Word, but Creation: breath itself. If Logos is breath as well as utterance, then speaking to your silence is an act of prayer, like arguing with God—whose notorious silence can seem such an indifference as to drive one to atheism.

I yearn to cry out "I am myself, not a ghost of parents or teachers or former lovers who drove you into silence by demanding that you speak in their dialects of possession. I am merely me, and it is you, merely you, I love and hunger to hear!"

You might reply "I am myself, not a ghost of parents or teachers or former lovers who drove you to performing as the sole way you could get their attention. I am merely me, and it is you, merely you, I hear and love, beneath whatever you say."

But how dare I assume that reply, since it has not been spoken?

It is possible to suffocate in such a silence.

█

Class plays its part in both articulation and silence, as well as in the different styles of expressing each. (Silence is an expression just as much as being apolitical is a political stance.) Accepted wisdom has it that verbal ease is a privilege of education and class (and what wisdom is accepted, in a patriarchy, but patriarchal wisdom?). Yet the candid, direct, metaphor-rich articulations of, for instance, working-class or poor women can throw into high contrast the repressed verbal style of middle-class women. In a group context, it can even intimidate them.

Culture, too, we are told, plays its part. As a European American, a white, apostate Jew who has lived most of her life in New York, and as a member of that financially insecure yet educationally enriched class the French term "intelligentsia," I acknowledge that my style tends to dramatize events, exaggerate states of being, and delight in conversation for its own sake, almost as an art form. (Sometimes you say you find this highly entertaining.) In another culture—a more Anglo one, for example—such forms of social congress may be judged as vulgar, prying, superficial, clownish, or stereotypically that of the "effusive American." (This ignores the considerable regional, ethnic, and urban / rural differences in the United States—

a common error made by those unfamiliar with the laconic Maine "Yup" and "Nope," the Mississippi front-porch yarn, the Chinatown "talk-story," the Harlem street-rap, *ad infinitum.*) In a classic gesture of psychological reductionism, it can also be labeled "psychobabble"—as if all U.S. residents lived in California granola-bins (that was unfair, I'm sure, to Californians). Whose, after all, is "the American voice"? Crazy Horse, Thomas Paine, Willa Cather, Zora Neal Hurston, Emily Dickinson, Ralph Ellison, Walt Whitman, Twain, James, Faulkner, Jeffers, Baldwin, Tennessee Williams, Erdrich, Cisneros, Hong Kingston, Morrison?

To me, obversely, such judges may appear in their forms of social communication to be cold, distant, haughty, secretive, and pretentious. My curiosity about an Englishwoman's life, her intellect and emotions, may seem to her rudely intrusive. Her restraint about inquiring into comparable details of my life, while for her an act of respect, may strike me as a mark of disinterest in—even contempt for—me, a lack of curiosity about wishing to know me at all.

Yet if class as well as culture are at this moment in history both constructs of patriarchy, then what would authentic forms of female communication entail? If women, in two different sexist stereotypes, are supposed to be chatterboxes or to remain silent, does that make me a collaborator with one stereotype and you a collaborator with the other? Or are your silence and my speech both facets of our feminist rebellion? Or is your silence male identification, as a survival mode—and is my loquacity male identification, as a means of controlling the expression between us?

What would a feminist silence sound like? What would genuine free speech say?

Age plays a part. I am sufficiently older than you to feel the press of time poignantly limiting, moment by moment, the chances for all I would and could say, all I am eager to hear. This particular aspect of human suffering is not attributable solely to patriarchy—which is politically inconvenient.

My tools as an artist are words—with all the inherent dangers thereof. A lifelong vocation addressing the silence of the unknowable reader.

If a pause can be pregnant, so can a phrase be aborted, or an idea brought to term, communicated, and grow to have a life of its own. What, then, would self-determination over one's own reproductive rights be in terms of silence, in terms of speech, in terms of living out loud?

It has taken me almost forty years of writing to realize that I live in an age where language is not only cheapened, but where the technology of modern communication has so shrunk patience and shortened attention-span as to make my tools perhaps as outmoded for an art form as a lute or virginal would be for a contemporary composer: quaint, possibly touching, a bit precious.

So I speak toward the beloved—toward you—out of a sensibility already weary with the pain of being a bad joke: "a word person" (so termed, affectionately, by a friend needing help with her electoral campaign literature); "so poetic, even in prose" (this, uneasily, from a colleague in publishing); "more of an intellectual than you think you are" (this astoundingly backhanded compliment from a long-time acquaintance tsk-tsking over the use of "big words" in my writing). I have learned to smile good-naturedly over such insults, even to adopt the safe defenses of caveat and self-deprecation in order to coopt such blithe definitions of my existence.

In the rare moments when I strike back, I am assured that it was well-meant teasing, that the teasers actually love me for (among other things) my words, that I mustn't lose my sense of humor. Yet one early sign of consciousness unfurled when women began to affirm losing our sense of humor over well-meaning jokes about dumb broads, frigid bitches, and mothers-in-law; when African Americans ceased to pretend shared amusement over watermelon and natural rhythm stories; when Jews and Italians, Poles and Hungarians confronted jokes about kikes and wops, Polacks and Honkies. When we decided to take ourselves ("too") seriously.

We know that humor is deeply political. There are those who claim all humor has an element of cruelty in it. Yet the humor of mutual recognition is not cruel, but revelatory. It resonates a joyful laughter—a communication of freedom. You and I have shared many such moments of humor, laughing until words fell into a happy silence of breathless gasps and aching ribs.

Consequently, I am loathe to censor—even, teasingly, to censor the teasing—into silence. Or to censor your silence into speech.

Meanwhile, the pain continues. To articulate the pain is, of course, to renew the entire process, and to invite more teasing—this time about one's hypersensitivity.

■

"You find it easy to talk about your feelings. I don't. Yet I feel as deeply as you do. I just don't flaunt it."

This seems to be a statement about powerlessness.

Then there is the infamous heterosexual cliché comment about two same-sex lovers embracing in public (surrounded by heterosexual lovers doing the same thing): "Look, I'm all for gay rights—but why must they flaunt it?"

If the two statements are related, which is a defense of power held (power decidedly *over*)? Are both?

■

If you say, "I am not given to verbal diarrhea," are you aware that what was merely your defense arrives with me as an offense?—and has the effect of silencing me. Besides, something snide in me wants to answer, the word is "logorrhea." But that would be to risk sounding elitist as a "word person."

If you say, "The difference is that you want me to change, whereas I love you the way you are," this sounds generous, mature, admirable.

(A short short story: a voyeur and an exhibitionist fell in love, moved across the street from one another, and lived happily apart ever after.)

Another truth is that wishing to preserve the status quo—in this case your silence / my speech—is the desire of the power holder: it preserves your inviolability and my accessibility.

Truth curls in nested boxes.

Still another truth is that all lovers fall in love with certain qualities of the beloved—which they then, idiotically, proceed to try and change.

Still another truth is that I want both of us to change, to find some third way between your art of silence and mine of speech, between the excess of the hidden and the surfeit of the revealed. Neither of us chose either of these dualities. (The truth is that you want both of us to change, too.)

Still another truth (a tiny box, this one, worn close to the bone) is that I fear being typecast as the repository of articulated emotion, the one who can be relied upon to Raise The Issue, hint / pressure / probe / nag / confront. Curiosity is, to me, an act of desire, of trust, all of a piece with what I've termed "erotic intelligence." Since, then, "wanting to talk about it" is to me one central form of loving—albeit the one traditionally and cross-culturally assigned to women—it can mean, in effect, feeling as if one is bearing more than one's share of the burden of emotional responsibility in a relationship. This is bad enough when dealing with a man. It is a delicate, hushed sort of madness when dealing with another woman.

■

After the Chinese Revolution, female cadres attempted to unwind the foot bindings of some of their sisters. But the tightly knotted, fetid bandages, which had reduced the human foot to the size of three inches, had sometimes rotted and grown into the flesh. Their removal caused insufferable pain, pain that had not been so experienced since the binding, because numbness had replaced sensation over the years.

Removal of the Padaung neck rings can cause suffocation.

How do I speak to you then, without violating your silence? How do I learn to believe you when you claim to love my speech? How do I strip myself of unnecessary verbiage so that my plainsong reaches you uncontaminated by my own defenses, manipulations, pretentions, or presumptions? How can I strain to hear you into speech—or hear what you wish your silence to tell me? How can I affirm your means of survival while not denying my own?

How do I speak to you in the act of love?

How do I love you in the act of speech?

■

These notes are only one side of the story. Which is, unfortunately, the point. It has taken me words to tell you these things, knowing as I do that the writing itself can be seen as an act of power, certainly of *hubris,* possibly even of revenge. But knowing, too, that these words have been brought forth with great care, risking more than a little, and leaving me raw in the process.

For fear.

For fear of being misunderstood. For fear of being misrepresented. For fear of never being answered.

O beloved voice: Have I just proven why you choose silence?

—July 1989

III

From the
1990s

A Massacre in
Montreal

*The following essay was originally written for the Op-Ed
Page of the* New York Times. *When the editor read the
finished manuscript, however, he decided that the piece
"made too many connections," and brought in too many
elements regarding violence against women from elsewhere in the world. We amicably agreed to disagree—since
I felt that the point of the essay was in making those connections, in emphasizing that the massacre in Montreal
was not an act existing in a void, but one committed in a
worldwide context of lethal, "normal" misogyny. Women
have no difficulty understanding this: December 6 is now
observed by the international Women's Movement around
the world as a Day of Remembrance.*

*The article was subsequently circulated in typescript
among feminists in Canada; it has been printed there, I
am told, in both French and English. Certainly the responses
I have had from Canadian women have been deeply moving and gratifying. Particular thanks is due to the Canadian feminist writer, activist, and scholar Greta Hofmann
Nemiroff, for her counsel and support during the writing
of this piece.*

*This is the first time this essay will appear in print in
the United States.*

"It's the women I've come for. You're all fucking feminists. I'm against feminism. That's why I'm here."

Those were his words, spoken in a quiet voice.

They were the last words ever heard by fourteen young women engineering students before they died, shot by a 22-year-old man who also wounded nine other women and four men during his semiautomatic-rifle rampage through the halls of the University of Montreal on December 6, 1989. His final act was to kill himself.

Newspaper and television reports carried the details. They seemed familiar; we read similar versions of the same story so often. He had purchased the rifle legally because he had no criminal or psychiatric record—no record despite numerous complaints by women neighbors and former girlfriends about his bizarre, sometimes threatening behavior. He was addicted to such combat magazines as *Soldier of Fortune,* to pornography, to movies about terrorism. He loved hanging around gun shops, talking with the boys. He was wearing combat fatigues when he went on his gynecidal spree.

The three-page letter found on his body was virulent with misogyny: females were to blame for everything that had gone wrong in his life—for his inability to graduate from college, his loss of various jobs, his failure to gain admittance to graduate school, the breakups of his friendships or romantic relationships with women. The letter also contained an "enemies list" of fifteen prominent Quebec women, presumably potential targets. Many of these women had not characterized themselves as feminists. But then, neither had most of the slaughtered students. That didn't matter. They were women: they were prey. They endangered men: they must be destroyed.

Honorable men find such violent attitudes and acts appalling. The guy in the street phones in to radio talk-back shows. The psychologists and sociologists write articles, initiate studies, give press conferences, issue quotes. And a further violence is wreaked—by precisely such honorable men. It is the violence of denial, evasion, collaboration. Every possible analysis of the massacre is promulgated—except that based on the spoken and written words of the gunman, Marc Lépine, himself.

Because Lépine was half Algerian, some of these gentlemen use the occasion to Arab-bash ("They're all so violent, you know."). Because he hadn't graduated college, some cite class resentment as his motive (although it was his own uneven scholastic record that failed him). Because the rifle had been manufactured in the United States, the importation of such products—and of "American violence"—can be deplored (as if Canada had no home-grown misogyny). Because the victims were women training for nontraditional jobs, there are the predictable sighs and pronouncements that "This is what happens when women refuse to stay home and have babies." Because his background included a "broken" home and battery, heads can be shaken over "the demise of the family" amid condemnations of abstract violence. Because he was raised by a woman, his "craziness" must be a reaction to her (when in doubt, blame mothers).

Why is it again left to women to notice a certain pattern evident in the facts of the case, a pattern the honorable men in their rush to self-serving judgment conveniently ignore?

The "broken" home *should* have been broken; it was a violent home, and the violence was not abstract, but specifically paternal. The father, Rachid Gharbi, tyrannized and battered his wife and two children for years—until the wife managed to divorce him and he returned to Algeria. That wife, Monique Lépine, reclaimed her name, raised both children on her own, became a nurse, and worked hard to support her family, even returned to school for a further degree so as to earn a better salary and improve their lot. In the transcript from her divorce hearing, she had testified that Gharbi repeatedly and unashamedly insisted women were not the equals of men, but were born to serve men. The son was seven years old when the father he so feared left; nevertheless he learned his lesson well. His father's attitude overshadowed the different context in which his mother tried to raise him. Because, subtle or blatant, that attitude was and is reinforced by the entire surrounding patriarchal culture.

Feminism. Yawn. Surely this is the "post-feminist" era, isn't it? Isn't the women's movement dead *yet?* How those damned women do yammer on about their marginal, neurotic complaints.

Once more then. With feeling. Because these "marginal" issues are about the majority of the human species, which happens to be female.

In North America, one out of three women will be raped; two-thirds of all women are victims of battering; a woman is raped every three seconds, beaten every fifteen seconds; one out of every four women experiences sexual abuse before age eighteen; nine out of ten endure sexual harassment at their schools or jobs. Two-thirds of the world's illiterates are female; women and children comprise ninety percent of all refugee populations and eighty percent of all poverty populations. One-third of all families on earth are women-headed. Less than a third of all women have access to contraceptive information or devices, and more than half have no trained help during pregnancy and childbirth. Complications from pregnancy, childbirth, and abortion—which kill more than half a million women per year—are the leading cause of death among women of reproductive age. With nonpregnancy-related reproductive tract infections (RTIs) factored in, the death toll rises to more than a million, with another 100 million women maimed each year. Women are one-third of the world's formal labor force, but receive only

one-tenth of world income and own less than one percent of world property. Outside the formal labor force—
whether as homemaker, prostitute, nun, fuel-gatherer,
water-hauler, farmer, or domestic servant—women's work
is regarded as unskilled, marginal, transient, or simply
"natural," and is invisible in the Gross Domestic Product
accounting of virtually all nations.* Nowhere does the work
of reproduction of the species itself count as "productive
activity."

This is violence.

So is the practice of *sati*—the forced "suicide" of a widow
on her husband's funeral pyre—still prevalent, though
outlawed, in the subcontinent of India. So is female
infanticide, still practiced, though illegal, in China. So are
the practices of bride sale, child marriage, polygyny,
abandonment, genital mutilation, and gratuitous hyster-
ectomies; so is the two-sided coin of forced concealment
in *purdah* and forced exposure in pornography. So is the
denial of two basic human rights—reproductive freedom
and freedom of sexual choice—to women by fundamentalists of all major patriarchal religions.

Feminism. Yawn. But that's why there's still a women's
movement, now worldwide, and growing.

The classroom doors of Montreal University's engineering school have glass panels. When Lépine ushered
all males out of the room and then shut the door, the men
stood in the corridor. *No one ran for help.* After shooting
the first women, he had to pause to empty and refill his
rifle magazine. The male teacher and male students did
not open the door and rush him, though they were many
and he was one. None of them made a move. *They watched
him through the glass panel.*

This is violence.

---

*See Marilyn J. Waring, *If Women Counted: A New Feminist Economics*
(New York: Harper & Row/HarperCollins, 1988).

Professor Elliot Leyton, a Canadian expert on mass murders, was quoted as saying "This is one of the very few mass-murder cases I know of in which women were specifically targeted." The brain reels. Jack the Ripper? Richard Speck? Theodore Bundy?

This is violence.

Canadian feminists tried to point out the obscenity of such erasure, such collaboration-by-analysis. Day after day, they mobilized, massing with pink armbands outside the Montreal cathedral at the victims' funeral, marching on the universities. Night after night, they consoled each other the way women do, by talking and weeping. They telephoned their sisters south of the border, and we phoned them, in shock at the capacity of most men to externalize the Marc Lépines as "other," to deny the commonality of masculinist aggression, to refuse acknowledgment of the banality of sexism, the pervasiveness of woman-hatred, the continuum of violence that creates a normality of terrorism in most women's daily lives.

As women do, we try to make sense of it through understanding, through "womanly compassion." A young woman lying in the hospital with her face half shot away murmurs that she'd like to forgive him, go forward, encourage other women to do the same. An older woman mourning her murdered daughter comments sadly that it does no good to hate, that Lépine was "a poor sick boy." Another bereaved mother says "I can't help but think of his mother. She must be suffering so." This is the human spirit reaching across grief to embrace commonality, not disavow it.

At such moments, every woman, whether she calls herself a feminist or not, shudders with fear and rage. At such moments, every woman secretly wonders why men hate women so. At such moments, every woman desperately reminds herself that men of conscience do exist, that there are men who actively reject the connection between violence and manhood.

But the honorable men make that difficult. The Québec premier, M. Robert Bourassa, refused women's petitions to close the legislature and universities on the day of the funerals. Such a day of official mourning was only called for, he claimed, "when someone important to the State had died."

Why, this is violence, nor are we out of it.

—*January 1990*

IN MEMORIAM

Geneviève Bergeron, *age 21*

Hélène Colgan, *age 23*

Nathalie Croteau, *age 23*

Barbara Daigneault, *age 22*

Anne-Marie Edward, *age 21*

Maud Haviernick, *age 29*

Barbara Maria Kleuznick, *age 31*

Maryse Leclair, *age 23*

Maryse Leganière, *age 25*

Anne-Marie Lemay, *age 22*

Sonia Pelletier, *age 28*

Michèle Richard, *age 21*

Annie St-Arneault, *age 23*

Annette Turcotte, *age 21*

Women in the
Intifada

In 1986, I spent over six weeks with Palestinian women in
the UNRWA (United Nations Relief and Works Agency for
Palestine Refugees in the Near East) refugee camps of Egypt,
Jordan, Lebanon, and the Occupied Territories of West Bank
and the Gaza Strip. That experience—and the intensely
moving first-person stories of those women—is detailed at
length in The Demon Lover.

As I wrote there, "I was to meet victims and survivors,
women who by their mid-fifties were already great-great-
grandmothers, women who bear the societal scars of having refused to marry at all, women who dare to love other
women. I was to meet Palestinian women whose sole means
of resistance is to wear keys on strings or chains around
their throats, keys to homes bombed or razed forty years
earlier. I was to meet highly educated Palestinian women,
sophisticated in the ways of patriarchal politics, who had
risen as far as possible within the PLO, only to hit the glass
ceiling of male supremacy." But the focus of the journey
was the women in the refugee camps, who suffer with every
breath they inhale. They are former peasants, teachers, ex-
guerrillas, artists, nurses, manual laborers, social workers, "housewives," doctors, organizers, students, mothers,
secretaries, factory workers.

I had insisted on women interpreters, knowing that the kind of communication I hoped to inspire would be impossible through male interpreters. This had never been done before; UNRWA had no female interpreters, but did manage to find Palestinian women among its own personnel who, although employed as educators, medical staff, or social workers, were able and eager to translate, never having been given the opportunity before. These women were extraordinary, and together we asked questions no journalist had ever bothered to ask of Palestinian women— and heard answers of such honesty and anger as to shock even the translators. Not surprisingly—although contrary to everything I'd been told—I found an omnipresent, open feminism, sometimes raw, often polished, albeit fortunately not so narrow as Western definitions thereof. These women's lives were also dramatic testaments to the indomitable and affirmative spirit of female human beings surviving in unspeakable conditions.

But if the conditions were virtually unspeakable in 1986, they were almost unthinkable in 1989, when I returned to the region—this time to focus on the Occupied Territories, specifically to investigate the impact of the Intifada (uprising) on Palestinian women.

The Intifada had begun in 1987, as a series of spontaneous street demonstrations and general strikes to protest the Israeli government's treatment of Palestinians, especially those in West Bank and the Gaza Strip. By March 1988, the Occupying Army (the Israeli government's term is "Administrative Authority") had posted an additional ten thousand troops on round-the-clock patrol in the two Territories; for three days at the end of that month, all 650,000 residents of the Strip—the most densely populated, poorest place on earth—had been confined to their homes under an "Iron Fist" policy of "collective punishment" curfew. There were over four hundred deaths and severe injuries in one week in Gaza alone. UNRWA, already overworked and understaffed (most UNRWA personnel in the field are Palestinian), moved to take emergency measures—keeping some clinics in Gaza open twenty-four hours a day, organizing special feeding programs, and more than doubling the international staff who direct the field offices. These temporary emergency measures were to become permanent, however, in response to the spiraling escalations of both the Intifada and the Israeli government's reaction to it. By August 1988, almost nine thousand Palestinians were in makeshift prison camps awaiting trial (including two thousand being held under "administrative detention" orders, which allow the suspect to be jailed for ongoing renewable six-month periods with no judicial review). Having already seen how Palestinian women not only share the conditions and anguish of their men but, in addition, bear the crushing burden of being female in a doubly intense patriarchal context (both Arab and Israeli), I could only imagine what the impact of even greater brutality on their lives might be.

What I had found in 1986 was a cauldron simmering with male violence and female suffering. When I returned in 1989, the cauldron had boiled over. The following essay is based on what I witnessed, heard, and felt in 1989; it is published here for the first time—with a postscript covering updated information through 1992—because during the intervening years various versions of it have been unable to find a home in print in the United States.

The first people I see, after the many khaki-clad, heavily armed soldiers clustered at the checkpoint border with Israel, is a four-block-long column of men in Gaza Town. They are kneeling on the cracked and broken sidewalks, hands on their heads, backs to the street, with faces pressed to the shuttered fronts of little shops. Some are bleeding, many have ripped clothing. Behind them stand soldiers, Galil rifles pointed at the back of the kneeling men's heads. I am told that "an incident" has just taken place—a stone throwing. These are the suspects, some caught in action, others merely picked up from a broad "sweep" of the area.

The second sight is of women—forty or fifty, perhaps—also on their knees, in the middle of the street itself. No, not on their knees; they are on all fours. Some are pregnant; some are old women; a few look to be little more than girls. All of them are weeping—some silently, some loudly. Other soldiers stand over them, semiautomatics at the ready. This is when I learn the new policy: that after demonstrations or "incidents," Palestinian women are rounded up and forced to clear the streets with their bare hands, picking up broken glass, chipped bricks, stones, still-smoking noxious tear-gas cannisters, spent bullets, sometimes a live Molotov cocktail. No brooms are allowed.

I know I am back in the Gaza Strip.

January nights remind me how close the Strip is to the savage cold of the desert in winter, and also to the damp of the Mediterranean Sea. A muscle-cramping chill settles in every evening. It is impossible to get the clamminess out of one's clothing, still damp from having been soaked through earlier by the daily rains. The sand—as roads, as pathways, as the floors of camp shelters approximately nine-by-thirteen feet and housing as many as fifteen family members—the sand has become churned mud. It sucks vigorously at my sturdy boots, almost pulling them off; what must it do to the rubber clogs or cheap sneakers worn by most camp residents? Open sewers in Rafah Camp overflow with rainwater, with run-off, with human waste. There is no heat in the shelters, and very few have any electricity at all. Punitive power cuts by the army, ordered with no advance warning, make even that unreliable.

I inquire about an impressive half-built edifice I've seen

on the drive into the Strip—a tall, modern building close to the beach. It turns out to be a pilot project for the Israeli government's plans to make the Gaza Strip into a Mediterranean tourist playground.

■

No news report can communicate the atmosphere of palpable fear, everyone tensed in apprehension of the next eruption of rage from one or both parties to the conflict. The ear quickly learns to interpret no shout as a greeting, no crackle of explosive as a car backfire; the eye learns to trust no scene as tranquil; there is no such thing as relaxing the alert, even for a second.

The faces of the men have changed. Relentless intense emotions seem to have distorted them into ritual masks. That reassuringly ill-disguised panic and confusion I had glimpsed on the faces of many young Israeli soldiers in 1986 has vanished, replaced by a smooth expression of contempt—though whether contempt for those they fight or for themselves no one can say. But it is clear that these young men have grown callouses over their feelings—over having any feelings, much less showing them—and now wear their discipline with tragic ease. Some do so with the indifference of professionals, others with the relish of fanatics. These expressions are strikingly twinned in the faces of the *shabaab*—the young male Palestinian militants. Except for the soldiers' array of weapons, and the blue jeans, T-shirt, and black-and-white-checked Palestinian *kefiyyeh* (neckerchief / scarf) worn by the *shabaab,* one could not tell them apart.

I suddenly understand the real reason why uniforms were invented.

■

Each of the 400,000 adult Gazans has been forced to exchange her or his old green identity card for a computerized, magnetic one issued by the army. The thousands of Palestinians standing in line to exchange the cards have been herded past soldiers carrying automatic rifles, toward rows of secretaries who punch the identity numbers into banks of IBM computers that instantly reveal all data such as outstanding tax obligations; each Palestinian must "clear up" such "problems" before being issued the new card—without which it is impossible to receive rations, register a marriage, obtain a driver's license or a birth or death certificate, accept a paycheck, do any banking, pass through the omnipresent army checkpoints along the roads, or go to seek or work at employment in Israel.

There is an "official policy" of no beatings. Yet everywhere in the camps now I see wounded, bandaged, and badly bruised men, women, and children. Each woman has stories. She—or her sister, her daughter, her mother, her aunt or cousin or friend—was beaten by soldiers: women in labor, old women, nursing mothers, toddlers, babies. Many point to the bullet holes in the walls of their shelters. The rate of miscarriages has risen precipitously—from beatings, from running after children or away from soldiers, from rising rates of hypertension and anemia due to malnutrition (because of food shortages), possibly from the effects of toxic elements in the tear gas, certainly from acute and unremitting stress.

The UNRWA clinics, many housed in decrepit buildings, their courtyards even more overcrowded with waiting women and children than in 1986, are as immaculate as they were then—with one exception: the smell of antiseptic has been overpowered by the stench of tear gas. It is a common occurrence for the army to lob gas cannisters into the clinic courtyards and into the clinics themselves. UNRWA formally protests such acts; the Palestinians denounce them as harassment; the army calls them, alternately, punitive actions in pursuit of a provocateur who may have taken shelter there, or simply "mistakes."

Used cannisters—still reeking acridity—are common-place sights. One sees them on the dirt roads, along the highways, in the muddy narrow lanes that pass for streets in the camps, in the city thoroughfares of Arab East Jerusalem. The United States officially states that it stopped shipping tear gas to Israel in the early 1980s.

The cannisters I see are clearly marked: USA 1988 Issue.

Most of the Intifada's daily "incidents" seem to constitute a war between children and adults. Confrontation after confrontation is between Palestinian boys, many as young as six and seven, throwing stones at Israeli patrols—each member of which is bedecked with a helmet, a pistol, a Galil rifle, an ammunition belt, a truncheon, a gas mask, and tear-gas cannisters.

At Al Ahli Hospital in Gaza, a haggard-looking doctor tells me that these days, when she enters the emergency room, she often thinks for a moment that, by error, she is in the pediatrics ward.

But the little boys no longer see themselves as children; they identify with their older brothers, the *shabaab*, their dead or living heroes. The little boys say they are "training for manhood." When one of them has been killed, the others speak admiringly of him as having become "a little man."

The women—both mothers and teachers—openly deplore this. At Nuseirat Camp, home to almost thirty thousand refugees, I have a reunion with teachers I had met three years earlier; I am surprised and moved that they remember me.

"Oh yes," Wafa smiles, "You are the American woman who cried with us. How could we forget that?"

Embraces, little cups of the ever-present strong Arab coffee, shared confidences. The teachers lament that they can no longer control their male students of any age:

"The army is not supposed to enter the camps. But you

see how, at the gates of every camp, there are soldiers—
entire encampments, tents, tanks. Just waiting. And they
come in and patrol. They swagger through, even though
they know it will provoke an incident. Sometimes the
shabaab do the provoking; they stand at the entrance and
shout curses across the road."

I nod, saying that I have already noticed how proficient
the young men—both Israeli and Palestinian—have
become in each others' languages, although their vocabulary is restricted to insults.

"If they studied more, they would know more," one
woman dryly interjects. These are, after all, teachers. I
am reminded of the Palestinian obsession with education; the pride that Palestinian women have the fastest
growing literacy rate of women anywhere in the Arab
world. Bassimah continues:

"The moment anyone sees them enter the camp, news
spreads. All it takes is four words—'The soldiers are
coming'—and the boys run out of the classroom. We cannot stop them."

More than one teacher had physically interposed herself between the boys and the door—and had literally been
run over.

And the girl students?

"They rush to the window to try and see what's happening," is the response. "Sometimes they join in. Sometimes they *lead* the demonstrations because the boys have
become more afraid of arrest. But basically the tragedy
of the girls is different. Do you remember what they used
to answer a few years ago when you asked what they
wanted to become as grown-ups?"

I remember well. They had said they wanted to become
teachers, doctors, nurses, lawyers, architects. Their faces
luminous with intelligence and hope, they had said they
didn't want to have more than two children—not like their
mothers, who have an average of six to eight. Some had

said they wanted no children at all; others said they never intended to marry or, if they did, it would be for love, not an arranged match. This, in the context of Arab tradition, had struck me as an incipient revolution.

Bassimah goes out briefly and returns with a student about twelve years old. The child is solemn, wears the *hijab* (head covering), has dark circles under her eyes.

"Ask her that question now," says Bassimah.

I do, and the response comes swiftly, in a flat voice:

"I want to be the mother of a martyr."

"But what if there is no need for martyrs by the time you are grown?" Wafa puts in. "What if there is peace, freedom, statehood? Then what?"

"I want to be the mother of martyrs," comes the monotone.

"You once wanted to be a writer, remember? You were so good with your essays. Remember how much you wanted to write books?"

The child looks confused.

"Try to remember," the teachers urge gently. "It still is possible for you. Your people need books, too, scholars, poets, storytellers. What will you do with your life after peace?"

For a moment there is a flicker in the little girl's eyes. Then the present closes down again, erasing past and future.

"I want to be the mother of martyrs," she intones.

The teachers and I exchange glances. The eyes I look into brim with tears.

Mary Khass is a widely respected Christian Palestinian educator; her specialty is pre-school child psychology and education; she is in demand as a speaker on the subject at international conferences. A woman in her late fifties, she looks ten years older than she did three years earlier. Her hands twist with anguish as she speaks to me.

"The children. My god, the children. You saw them before—their games, their laughter—even in the camps, even in the midst of poverty, crowding, danger, humiliation. They were still children. But now? Now their favorite game is 'Intifada.' They take turns playing soldiers and Palestinians—like cowboys and Indians. They play at gassing, arrests, detention, beatings, roundups. They are brutal with one another; it has become their fun. Nothing dissuades them—not coaxing or promises, not talkings-to or discipline. They are saturated with violence."

I ask about the pride the Intifada has undeniably rendered the Palestinians, a pride in fighting back, in ceasing to be victims.

"The adults may feel the pride. The men, certainly. But what is happening to the children is forming a legacy we will have to live with for generations. The leadership must be brought to understand this, to comprehend that these children are being drenched in violence and vengeance. Many can no longer imagine any other way of living. The adults know that in five years, ten years, there *will* be a two-state solution. Any sane adult, Palestinian or Israeli, admits that. But how will these children deal with peace? They no longer have any context for relating to it. These children will carry the scars—scars of euphoria at bloodshed—for the rest of their lives. And infect *their* children. We are recreating Northern Ireland all over again, here and now."

■

But the pride is there, too, and fiercely cherished as the sole possession of a desperate people. It differs in its expression. For the men, it is a pride in manhood—best expressed in martyrdom. For the women, it is a pride in keeping what little they can alive.

Everywhere they have organized into neighborhood women's committees. The women manage to secure and share food even under curfew. They care for the wounded.

They try to rescue and hide children about to be arrested. They help one another survive—the newly widowed, the deserted and abandoned (by men who have disappeared—to detention or deportation, or to fight or to flee). They share their already overcrowded shelter-homes, giving refuge to families whose shelters have been bulldozed (the policy of collective punishment permits the destruction of a shelter if the soldiers think a family member has thrown a stone).

In 1986 the just-budding women's committees had been focused on adult literacy, on skill-sharing, on small income-generating projects. Now they are full grown. But now they are focused on community survival.

And the Intifada has had its own effect on the women. The boldness that was evident in private, with only other women present, has gone public. They no longer ask permission of their men to receive a guest or to go out— even at night. They say that the men don't like this but can do nothing about it. Even the men know the women are the lifeline of survival.

The women are excited by their newfound relative freedom, and amused by the men's reaction. They seem on the whole to have retained a sense of humor that the men appear to have lost.

Rula, in Kalandia Camp in West Bank, is witty in her description of women's plight under the Intifada:

"Well, of course there is the terror, and the special hardships in getting food, water, basic necessities. But I sometimes think that the worst of it is the presence of the men. Before, the men would leave after breakfast and not return until dark. If they had employment, they'd go to work; if they were unemployed, they'd be out looking for jobs. And there was always a coffee house, no matter how dilapidated, where they'd sit for hours and talk. Meanwhile, the children would be in school. This of course meant that the women could get on with life—the washing and cleaning and cooking—and maybe even have a minute to sit with a friend and talk. But *now* . . ." Rula rolls her eyes in mock despair. "Now—between the curfews and school closings and job firings called for by the Israelis, *and* the general strike days and school closings called for by the Intifada leadership—there are sometimes days on end when all the men and children are home. *All day long.* It's a nightmare: they're underfoot all the time, wanting this, demanding that, whining about something else. The woman must cook three full meals a day—when and if there's food. She has no peace, even for a moment."

The neighborhood women's committee near her, Rula says, organized an ingenious solution. There was one battered black-and-white television set in the area and, whenever the power was on, the women marshalled all the men and children, parked them in front of it, and then went on about their lives.

■

On my first trip into the region, mobility in and between camps had been difficult at times, but always possible. I could start out talking with women by 6 A.M., spend the entire day at one camp or visit two or even more, and continue until late at night, sometimes "changing shifts" of exhausted interpreters.

This trip, mobility is severely restricted. Camps are "sealed" with absolutely no notice, leaving one at the entrance trying to get in—or inside trying to leave—for hours, or days. Absolute curfew in the Occupied Territories is lowered at dusk; the streets in Gaza or in East Jerusalem look like ghost towns. Any vehicle caught driving—even with UNRWA credentials—may be subjected to thorough stop-and-search tactics, harangues, threats, frisking of the occupants.

In some of the tiny Palestinian villages, to move at night is to risk yet another danger: the assumption that the car headlights presage an army transport. A shower of stones is likely to greet such a vehicle.

But there are women I promised to see in one such village, and the only time to do so is at night. Under cover of darkness, they conduct now-illegal literacy classes for adults and for children who have fallen behind in their school work because of forced school closings.

I do not travel in an UNRWA car. A Palestinian woman drives me in a borrowed, battered private car. And as we pass through the villages, she blinks her headlights in a particular signal.

"How come the authorities don't pick up on the signal?"

I cannot see her smile in the dark, but I can hear it in her voice:

"They try. But the signal is changed from day to day."

I do not ask how.

■

In West Bank, I go to Ramallah, to the Ramallah Women's Training Centre, which I had written about earlier as "an oasis of sanity and hope." Three years earlier, the spacious grounds, the spotless classrooms, the tidy dorms—all were filled with young women (288 vocational students, 350 teacher-training students), talking animatedly, laughing, walking arm-in-arm, proud and beautiful. This was the first vocational training center for women in the entire Middle East, and a source of enormous pride to Palestinian women.

In 1989 the grounds are deserted, the classrooms and dorms empty. I learn from the school's principal, Ms. Lamis El Alami, that the school had been closed by the Occupying Authority for over a year.

"All the Palestinian institutions of higher learning—like Bir Zeit University, like this one—have been forcibly closed," she tells me. "Accusations that they were hotbeds breeding student radicalism, you know. The irony is that here, the girls glimpsed a peace they had never known—

peace not only from Occupation, but from the constraints of their own fathers and brothers. Here they learned skills for the future, and how to pass on those skills. From here they would go home questioning everything: violence, religious fundamentalism, multiple pregnancies, arranged marriages, all the patriarchal traditions. For that kind of consciousness, yes, we were a hotbed, a breeding ground. Now . . ."

I ask when the school might be permitted to open again. She sighs.

"Who knows? We petition regularly. It could be next week, next year, never. We try to use the time constructively, even with a skeleton staff. We are fund raising to build a new department, to train women physical therapists." Her eyes begin to gleam with excitement. "There is discrimination against female patients who need physical therapy, you see. And as you know, there are many in need of physical rehabilitation, many wounded, paralyzed—from beatings, from bullet wounds, even from the so-called merciful rubber bullets. All the Arab physical therapists are men. But tradition has it that women's bodies ought not to be touched by men other than their husbands. So the male patients get rehab but many female patients go without. It's tragic. This new department will begin to address the problem."

Together she and I stroll slowly through the deserted grounds. I comment on how beautifully they still are kept up, the flower beds neat, the grass mowed, the bougainvillea still cascading its crimson brilliance, the climbing white roses perfuming the air, indifferent to whether an Arab or Israeli or U.S. visitor breathes in their fragrance.

"Oh yes," Ms. Alami smiles, "Volunteers. Mostly women, of course. We will not fold up and go away. We will outwait this, so the girls have us to come back to someday." Her face clouds over. "But I grieve for the ones we've lost. Some of the girls refused to leave the dorms; the soldiers dragged them out. They were desperate not to return to the camps, to their families—they knew they were of marriageable age and that their fathers . . . many of them are already lost now, married, pregnant, trapped in reliving the lives of their mothers and grandmothers. Still," she sighs, drawing herself up again by sheer will, "we will outwait this. We will not go away."*

■

In an attempt to meet the demands of "the emergency," UNRWA has created a new post in the camps: Refugee Affairs Officer, or RAO. These RAOs, staffed by internationals, not Palestinians, have no actual legal authority to intervene in an altercation, but they exert a "moral presence." Totally unarmed, working in two-person teams with Palestinian RAA's (Refugee Affairs Assistants), wearing UN armbands and carrying two-way radios to alert the field headquarters about a crisis, RAOs drive or walk through the camps. An RAO may, for example, stand between advancing army patrols and bands of *shabaab;* try to dissuade soldiers from making an arrest; try to calm an enraged crowd; rush a bleeding child to the nearest clinic if the camp is sealed and no ambulance is permitted in.

The previous year, when camps in the Strip had been sealed for as long as a month, with no fresh food supplies permitted in, the then-deputy field director of the Gaza Field, a remarkable Englishwoman, Angela Williams, defied the army and ordered in a truck convoy of food supplies on her own authority. She is now based in Vienna, as director of Relief and Social Services—which means she travels regularly to and through the camps in the field. It was a subtle diplomatic solution.

One of the first acts Williams took in her new post was to increase the number of Women's Program Centers in

---

*The Centre reopened in 1991, and some women who had been married and become pregnant (or even had borne children) in the interim were readmitted to complete their studies. This was a first: married or pregnant women attending college is almost unheard of in the Arab world.

all the camps, and to create special Women's Program Officers in each field.* And in January 1989, UNRWA got its first woman RAO—a Swede, who worked the Gaza Strip.**

▰

Western newspapers regularly decry the "rise of religious fundamentalism" among Palestinians, formerly the most secular of the Arab peoples. This increase is said to be most pronounced in Gaza.

Yet what I find in Gaza makes this "rise" eminently explicable.

The Israeli government has outlawed any large political meetings of Palestinians, just as it has outlawed any flying of the Palestinian colors. (Yet the colors appear mysteriously, overnight, waving from a lampost here, a street sign there.) The Israeli government prides itself, however, on freedom of religious expression. Therefore, is it surprising that hundreds suddenly congregate with impunity in the mosque?

To be sure, Hamas—the fundamentalist Muslim group—is delighted at this, takes credit for it, and boasts about attendance. Hamas has tried to challenge the secular leadership (both indigenous and PLO) of the Intifada with its own strikes, hazings, demonstrations. But the bulletins from the Intifada secular leadership—which also mysteriously appear as daily handouts—denounce the mono-religiosity of Hamas, reminding their constituents that this is not a *Jihad,* not a religious war; that there are Christian and Druse and agnostic Palestinians; and that the liberation fight is for *all* Palestinians.

I ask woman after woman if she believes fundamentalism is on the rise. And woman after woman admits that

* As of 1992, the number of centers had tripled and the number of women attending them had quadrupled.

**By 1992, ten of the twenty-one RAOs in the Occupied Territories were women.

Hamas is feared—but as for the reported rise in the number of its adherents, woman after woman laughs.

As I write these words, two bullets lie in a shallow dish on my desk. These are the much-publicized "rubber bullets" that the Occupying Authority claims are used—even at risk to Israeli soldiers—rather than live ammunition. Because they are so "safe," they are fired at point-blank range.

The bullets are not light, as one would expect from rubber. This is because they are not rubber through and through. I have taken a razor blade and cut slices from each, so as to see into the interior.

In one, the interior is a solid steel core.

In the other, there are hundreds of tiny iron fragments.

It becomes clear why a tour of any hospital or clinic in the Occupied Territories reveals such patients as a woman blinded by a rubber bullet, a six-year-old girl paralyzed by a rubber bullet's fragments imbedded in her spine, an old woman dead of suffocation because a rubber bullet was shot into her throat when she opened her mouth to scream.

How I came by the bullets is simple: in some camps, they litter the ground, there for the picking.

How I got the bullets out with me past security at Ben Gurion airport, so that I could show them on television in the United States, is another story—a story that will have to wait for a day when I never intend to return to Israel/Palestine.

In Dheisheh Camp in West Bank, south of Jerusalem, I arrive to find I am invited to a wake. A young man, eighteen years old, was shot and killed the day before. Both my interpreter and I demur, expressing misgivings about imposing on a family's privacy and grief. But we are pressed, and it would be rude not to accept the hospitality.

The family home is a two-room concrete shelter. In the outer room, about thirty men are congregated, some sitting in rickety chairs, others standing, all of them talking, smoking, drinking coffee served by young boys of the family. A large photograph of the dead son—the martyr—is taped to the wall, framed by paper streamers of green, red, black, and white, the forbidden colors. Under it sit the father and *mukhtar*—the camp elder. The grieving father is being lionized by the visiting men who file past him, slap him on the back, embrace him, pump his hand in congratulations. The father is now beaming; he has prestige.

We are ushered to and through this room, into the second room.

It is filled with women, sitting on the floor, backs to the wall, all around the edge of the room. At the far wall sits the mother, flanked by her daughters and other female relatives. It is explained who we are, and through the interpreter I offer my condolences. The mother accepts them with dignity, and thanks us for coming to pay our respects. Then she falls to talking about her son. Suheilya, my interpreter, whispers the translation.

The mother and other women are sharing memories. How lovely a child the dead boy was, how his name, Jamal, means "beauty," how he had laughed with joy the day he took his first halting steps—remember?—how smart he had been at school, how handsome he was becoming, how he never balked at helping his mother, how he had worked with his sisters on their homework, how hard he had studied, how excited he had been on winning the scholarship, how he planned to become a lawyer some-day . . .

It is so simple and natural a thing to weep, that I don't notice how we all are crying softly. This woman's son and my son—safe as a student back at his music conservatory in Boston—are the same age. Suheilya and I sit cross-legged like the rest of the women, on this cold floor strewn with threadbare blankets, holding hands.

The *mukhtar* bursts into the room, his rheumy eyes flashing, his bony finger pointed accusingly at the mother, his voice loud in furious denunciation. Suheilya is transfixed at his ranting; I tug at her sleeve for a translation. Rapidly, in a low whisper, she tells me that he is berating the women for mourning, reminding them that this is a day for great celebration, that they should be honored to have known a glorious martyr, that female tears scald the soul of one so elect, that they insult and dishonor his memory by their womanish sorrow. All the women fall silent; all except Suheilya and I dutifully draw fixed smiles across their faces. Satisfied, the *mukhtar* leaves.

There is a silence after his departure. Then, with a look of contempt at the door by which he left, the bereaved mother tears open the front of her dress, snatches the veil from her head, rends it in two, beats at her bare breast with her fists, and keens in a wild grief, "My son, my son! See how I am not even permitted to mourn you . . ."

And then all the women are free to cry.

Later, Suheilya, still trembling, as I am, says to me, "What we saw is the Intifada *within* the Intifada."

Zahira Kamal has violated curfew to come and see me at my West Bank lodgings, in a Jerusalem convent just outside the gates of the Old City. It is very good to see her again. In her early forties, she is one of the new generation of Palestinian grass-roots woman leaders. No men appointed her to a formal post heading a "women's auxiliary," nor does she spend her time doing charity work, winding bandage rolls, or organizing parcels for men in prison. She proudly calls herself a feminist, and her work is with women—in prison, in the camps, in the villages.

In 1986, when we first met, I had been impressed by the Women's Work Committee that she and five women friends had been building for a decade—a network of more

than nine thousand women in over seventy groups across
West Bank and the Strip. The WWC, mindful that most
women couldn't come to any center because of fathers or
husbands forbidding it, made a practice of going to where
the women were. Literacy classes ensued, sewing classes,
knitting and embroidery instruction, typing classes—all
aimed at skill sharing, all aimed toward empowerment,
toward an economic self-sufficiency that might be gained
by paid employment. A fluid, semi-visible, dynamic network.

"If a woman doesn't show up for a meeting, we visit
her where she lives," Zahira had told me, "We prod her,
gently, to find out why. Usually she is being beaten and
is ashamed to tell us. We talk together with all the women
of the family, to build support for her—and we suggest
ways in which the women might argue tactfully with the
men. For instance, if the men use koranic texts to justify
beating women, we suggest that the women question
whether the texts have been correctly interpreted. We try
to get women to challenge the power structure in the
family. *And they do.*"

Zahira had then been under town arrest for six years;
this had not changed, three years later. She cannot get
permission to attend international women's conferences.
She has never married, was trained as a physicist, and
has put all of her younger sisters through school and college.

Now, during the Intifada, she and I sit together again.
All of the contradictions inform her conversation, and
show in the new lines of her strongly boned face: pride
at the uprising; frustration at Palestinian fragmentation;
rage at the Israeli government; fury at PLO leadership for
not always acting wisely; heartache at the violence, the
counterviolence, the glorification of death. But now the
WWC has expanded into the Palestinian Federation of
Women's Action Committees.

And she radiates pride about "her" women. Even more excitedly, she tells me that she and other women have already begun meeting to draft articles of the proposed Palestinian Constitution, toward the someday-state of Palestine.

"Oh it will be a while yet, I know. But it *will* come. And when it does, it is vital that women are covered by secular law, not by *sharia,* or religious law."

The full impact of this is borne in on me slowly. Such a new state would be the first Arab country in which women were totally, not partially, protected by secular law. She follows my train of thought:

"Yes. There will be tremendous pressure brought to bear by the entire Muslim world for Palestine *not* to do this. The other Muslim countries will be terrified that it will be contagious. Even in Israel, as you know, divorce, marriage, and custody all are under the authority of the rabbinical courts. But this is the moment to begin, so that the revolution cannot use us and then betray us, as it did in Algeria and everywhere else. That is why we are working on—and already lobbying for—such assurance *now.*"

We are joined by a shy woman, a little over five feet tall, in her late twenties, whom Zahira wants me to meet. Amal tells me her story quietly, without drama: how she was detained without charge but knew it was because her husband had been politically active; how she was kept for six months in solitary detention; how when she refused to give information on his whereabouts she was tortured—hung by her wrists and beaten on the soles of her feet until she could not stand; how she was kept for ten days and nights in "the cabinet," a compartment so small that even a woman of her size was unable to lie out full length or stand up straight; how they broke her arm; how they would not let her mother bring her baby daughter to visit.

As always, there are tears, and embraces, and even

laughter. They implore me to "write about us, tell the world we exist." Eventually, they take their leave, and I watch them go into the night, risking their safety during curfew to have met with me.

But as I turn to go to my room—perhaps because the Intifada has now numbed me, the visitor, with its atrocity stories—I find I am thinking not of the woman who suffered torture for the sake of her husband and her people, much as I stand in awe of her courage and endurance. Instead, I find I am thinking of the women who are, against all the odds imaginable, already organizing to ensure the secular, legal freedom of female citizens in an eventual new state—right in the heart of the Middle East.*

Rita Giacaman, only in her thirties, is the leading Palestinian scholar on women's health, and an autonomous feminist who has dared reject alliance with any political faction of the male Palestinian leadership. She receives me in her West Bank apartment, despite being late on her deadline for a scholarly paper. She comments humorously on how much time she has on her hands, now that Bir Zeit University, where she teaches and does research, has been closed by the Israeli government.

She speaks with her characteristic rapid energy—about the sometimes cynical use of women's neighborhood committees, women's life-saving actions, women's devotion, by the various male leadership factions.

"There must eventually be a totally autonomous women's movement of Palestinian women, or—no matter how we prepare for 'after liberation'—we will be betrayed."

---

*In 1991, Zahira Kamal would be part of a delegation of Intifada leadership that would fly to PLO headquarters in Tunis to negotiate with PLO leader Yassir Arafat for a strong indigenous presence from the Occupied Territories at the Madrid Peace Conference. Later that year and in early 1992, she would travel to Madrid and to Washington, D.C., as a member of the Advisory Panel to the Palestinian delegation at the U.S.–Russian-sponsored peace talks.

Such a radical position leaves her very far out on a limb, with virtually no support.

"Well," she shrugs gamely, "a feminist is used to such a position, no? After all, if women on both sides of this conflict held real political power, we probably would have had peace a long time ago. I prefer to recognize the truth and speak it, no matter how painful or unpopular. Perhaps I'm just a little ahead of my time . . ."

Events in the Middle East seem to move at once in slow motion and with the rapidity of a vertical curve. More will have changed by the time you read this. But while "experts" debate the outcome of the Intifada—has it run its course? can it be contained? who are the emerging leaders? has it become counterproductive? has it degenerated into mindless bloodletting of self-proclaimed militant against accused collaborator?—I think of the women, and how for them there is no going back. The experts still overlook them, ignoring their deaths as they have ignored their lives. Yet in these ignored women resides the real hope for any lasting peace in the region.

—1990

Postscript

I have not written here about the way the Gulf War screamed down on the already barely endurable lives of these women; how the Israeli government did not send warning sirens about SCUD attacks into the Occupied Territories; how Palestinians in West Bank (those who had telephones, that is) could at least rely on principled Israeli peace-activist friends to ring them up and warn them that the sirens were wailing and they should take shelter, but how there was no such alternative in Gaza. Or how even after the Israeli High Court overruled the government's position that gas masks should not be distributed to Palestinians, the masks were not forthcoming. Or how after two children had died, Palestinian teachers and UNRWA personnel in the Strip fanned out even after curfew, to warn panicked women in the camps not to put plastic bags over the heads of their children in the hope of protecting them from the rumored SCUD gas. I have not written here how, in the heat of the Gulf War crisis in December 1990, Palestinian feminists gathered in Jerusalem in an unprecedented women's conference dedicated to pluralism, democracy, anti-sexism, women's status since the beginning of the Intifada, and the birthing of an autonomous women's movement. Women activists from all segments of the Palestinian movement united in condemnation of religious fundamentalist attempts to reinstitute the hijab, *male leaders' resistance to women's presence in the decision-making process, family pressures and traditions responsible for a rise in the numbers of female high school and university drop-outs, and the particular brutalities visited on women prisoners.*

I have not written here how, at the height of the SCUD attacks—when Israeli and Palestinian male reconciliation activists broke off dialogue and returned to their respective adversarial positions—Palestinian and Israeli women held a peace march together. And were gassed—not by Iraqi missiles, but by U.S.-manufactured chemicals thrown from Israeli army vehicles.

I have not written about the much praised Israeli airlift of Ethiopian Black Jews—who were immediately housed beyond the Green Line, where they are both out of sight of white Israelis and in sight (and stone-throwing range) of Palestinians outraged that these newcomers were being planted in soil from which they themselves, after generations of living there, have been uprooted. (The Black Jews, of course, have no idea of the game in which they are the pawns.) Nor have I written about how the recent influx of Russian Jews—also much heralded—has strained an already fever-sick economy; how peace-oriented Israelis worry that these emigrés may constitute a new voting block for the sabre-rattling conservatives who would permanently annex the Territories for a "Greater Israel"; how more than half of the "dirty jobs" in Israel, once reserved for the Palestinians, are being taken away from them and given to the new arrivals; how Palestinian employment in the Territories now is between 35 and 40 percent; how hunger is a daily fact of life; how there is a growing number of women begging in the streets. I have not written about the rise in numbers of Palestinian women being deported from the Occupied Territories; these women, who were born outside the Territories but whose husbands live and work there, are ostensibly granted renewable permits to remain in the Gaza Strip or West Bank. By late 1991, the military administration was revoking or not renewing many such permits, with the result that an estimated 120,000 Palestinian women and children now live illegally in the Territories under threat of summary expulsion.

I have not written about Rashideyeh Camp in Lebanon, where the hunger became so great that, after the rats had been caught and eaten, the men petitioned the mullahs for dispensation to eat human flesh. No one asked who would cook it. Everyone knew that was the job of women, who were already "unclean."

I have not written about what Palestinian feminists are calling a new male backlash in their own communities: men who, frustrated at unemployment, powerlessness, and continual chaos, and irritated at the newfound independence of their wives and daughters during the Intifada, are taking out their rage on those women; how domestic violence has risen precipitously in the past year; how men are now taking second wives (previously a rarity among

Palestinians); how fathers are selling their daughters to be *second wives "because of the shortage of eligible husbands" due to death, detention, and deportation; how "honor murders" have been spreading in both Gaza and West Bank—cases of brothers killing sisters they suspect of having had an affair, or even of dating a man without family knowledge and permission. Whether or not these young women have actually done so is irrelevant; the mere suspicion was sufficient to justify one young man slitting his sister's throat in Nazareth, and another—in Gaza's Maghazi Camp—locking his sister inside a large freezer for five hours while he sat outside and waited for her to die.*

But I also have not written of how the women are rising to meet this backlash*: of how a new group, Al-Fanar, formed in 1991, has marched publicly to denounce these killings. Such a march by women—in the context of the tradition of "family honor," and furthermore in the context of required Palestinian solidarity during the Intifada—is itself a startlingly radical act.

I think of Miryam, in Beach Camp, who is congenitally blind, the offspring of an arranged cousin marriage, who grinned and told me, "Women? We are as realistic as yesterday and as inevitable as tomorrow."

I think of Rita, who has recently given birth to a baby girl, laughed in the face of death, and announced proudly, "Another Palestinian feminist in the world!"

And I think of Ablah, secretly teaching women and children to read under cover of darkness in a West Bank village, smiling up at me across the frail glow of candlelight and saying, "This is the Intifada, my sister. And beyond it, next, comes the real one—the women's *Intifada."*

—1992

*See Rabab Hadi, "The Feminist Behind the Spokeswoman—A Candid Talk with Hanan Ashrawi," *Ms.*, Vol. II, no. 5, March/April, 1992.

Two Essays on Another Just War

In January 1990, I returned to Ms. *Magazine as editor in chief (I had been a part-time contributing editor from 1974 to 1987). My return was based on three assurances: that the magazine would no longer carry any advertising, that it would be absolutely autonomous editorially from any publisher-owner, and that I would be free to develop it in the direction of an international consciousness.*

Against all "industry logic," the eventual product—debuting in July 1990—became a remarkable success, proving that readers were, as their letters put it, "famished for real sustenance and weary of junk food." Indeed, the premiere issue sold out within two days—and a second print run of that issue subsequently sold out within days, as well. (As of this writing, in 1992, the new, reader-supported, "liberated" Ms. *is, ironically, already more successful than its commercial predecessor.)*

In the first issue, I promised readers "the most passionate editorials" I could write—not coy "editor's notes" in the manner of most traditional women's magazines; I vowed to write "about religious fundamentalism and toxic groceries, female sexuality and children's suffrage, how debt affects women struggling to farm in Iowa (and in Brazil). About making: connections, sense of it, change, love, mis-

*chief, a difference, merry. About peace budding in the
northern hemisphere [the U.S.S.R. and Eastern Europe had
just begun their transformations], nuclear-free zones flow-
ering in the southern hemisphere, consciousness ripening
in both hemispheres of our brains. About what all this might
mean for women ..."*

*Then, one month after the premiere issue came out, Iraq
invaded Kuwait.*

*In one form or another, the next four editorials focused
on the Gulf War. What follows are the original, longer versions of two of those editorials.*

Between the Lines

What could be more peaceful than a rainy weekend morning, a leisurely second cup of coffee, and a spread-out
Sunday paper?

Yet within an hour I feel anything but peaceful.

It's not just the headlines and lead stories—familiar lies;
tragedies large and small; tribal / national / economic /
ethnic / religious / geopolitical rationales for violence.
That's only half the story. Which is the point.

Remember when you were a child and played "What's
wrong with this picture?" You know, where you're presented with what looks like a perfectly normal drawing—
of a seascape, or a small town—and only after careful
scrutiny do you notice that a seagull lacks one wing, or
that a "Way Out" sign leads to a dead-end street, or that
one cottage has no door? Well, that version of reality is
what passes for news. Which leaves me and millions of

other women (and some men of conscience) playing "What's wrong with this picture?" every time we pick up a newspaper—and also has us talking back to our televisions and radios in a one-way mutter. For example:

The headline: "Iraq Invades Kuwait." The text sets forth the news priorities: oil interests alarmed; gas prices rising; Arab summits attempted; boycotts threatened; rumors that Iraq will invade Saudi Arabia; Saudi troops massing at *their* border; old manipulations and new pronouncements by the superpowers. Important men—scholars and experts—analyze the faults or merits of an absolute hereditary monarchy as compared to a totalitarian military dictatorship. They do this quite seriously.

And between the lines?

The Iraqi Women's Federation (which exists precariously at the government's indulgence) makes as many waves as it dares on behalf of women's rights. Recently, it donated financial support to *Al Raida*, the journal of the Beirut-based Institute for Women's Studies in the Arab World. The Federation even has some extra-courageous members who demonstrate for peace. This is a life-risking act. In a country that is the world's biggest arms buyer, to advocate peace even privately can be regarded as treason. Yet Iraqi women have suffered a ten-year war with Iran, the loss of thousands of husbands, sons, fathers, and brothers, and a war-devastated economy. Clearly, they do not enjoy this. Some, to be sure, are swept up in patriotic fervor; most merely endure and mourn. But a few take a stand against war; they have been doing this, amazingly, with no press attention, for years.

Meanwhile, in Kuwait, women still don't have suffrage. We're not discussing Saudi Arabia—where *nobody* has the vote. The vote does exist in Kuwait. But only for literate male Kuwaitis over age twenty-one who are "first-class" citizens (defined as being related to residents of the country who can prove that they or their ancestors were there before 1920). This means that less than four percent of the total population are qualified voters, because "non-Kuwaitis" (cheap imported labor) compose *almost 59 percent* of the country's residents. Women, however, have a less complicated status: whether "first-class" Kuwaiti or non-Kuwaiti, women cannot vote at all.

Not that they haven't tried. Kuwait became a sovereign state in 1962, and within a year the first women's organization had been founded to lobby for suffrage. Twenty years later, the Arab Women's Conference held in Kuwait issued a unanimous call for a minimum marriage age of sixteen, equal rights, abolition of bridewealth (dowry)— and the vote. Finally, in 1981, the prime minister promised that women would soon be allowed to vote in parliamentary elections (but not run for office). The following January, however, a bill to grant suffrage to Kuwaiti women came out of committee with a recommendation that it be rejected because the time was inopportune "in light of well-established traditions"; the bill was defeated, 27 to 7. One week later, 10,000 women marched through the streets of Kuwait City in protest. (This demonstration also did not make headlines.) There have been some victories: in 1982, Kuwait became the first Arab nation in the Gulf to legalize abortion. But to this day, an active women's movement, including the Kuwait Women's Social and Educational Society, lobbies for suffrage.

Were Iraqi women consulted about the decision to invade Kuwait? Do Kuwaiti women have a voice in their nation's policies? Wouldn't a more accurate headline have read: "Half of Iraq Invades Half of Kuwait" (while both "other halves" are forced to suffer, respectively, the sacrifice and the occupation)? And were U.S. women asked permission as Bush decided to "intervene"? (Were we considered with regard to the "interventions" in Libya, Grenada, or Panama? Were we *heard* when post-intervention polls showed a gender-gap of women's disapproval?)

And when will I learn not to ask absurd questions?

That women tend to oppose militaristic solutions and the cavalier loss of life is hardly news. What *is* news is the consistency of this trend—and the growth of the gender gap.

In a December 7, 1990, *New York Times* article titled "The Gender Gulf," U.S. pollster Louis Harris noted the "enormous difference" between female and male attitudes regarding military intervention. Recalling that both women and youth had opposed the Vietnam war (generally, men and older citizens had supported it), Harris noted that in the Persian Gulf crisis the "generation gap is less evident and the gender gap is more acute."

His polls showed that people in the United States opposed military action in the Gulf by 61 to 35 percent (four percent undecided). But the gender breakdown was even more dramatic. For instance, according to Harris:

- 48 percent of men favored attacking Iraqi forces occupying Kuwait, while an equal number of men opposed it. But women opposed it by 73 to 22 percent.
- Overall support for "surgical" air strikes against Iraq dropped from 65 percent in September 1990 to 43 percent in December—but, while men still advocated such bombings (57 to 40 percent), women opposed them by 63 to 29 percent.
- Interestingly, Harris found that women and men were in essential agreement on Gulf strategies that did not involve killing or dying; for instance, a majority of both women and men wanted the United States to wait and let the embargo against Iraq take its longer-term effect.

Harris concluded that, since those under age thirty seemed only slightly less inclined to support military action than their elders (a marked difference from the Vietnam period), this meant that "for the first time, women alone might turn American public opinion about a war" and "sway the polls against President Bush's using military force in the Gulf." (Indeed, in almost all cases where the gender gap narrows or even closes, it's women who have influenced men, not the reverse.)

Tragically, the men in power did not listen to the polls—or to women.

"All politics is a struggle for power," wrote C. Wright Mills in *The Power Elite,** "and the ultimate kind of power is violence."

"Power and violence are opposites," wrote Hannah Arendt in *On Violence,*** as if in direct reply to him. "Violence appears where power is in jeopardy, but left to its own course it ends in power's disappearance. . . . The chief reason warfare is still with us is neither a secret death wish of the human species, nor an irrepressible instinct of aggression, . . . but the simple fact that no substitute for this final arbiter in international affairs has yet appeared on the political scene."

That substitute has now appeared. As with every major shift in human history, it manifests itself at first almost naively, from an unexpected (and even ridiculed) direction. Only after such a shift has demonstrated its energy as a transformative wave does it in retrospect seem obvious and inevitable.

That substitute—that transformative wave at this stage in the saga of the human species—is women as a global political force.

The vast majority of women, cross-culturally and through history, have suffered from and appeared to disagree with Mills's definition of violence as "the ultimate kind of power." It is both fact and tragedy that the majority of men, cross-culturally and throughout history, also have suffered from that definition—but appeared to agree with it.

*(New York and London: Oxford University Press, 1956).
**(New York and London: Harcourt Brace Jovanovich, 1970).

If I had to name a single quality characteristic of patriarchy, it would be *compartmentalization,* the capacity for institutionalizing disconnection. Intellect severed from emotion. Thought separated from action. Science split from art. The earth itself divided—national borders. People categorized: by sex, age, race, ethnicity, sexual preference, height, weight, class, religion, physical ability, *ad nauseam.* The personal isolated from the political. Sex divorced from love. The material ruptured from the spiritual. Law detached from justice. Vision disjoined from reality. We have all of us—female and male—been wounded by these dissociations.

If I had to name a single quality characteristic of global feminism, it would be *connectivity*—a capacity dangerous to every status quo, because of its insistence on noticing.

So it isn't coincidental that all over the world, women continue to press for substitute solutions to conflict, from El Salvador to Sri Lanka to Southern Africa's Transvaal Province. All these women see clearly—and articulate plainly—the connections between war and economic impoverishment, conquest and rape, munitions and environmental devastation, militarism and masculinism. And back in Illinois, Stephanie Atkinson, the first woman in the history of the United States to go publicly AWOL on peace principles, saw the connections clearly, too.

The Gulf War will someday be "old news." But the women on both sides of the lines will still be invisible between them—a major, ignored story: female human beings struggling for dignity, freedom, and peace. News of such women shadows every story.

The only way headlines of violence might ever change is if the space between the lines becomes visible. Which is where you and I come in.

With every news item we read and hear, we can search and listen for and learn about the missing reality, the other half of humanity. And we can *pass it on.*

Because the truth is that we are the other wing of the seagull. We are the way out of the dead-end street. We are the door.

—August 1990

Digressions

This is what they do to us, the men in power; this is how they dominate our discourse. I wanted to write about many other things, and instead here I am, writing about war again.

So just when we thought it was safe to come out of the cold one, they gave us a hot one—a Nintendo War, a high-tech videogame version of ritualized mutual murder that one side terms "Holy" and the other terms "Just." One side calls for rivers of blood. The other uses phallocentric rhetoric ("penetration," "softening up their hardened bunkers") and jolly football-game metaphor. (Is it a digression to note that a recent study found violence against women in the United States rises dramatically during Superbowl weekend?)

Meanwhile, saturation bombing is dutifully rendered in saturation media coverage. But despite the public's hunger to know what's really happening and why, most reporting remains repetitive and shallow. During World War I, the British prime minister Lloyd George confessed that "If people really knew, the war would be stopped tomorrow. But of course, they don't know, and they can't know." So we become resigned to coverage blatantly labeled "Censored by the U.S. / Saudi / French / Iraqi /

Israeli Military" with the impeccable rationale that censorship saves soldiers' lives. (Is it a digression to recall how feminists who protest that pornography claims women's lives are denounced for promulgating—you guessed it—censorship?)

A truly free press might teach us many things.

It might explain how "borders" in the Middle East are arbitrary, imposed early this century by the British, across tribal, ethnic, and geo-political boundaries. It might remind us that the first use of gas in warfare began with riot or tear gas introduced by the *Allies* in World War I— "to save lives"—then escalated to lethal gas used by the Germans. (At this writing, the United States is considering introducing riot gas again—"to save lives"—in ground combat in Kuwait.) A free press might actually educate us. Or is it a digression to note that General Electric, the awardee of U.S. government contracts to manufacture "Peacekeeper" MX missiles, now owns the National Broadcasting Company?

I've had this fantasy lately, about a press not only free but creative: Since heads of state now seem to communicate with one another more swiftly via Cable Network News (CNN) than through diplomatic channels, what would happen if CNN imaginatively declared that Washington had just announced a truce, Baghdad had just called a ceasefire, and both sides were eager to talk peace? Would life imitate art?

Of course, even if the media were that witty, they still might not cover the invisible half of humanity; it would be considered a "digression" to focus on the majority of the populations in all the countries concerned: women.

Yet digressions help us make connections. For instance:

· George Bush and Saddam Hussein have more in common than a mutual preoccupation with manhood and oil. Hussein doubtless understands the Reagan / Bush assault on women's reproductive freedom. In 1987, during the Iran-Iraq war, the Iraqi president proclaimed that it was the duty of every Iraqi woman to bear at least five children; in 1989, he declared not only abortions but contraceptives illegal. Even condoms were withdrawn from sale and confiscated from visitors' baggage. Within the past year, three Iraqi doctors have been publicly punished for having performed secret abortions. Every patriarchal state needs to control sexuality and reproduction, because every army needs cannon fodder.

· Wouldn't it be interesting if our understandable concern for the safety of female POWs be extended to a comparable concern for battered women held captive in abusive relationships? If the alarm about women risking injury or death in a combat zone included the realization that for most women daily life *is* a combat zone? (As U.S. Army Staff Sergeant Valerie Shidlowski put it, "We're here fighting for freedom, and we have none ourselves.") Has anyone wondered if the Asian and Kuwaiti survivors of Iraqi army rapes, or the women picking their way through the blasted rubble of their Baghdad homes, are covered by Geneva Convention rules about "civilized behavior" in war? They're not.

· There is one point of agreement, though. Everyone is trying to avoid "repeating the mistakes of Vietnam." We have been assured that this war will be over quickly, that this is not another Vietnam—as if the only thing wrong with the Vietnam War was that it took too long. Even antiwar activists, anxious not to alienate, chant "We Oppose the Policy, but We Support the Troops." (It does them no good anyway; the Right Wing calls their bluff and middle America remains suspicious of them as "peaceniks.") The illogic of the statement, as well as its moral laziness, gets conveniently overlooked. It was William Butler Yeats, the great Irish poet, who wrote, "How can you tell the dancer from the dance?"

"I'm only doing my job," they say, these young men and women—and the heart cracks at how frightened they look. "Ignorant armies clash by night," another poet, Mathew Arnold, wrote. But an ignorance that defends "doing a job" on behalf of wealthy white men who haven't done *their* job of statesmanship properly is no longer acceptable as an excuse for lacerated flesh and fragmented minds. This century has given us much to mourn, but something to learn: the Nuremburg Trials ruled once and for all that "I was only obeying orders" absolves no one of responsibility. Remember the saying "Someday they'll give a war and no one will come?" They couldn't give a war if the troops simply wouldn't come. Contorted logic to the contrary, the only way to support the women and men in the armed forces is—as an older peace chant demanded—to bring them home, *now.*

· Deep down, we all know why they volunteered in the first place, don't we? There are really three prerequisites for a "volunteer" army.

The first is practical, requiring that a segment of the population be economically disadvantaged. (In a society still racked by sexism and racism, we know who the poorer segments of the population are: this is why almost a third of the U.S. forces in the Gulf—and nearly half of the 27,000 women—are African American.) Most people enter the armed forces for basics they can get nowhere else—a guaranteed income, decent housing, free medical and dental care, a higher education. In effect, the Pentagon practices *(shhh)* socialism. The U.S. Department of Defense is the largest centrally planned economy outside the Soviet Union—and given the current state of the Soviet economy, the DOD probably tops out.

The second prerequisite for a volunteer army is political: the promise that equality and power in the society are gained by participation in military service. Yet the people who do the killing and dying still aren't the wealthy white male people in power who make the policies.

The third prerequisite is psychological: the mystique that has been created and attached to the wearing of a uniform and the bearing of arms—the mystique of bravery, sacrifice, heroism.

The only way the first incentive to soldier will disappear is by eradicating sex, race, and economic bigotry. The only way the second will vanish is by redefining power and empowering ourselves. The only way the third will become obsolete is by refusing to "support" the mystique. We *don't* need another hero.

It is for such "heroism" that human lives are sacrificed—the soldiers, the civilians, the onlookers. For this, Asia may lose its monsoons to the giant cloud of "petroleum winter" toxic ash drifting from the burning oilfields; upwards of a million people whose agrarian lives depend on the monsoons will starve and perish. For this, the creatures of the Saudi and Kuwaiti deserts—jackals, sand cats, hares, reptiles, insects, and birds—will be struck deaf by the roar of tanks, planes, and bomb bursts, will be cut by or entangled in the mounds of plastic and aluminum litter left by the armies, will be maimed or killed for years to come by the buried land mines, will be poisoned by the chemical and human waste left behind. For this, the wild cormorants, innocent of borders or conquest, suffocate in oil, and stagger wingspread onto the beaches of the Gulf to shudder and die.

I had wanted to write about other things. But we have much work to do, my friends, and little time. Please take my hand.

—January 1991

400 Years in the
Convent and 50
Years in Hollywood:
The Philippines

In October 1988, I journeyed to the Phillipines at the invitation of the Philippine women's movement. A delegation of five women had been invited—all of us members of the Sisterhood Is Global Institute.* The delegation—Mahnaz Afkhami of Iran, Keiko Higuchi of Japan, Madhu Kishwar of India, Marilyn Waring of New Zealand, and myself—were to spend ten days in Metro Manila, investigating the conditions of women in the urban area, in private meetings with women's groups, and in public panels with representatives of those groups. We were then to split up and for another week or so travel to rural areas of the country for the same process, returning to Manila for a major press conference, more public panels, a march, etc. (There was

*The Institute was founded in 1984, as an activist continuation of *Sisterhood Is Global: The International Women's Movement Anthology* (New York: Doubleday / Anchor, 1984), which I had compiled and edited. Co-founded by the contributors to the anthology—the late Simone de Beauvoir among them—it is the first international feminist "think tank," operates a global female human rights Action Alert System similar to that of Amnesty International but focused on women, and periodically sends teams to various trouble spots specifically to investigate the condition of women. The Institute, which moves its headquarters periodically so as never to be under the hegemony of any one country, is currently (as of 1992) based in New Zealand.

also to be a meeting with President Corazon Aquino—but when the president's office learned that our delegation, not surprisingly, affirmed reproductive freedom and a woman's right to divorce—both of which are illegal in this intensely Roman Catholic country—the audience was cancelled.)

I arrived a week earlier, in order to journey to the north— the mountainous Cordillera region—to meet with women who were semi- and fully underground in the NPA (New People's Army), and with indigenous women (primarily of the Igorot, Ifugao, and Kalinga tribes). Later, my rural "assignment" was to Davao, in Mindanao, the Autonomous Muslim Area, a hotbed of rising religious fundamentalism, site of the worst human-rights abuses according to Amnesty International, and a region of virtual civil war not only between the peasants and the military but between the peasants and right-wing vigilante groups, as well as between contending Muslim factions.

This essay was my contribution to the institute's later report on the mission. It has never before appeared in print.

The South Asian archipelago called the Philippines is Graham Greeneland: suffocating heat layered by visible stripes of sluggish, polluted air; extremes of impoverishment and abundance that make understatement seem hyperbolic; and the omnipresence of post-colonial despair and neo-colonial corruption that have become a way of life. Last, but central—despite the pretense of a somewhat cynical democracy ("bequeathed" by U.S. colonialism)—real power is shared between the general and the cardinal. The former's name is Ramos (later, in 1992, elected President); the latter's name, aptly, is Sin.

Heartbreakingly proud to call itself the only Christian country in Asia, the Philippines everywhere bears the scars of repeated colonizations. As the Filipinos put it, "We have spent four hundred years in the convent [the Spanish hegemony] and fifty in Hollywood [the U.S. control]." Twenty-two major U.S. military bases have pockmarked the country since 1901; two of them (Clark Air Base and Subic Naval Base) the largest U.S. bases overseas anywhere in the world. The culture is saturated with U.S. pop music, movies, trends, and fast foods. Some sixty indigenous groups throughout the seven thousand islands have been occupied for centuries by various conquerors; the diverse population—a mix of indigenous overlaid with Chinese, Indonesian, Malay, some Indian, some Japanese, much Spanish, and much U.S. (both European American and African American)—itself shows the genetic mix. (To a feminist eye, this translates as waves of rape.) Those with a "purer" Spanish heritage or a "pure" Chinese ancestry are openly or covertly considered the elite. Economic power resides basically with ten families, mostly intermarried to preserve their hegemony, who control over 90 percent of the country's wealth. Corazon Aquino— who came to power in 1986 when the "People's Power" revolution overthrew the twenty-one-year dictatorship of Ferdinand Marcos—is herself a daughter of one of the ten families and the widow of a member of another. That her administration, on which the hopes of the nation rested, is now regarded as inept and in places more corrupt than that of Marcos's regime, comes as less of a surprise when one learns that her brother owns the largest sugar plantations in the nation.

My first brush with authority comes at customs, on arrival. Buried in my luggage are four menstrual regulation kits, sometimes called menstrual extraction devices, each sterile and complete with cannula, each equipped to perform, in the right hands, up to 300 abortions. When I had asked Filipina feminists what they would like me to bring, this was the reply. But my luggage is searched, and the customs inspector is not only the representative of the border authority; here the inspector represents the law, the military, tradition, and the Church. Fortunately, this particular inspector is also a man. At such moments, ancient feminine wiles become activated as part of a feminist's "by any means necessary" repertoire. I drop my gaze from his, and shyly mumble something about "personal use."

"Female troubles," I murmur, with a vague wave of the hand.

Wondrously ignorant of female anatomy, and desperately unwilling to receive a private tutorial in a public place, the inspector coughs with embarrassed efficiency, smiles in superior masculine pity, and gestures for me to pass right on through.

The North: Luzon

The mountainous Cordillera region has a single two-lane highway that weaves through a countryside redolent of scenic beauty, now a metaphoric and literal battlefield. Logging industries for export to Japan have gashed the hillside forests. Half-built schools and community centers stand as mute testimony to abandoned "development" schemes, in the midst of villages subsisting in a depression of extreme poverty. Here, as in similar villages throughout the world, I am informed that the women "don't work." And here, as in similar villages throughout the world, the men sit drinking cheap beer in the local lean-to tavern, staring out with lackluster eyes, while the women seem never to stop moving, except to nurse an infant at the breast. Otherwise, they are selling meager wares—handicrafts, weavings, baskets—in the small marketplace, or carrying loaded pots or baskets on their heads or their backs, or squatting beside open cookfires, or bending over the rice paddies through which they wade, ankle-deep in water, or hunching above mountain streams, pounding laundry clean with rocks and their fists. In every activity, each woman is usually surrounded by three or more children, stair-stepped in age, hungrily clamoring for attention.

The government, the district authorities, the international aid agencies—all may be confused about the best solution to these villagers' problems. But the village women are quite clear about their needs.

As early as the 1960s, indigenous women of the region managed to stop construction of a huge government-backed dam—the Chico Valley project—intended to be the largest in Southeast Asia. The dam would have diverted the river (source of irrigation for the rice paddies) and flooded ancestral tribal lands; it meant resettlement for the Kalinga people. Igorot and Kalinga women had been "drafted" as guides, cooks, and washerwomen for the project surveyors. In order to stop the project, and also to stop their own menfolk from traditionally violent means of resistance the women knew would lead only to bloodshed and defeat, the women devised a plan. Each morning they watched the surveyors lay out their stakes; each afternoon, they stripped naked, pulled up the stakes, and burned them in full view of the surveyors. Neither the surveyors nor the tribal men dared touch the women because they were naked—in effect, tabu. (Among the Kalinga, women are honored and treated with great respect; to mistreat a woman is to endure eternal loss of face.) At last, the government, and even the World Bank, gave up. Near the site of what would have been the Chico Valley dam stands a plaque, commemorating the pledge to the indigenous peoples of the region by the Marcos government to discontinue the project.

The women know very well what they don't need— and what they do.

In Bontoc (the "main town" of the mountain province),

the local women ask that when I meet with women sen-
ators and congressional representatives in Manila, I should
please remind them of their campaign promise: a pigsty
for the Bontoc women's farming co-op. It would cost perhaps only five or six hundred U.S. dollars, and it would
change these women's lives. They had already been
waiting for the campaign promise to be fulfilled for seven
months.

In the village of Sagada, one woman, Dr. Geraldine
Cayambas, is the only physician ministering to a surrounding mountain population of 250,000 people. It bog-
gles the mind. What does *she* need most?

"Everything," she smiles wearily, "and anything. Aspirin, cotton swabs, even rubber gloves." Most of the ill are
women; most of the illnesses are related to poverty (anemia, diarrhia, malnutrition) and to multiple pregnancies.
But there are also gunshot and machete wounds. Sagada
is "contested territory": just the night before, in fact, there
was a government raid on this New People's Army-con-
trolled area—shootings, arrests, disappearances. Outside
Sagada, in a meeting, the NPA women are properly
guarded in conversation, but during our talks a fragile
trust flowers. One—the only female field commander in
the NPA—admits her rage that the NPA Central Committee, which is male, has so far refused to add the rights to
divorce, contraception, and abortion to the NPA political
platform.

"The men claim it would alienate the people," she
fumes, "because of the Church's hold over everyone. To
which the female cadres reply, 'Alienate *which* people?
Certainly not women!' As it is, Filipinos are a la carte
Catholics: we take some elements, leave the rest; commit
our sins, then confess them. There hasn't even been a
proper study done on how many hundreds of thousands
of women die in this country every year from backstreet
illegal abortions, from poisonous home remedies, from

knitting needles, from pouring lye into the vagina. Right outside the major cathedral in Manila, there are street stalls selling illegal—and dangerous—abortifacients. *And,"* she adds, pointing a finger at a female comrade for emphasis, "I'd like to know why it is that radical men don't worry about 'alienating the people' when it comes to advocating land reform in the guise of collective ownership! Or is their position on women totally compromised by their alliance with Leftist priests?"

The conversation turns to battery, as common here as everywhere else. I am told of the Filipino proverb that goes, "I beat her because I love her"—and I can't help commenting that I've heard versions of the same proverb as evidence of "local tradition" in Peru, Egypt, Italy, and Japan, as well as in Texas. The women laugh in recognition. The woman commander—separated from her husband, a high-ranking NPA man who had beaten her—successfully fought being purged for her refusal to remain with him, and even managed to accomplish *his* purge from the leadership, on the grounds of his domestic violence. In the context, this is a staggering feat. (Privately, I think to myself that she must be one hell of a field commander, whose skills the NPA simply dared not lose.) But her personal grief wells in her eyes when she speaks of her two children, who live with distant relatives, and whom she can visit in secret only once or twice a year. She asks me for books—specifically feminist books—to be sent to a safe-house address. It's wise to write nothing down in the circumstances, so I make mental notes: books, safe-house address, aspirin, swabs, cotton gloves. . . .

The Cordillera Women's Education and Resource Center is based in Baguio City, but actually functions out in the remote villages of the region. (There is another "women's center" in Baguio, to which few women relate; it is run by a Catholic priest who formerly commanded an NPA battalion and then switched sides to work with the army.) Baguio is the nation's summer capital, with a population of 120,000, public flower gardens, a hot springs, a golf club—and a U.S. base and "rest and recreation" area. Baguio is also the site of the Japanese community, and the place from whence many of the Filipina "mail-order brides" are recruited—a tragically high number of whom are destined for sex-tourism brothels. The Cordillera Women's Centre does some organizing in Baguio, and Vicki Corpuz, the center cofounder and director, manages to publish a little news journal on the activities of local women and women's groups. But most of the center's energy is spent on taking its humble programs— primarily literacy and advocacy—out into the hills and rice paddies.

We go out into one of the tiny rice-paddy villages, actually a cluster of six open-sided huts. It is a day's trek, first by minibus from Bontoc, then by foot: hiking down one steep hillside, across a rather intimidating rope bridge over the river far beneath, up the other steep hillside, onto a plateau, and along the thin strips of earth—tight-rope-style, one foot in front of the other—that divide the paddies. At last we sit on the mud floor of one of the huts, drinking peanut coffee from a shared tin cup. Most urban Filipinas speak English and some also speak Spanish and / or Chinese; the city women speak only a little Filipino (Tagalog), the language of "the common people"; the tribal people of the north have their own languages and dialects. One woman translates.

Gunnawa, the woman in whose hut we sit, comes from a family of peasants who have lived on this land for centuries. She is the mother of seven children, many of whom crowd around us as we speak. She is in her thirties, but looks like a woman in her sixties. Her teeth are rotting; her skin, tanned to leather, is stretched across a gaunt frame. But her eyes gleam with intelligence.

She is proud that her children are learning to read; a

woman comes as often as possible—sometimes once a week—from the Women's Centre to teach them. Her greatest regret is that she herself never learned to read or write. We talk about her dreams for a better life. The longing in Gunnawa's soft voice is clear even before the translation reaches me in another woman's voice. What did she want, more than anything? To learn to read, comes the quiet refrain. Not more food, better housing, some easing of her intense labor? No, Gunnawa insists with dignity, to read.

"Because, you see," she continues, a shy smile flickering across her weatherbeaten face, "someday I might go somewhere. I hear that there are signs on the roads. If I could read the signs, I could know where I was. And I could know where I was going."

Later that afternoon, high above the river, each of us clutching at the ropes of the swaying bridge, Vicki shouts to me that somehow, some way, she will start an adult literacy program for Gunnawa and the women of this rice paddy.

But there are some rice-farming peasants in northern Luzon who do know how to read and write—and who display these skills in an astonishing fashion.

The rice terraces of Banaue—proudly referred to by locals as the eighth wonder of the world—were built some two thousand years ago by the Ifugao people, literally carved by hand with primitive tools out of the mountainsides—broad stepping stones that rise well over 1200 meters high. This in itself is an impressive sight. Then one notices that the rice on many of the terraces is planted in sophisticated patterns: swirls, nested triangles, geometric designs bordering concentric circles, "Greek key" motifs—the same types of patterns seen on the hems and sleeves of clothing made by Ifugao women, and worn by them as tatoos. But to execute such intricacy on such a scale! Awe is the only response, awe at how stubbornly sublime the human spirit is in its hunger to invent some means of expressing beauty and form in infinitely creative ways, no matter the deprivations suffered. *Then* one notices what at first seems a hallucination, as if the complex configurations had squirmed into the letters of a message against one's squinting eyesight in the sun. With a shock, one realizes it is no hallucination. Here, where for two hundred centuries the indigenous peoples have endured encroachment and oppression; here, in the heart of the "contested areas," where ignorant armies of the NPA and the government clash by night; here, where Gunnawa's longed-for road signs might tell her where she is and where she is going, the rice is planted for the world to see, in clear messages—and in English.

One reads *Revolution.*

The other reads, simply, *Love.*

■

Manila

Being a New Yorker, I am hardly unused to air and noise pollution, but parts of Metro Manila can make Manhattan smell, sound, and even look like a bucolic island. The heavy, sweetish stench of gasohol, fuel of the omnipresent jeepneys, is everywhere, and exhaust pipes belching out clouds of this visible poison make the chronic traffic jams more than metaphoric headaches. Each jeepney— a cross between a jeep and a small bus—is a testament to the Filipino sense of humor and ebullience: painted and bordered in different vivid primary colors, decorated with flags, flowers, lights, metal birds, animals, and pinwheels, and named after one or another Catholic saint. Parts of the city are undeniably beautiful—and deliberately lavish, with cultural, business, and tourist centers, museums, parks, broad avenues, (many) churches, and five-star restaurants and hotels (plus a well-groomed U.S.

military cemetery, final resting place for 17,000 U.S. soldiers from World War II). Nor is Manila different from any other metropolitan center in having its share of slums—except that here both the opulence and the poverty are at *acute* extremes, with little middle class between.

Not since Brazil's Rio de Janeiro and São Paulo have I seen entire districts of a city walled off, with private police to guard the inhabitants against feared forays by the poor. I am not speaking about Manila Intramuros (the Old City, with its fortress walls dating from the 1500s) but about certain residential areas elsewhere in the Metro Manila sprawl. One borders on the business district of Makati; it is the site of mansions with lake-and-fountain-landscaped grounds rivaling small parks—a stunning contrast to the Tondo community, where almost 200,000 people, many of them tubercular, live in approximately 18,000 tin shanties in less than a three-mile territory.

On one visit to District 3 in Quezon City (itself a section of Metro Manila), we file through a maze of culverts and alleyways into another slum, a warren of fire-trap huts reeking with the filth and despair of an urban poverty that, by sheer contrast, could make rural impoverishment seem almost wholesome. A male resident responds to the question (asked of a woman) about the population; approximately forty families live here, he interrupts to tell us. The crowd of curious, friendly people who have come to meet us belies these figures. But it turns out that the man is defining "family" as male-headed; actually, over one hundred families live here—but they are woman-headed and so don't count. At this, all the women, residents and visitors alike, exchange glances of sardonic amusement.

The whirl of meetings with women's groups, large and small, is exciting, exhausting, and more than a bit bewildering. All movements endure schisms, but the women's movement here is special: even I have never seen such fragmentation. This is in part because of class, economic, and ethnic differences; in part because of political factionalism and polarization fostered by years of colonization and then dictatorship; and in part because of the Church's "charitable" control over much service-oriented progressive activism. But whatever the causes, there are literally thousands of different groups—some of them reinventing light bulbs already set aglow by others, and more than one of which is composed of, as a local feminist put it (in U.S. lingo), "all chiefs and no Indians."

There is GABRIELA, the largest, an organization in itself with over forty-five other large and small NGOs (nongovernmental organizations)—including KMK (the women's labor group) and AMIHAN (the women farmers' and peasants' alliance)—under its coalition umbrella. GABRIELA has task forces on most issues, from prostitution to sexual abuse to health to employment to domestic violence, etc., and operates refuges, runs literacy and advocacy programs, conducts international campaigns over human-rights abuses, and organizes demonstrations; its grasp barely manages not to exceed its considerable reach. It has been red-baited consistently, harrassed by the government, and accused of being "in collusion" with the Left—which in this country is defined as anything from insurgent political parties to NPA guerrillas.

PILIPINA, organized in the early 1980s by four women (including a feminist nun), is supposedly more "centrist," with many affiliates who hold government or academic positions. WOMANHEALTH is another, newer, coalition of NGOs working on reproductive rights, AIDS and STDs, and other related female health issues. KAIBA is a women's political party that has so far managed to elect one candidate, the glamorous, wealthy, and liberal congresswoman Anna "Nikki" Coseteng (who also hosts a television program, "Womanwatch"). There are the more "traditional" women's groups, such as the National Commission on Women, the National Federation of Women's Clubs, and others. Then, too, there is the Center for Women's Resources *and* the Women's Research and Resource Center *and* the Women's Studies Consortium, the Women's Media Circle, the Women Artists and Cultural Workers, the Women's Spiritual Community, the Third World Women's Movement Against the Exploitation of Women, and innumerable activist religious women's groups. On the so-called far Left, there is MAKIBAKA (which had its founding some years ago in protest against the Miss Philippines Pageant and now is semi-underground because of suspected links with the NPA women), KALAYAAN (which tries to organize women plantation workers), SAMAKANA (voice of urban poor women), and still others. There appears to be more than a little group-hopping, as well as joint membership in different groups, a phenomenon certainly not restricted to the Philippines. Often there are splinter factions within each group, yet since the entire political climate is variable, alliances seem to shift constantly, with actual political differences often taking second place to personality differences and /or conflicts or resolutions between (literal) cousins. It is important to keep in mind those above mentioned ten dynastic multi-branched families: former generations may have spent their lives building their fortunes, but at least half of the current generation, despite their elite status, seems bent on various forms of revolution—an irony that the splendid Filipina writer Ninotchka Rosca has explored in both fiction and nonfiction. This means that most Filipina feminist leaders have servants (sometimes entire families in service, in fact), which is startling and discomfiting to a North American feminist organizer like myself. But at least they can't be accused of resting on family laurels *or* plantations.

All this grouping and regrouping—plus the tendency of some to start new groups at the drop of a funding peso—means that there are perhaps as many women's movement groups in the Philippines as in the United States (this in a nation of about 55 million people, one-fourth that of the U.S. population). And while the gravity of most Filipinas' lives definitely warrants such attention, it is not clear that this hive of activity always manages to address that gravity effectively. Still, while visitors might feel somewhat lost in the fog of political confusion engendered by this situation, Filipina feminists appear cheerfully comfortable with it, and committed to going about their business of making as much of a revolution as possible. And indeed, it soon becomes clear to our small international delegation that one of the reasons we have been invited here is to serve as the catalyst, the "glue," for meetings between groups that have for years refused to communicate with each other. We are the excuse for private individual reunions and public group coalitions.*

They are a wonderfully bizarre mix, these women, as in every women's movement everywhere: Nelia Sancho, a former beauty queen, now a leader of GABRIELA; Petite Paredo, an activist and artist who produces exquisite dimensional collages, both representational and abstract, later to become head of GABRIELA; all-around-skilled Gertie Terona from KAIBA; the women from MAKIBAKA who must here go unnamed for their own safety; the fifty or so fatigued but exuberant women—too many to name here—who had worked for months to organize the Sisterhood Is Global Dialogues in their country; Anne Leah Sarabia and Alma S. dela Rosa of the Women's Media Circle, who conceived and organized the entire visit, and who steadily do remarkable work in trying circumstances while managing to keep a sense of humor and proportion.

Then of course there are the few feminist women in

*This was a politically savvy strategy on the part of the Filipina organizers. As of 1992, they tell me that the general coalition of all groups forged at the time of our visit has held—shakily at times, but together nevertheless.

electoral politics—less supported, perhaps, by this fragmented, lively, quarrelsome movement than their paral-
lels in Western nations are—but burrowing from within
nonetheless. Chief among these is Letitia Ramos-
Shahani, a former United Nations assistant secretary
general, herself secretary general of the 1985 U.N. World
Women's Conference in Kenya, and now a senator. Letty
Shahani—despite being the sister of the extremely powerful General Ramos—maintains the same independent,
principled stance that took her into *de facto* exile during
most of the Marcos years, and led her to declare support
for Corazon Aquino and the democratic upheaval before
the People's Power Revolution, before such an idea
became acceptable, even chic, to the rest of her class.
Raised as a member of the elite (but of a Protestant family) and trained as a diplomat, Letty Shahani's effective-
ness is undeniable; her quiet, "ladylike" voice and weary
eyes are the only visible signs of what must be hidden
psychic scars from trying to translate her complex global
politics into even the simplest local action.

The chaos of culture, politics, religion, and economics—the colonial legacy and neocolonial reality—that these
women must deal with in this country is a staggering
challenge; it makes for a social climate as volatile as the
archipelago's thirty-seven volcanos, seventeen of which
are classified as active.

For example, I attend a march and rally near Malacañ-
ang Palace, site of the presidential residence and office.
A few of the women's groups have elected not to attend,
but representatives from many are there. It is a small
gathering, perhaps only three or four hundred women.
But some have come from the Tondo slum, some from
outlying provinces, some were driven there in air-con-
ditioned cars with chauffeurs, some have walked from
the university. There are the omnipresent Catholic activist nuns, the schoolgirls, the mothers with children slung
on their hips, the crisply efficient organizers, the radical

activists brandishing fists and red banners, frowning mil-
itantly beneath their red headbands. There is singing,
guerrilla theater, dancing—an air of affirmation against
absurd odds. The rally takes place at an intersection a
block or so away from the palace. A movie theater mar-
quee at the intersection blazons "Rambo"; signs outside
a drugstore advertise Marlboro cigarettes and Revlon lip-
stick; a record-store window displays the latest Madonna
and Michael Jackson cassettes. I have been asked to speak
at the rally. I am not eager to do so, but it's difficult to
deny these women the, they say, rare support of a U.S.
citizen who agrees with them that the U.S. bases are an
abomination that must go.* The women's warm reception for my few remarks is moving; such gratitude for so
very little. They are especially pleased that I address them
in Tagalog, since more than half of those attending speak
no English or Spanish.**

But the air of celebration evaporates rather quickly as
the boulevard between us and the palace suddenly begins
to fill—with the army. Jeeps, trucks, and buses disgorge
soldiers in full mufti, with bayonet-fixed rifles. An army
firetruck pulls up, its personnel leaping out to unravel its

*In 1991, the eruption of Mount Pinatubo buried Clark Air Base in vol-
canic ash, forcing the United States to abandon it. That same year, because
of public protests—led by women—the government rejected a lease renewal
for Subic Naval base, requiring the United States to withdraw from it by
the end of 1992.

**This has been a personal practice for years in my travels through the
international women's movement. In advance of going to a country whose
language I do not have, I seek out women of that country kind enough to
translate for me (and teach me how to pronounce) certain phrases, senti-
ments, and basic cross-cultural feminist political positions. After as much
practice as possible (and relying on the merciful forgiveness of the audience for any mispronunciation), I press these paragraphs into use at the
beginning and end of every public appearance. It is well worth the effort,
and highly practical, for at least two reasons: it is intended (and received)
as a gesture of courtesy to the women of the country and language I am
visiting, and it makes it very hard for the local translator—or perhaps press—
(by intent or error) to distort my politics. Considering my country of origin,
this is particularly important.

hose—pointed toward us. We have a single bullhorn; they have a mobile public address system, through which they order us to disperse.

And suddenly the importance of the eclectic mix of demonstrators becomes clear. A university professor, two nuns, a schoolgirl, a media activist, an artist, and a rural mother form an instant delegation, walking together calmly toward the army commander, carrying a permit for the demonstration and also a petition (about female human rights abuses) to the president. If "people power" has been coopted and betrayed since February 1987, here at least it is still alive and well. The women stand talking with the army officer for a few minutes, returning to brief the rally. We are not allowed to tender the petition ourselves, nor are any of our chosen representatives. We must disperse or be attacked. But the officer swears by the Virgin (no small thing in the Philippines, especially in the presence of nuns) that he will personally see that the petition is delivered to a presidential aide. The consensus of the rally is to accept the deal, and we gradually disperse after the small delegation treks back to the officer and hands him the petition. Everyone beams, including the officer. It is surreal—and very Filipino.

But Olongapo, the "rest and recreation" playground for the U.S. Navy's Seventh Fleet base at Subic Bay, is also surreal—and very "American," in the worst possible sense. About a three-hour drive from Manila, this town, whose mayor actually holds U.S. citizenship, is a Hieronymous Bosch hell done up in neon. Street after street boasts only bars, pubs, book and video porn shops and porn movie houses, massage parlors, nightclubs, dance halls, display arenas where women box and wrestle nude, and "hospitality hotels." Thirty percent of these enterprises are owned by ex- or current servicemen. Tourist guidebooks euphemize Olongapo's image as "the Fun City of the Philippines," and some more honestly describe the town's annual $500 million principal industry as prostitution. But what they do not say is that most of the smiling, empty-eyed women who line the streets, lounge in the door-ways, and perch on the barstools are teenagers. Some are children as young as nine, ten, and eleven, who are third or fourth-generation prostitutes. What the guidebooks do not say is that in the back streets GABRIELA and WOMANHEALTH and the Third World Women's Movement Against the Exploitation of Women run shelters for these women when they are battered for trying to run away from pimps, bar proprietors, or brothel owners, clinics for them when they sicken, and hospices for them when they are dying of untreated venereal disease or from AIDS. What the guidebooks do not say is that the bars are not only rank segregated (for commissioned officers or NCOs) but also race segregated (for African American, Latino, or European American sailors). What they do not say is that if a woman tests HIV-positive during one of the periodic Philippine government "sweeps" of "hospitality girls," the bar owner where she works is informed, the Navy is informed, and every disembarking sailor is given a flyer with her photograph, description, and name on it, but *the woman herself is not told.* She learns slowly, by ostracism—and then by starvation.

Prostitution is of course formally illegal in the Philippines. But Olongapo is only one of many R&R centers; they surround each of the U.S. bases. During the Vietnam war, the R&R cities of Angeles and Olongapo "hosted" 10,000 U.S. servicemen daily. In the red-light district sur-rounding the U.S. base in Okinawa, 99 per cent of the female sexual workforce is Filipina. Manila itself is noto-rious as a sex-tourism center, and in fact one sees bus-loads of Japanese businessmen (over 80 percent of whom are sex tourists) wearing party hats as they careen through the city on their lecherous holiday. Mainstream Manila hotels give such guests discreet leaflets (in Japanese) at check-in, informing them of reliable "contacts" and house rules regarding the "hospitality ladies"—who must arrive via the delivery entrance after dusk, who must not be taken to public parts of the hotel, and who must depart by eight in the morning. That the prostitutes must engage in regular pay-offs to the police and the hotels is taken for granted. That "specialty requests"—such as the desire to whip a woman, to urinate on her, to torture her, or the desire for a girl-child (or boy)—will be met quickly and efficiently is also taken for granted. That a woman or child can be "rented," say for a weekend, week, or month, and taken to one of the tourist islands, such as Boracay in the Visayan Islands, along with the rest of one's luggage, is also taken for granted.

Asian Women United, a coalition of Japanese and Filipina feminists, have for more than a decade been working in coalition to stop the flow of sex tourism, and with some success. But they have formidable adversaries: the current wealth of most Japanese men, the chronic poverty of most Filipinas, and the hypocrisy of a Philippines government that outlaws prostitution on the one hand and, on the other, factors prostitution's considerable earnings in foreign currency into the Gross Domestic Product.

The South

Mindanao—the name of South Pacific legend—is the second largest island of the Philippines; its capital, Davao, is the largest and fastest growing city in the entire country after Manila. Davao is a city surrounded by vast multinational plantations owned and operated by Dole, Del Monte, and other multinational agribusiness corporations.

The "Propagation of Islam" spread through Mindanao

and the neighboring Sulu Islands in 1380, and the majority of Filipino Muslims still live in this area, where they have for decades waged a campaign to create an autonomous Muslim state. Various armed Muslim groups—the largest and oldest of which is the Moro National Liberation Front (MNLF)—clash with government forces, NPA cadres, paramilitary vigilante groups, and private armies operated by the plantation owners. Before Aquino came to power, the NPA had controlled large parts of Mindanao surrounding Davao and Cagayan de Oro. These were "liberated zones" where the military dared not go. After Aquino's ascendancy, paramilitary groups were encouraged by the administration, in order to counter the popularity of the NPA.

Davao is, in fact, now notorious for being the site of the first Aquino-government-approved vigilante groups, Alsa Masa and Nakasaka, dreaded for their harrassment, torture, murder, and hamletting of poor farmers. There is nothing particularly secretive about these groups. At a squatters' demonstration to protest the lack of housing— a little "tent town" built of cardboard and large plastic trash bags in the small park in front of city hall—submachine-gun-armed vigilante men in civilian clothing patrol menacingly, scrutinizing and memorizing the faces of the demonstrators. Then, when the paramilitary notice international visitors (and my camera aimed at them), they leap into a jeep and speed away. The government and the army claim that they cannot control the vigilantes and in no way equip them. Yet the weapons are army-issue, as is the jeep.

In the midst of all this, Davao City has sprouted several lush tourist resorts, to which Japanese businessmen, European tourists, and U.S. military officers flock, conveniently oblivious of the surrounding political and social climate.

But the stilt city at the waterside tells a different story.

Here, hundreds of families—most woman-headed (from abandonment or widowhood)—cling to life in precarious lean-tos built of scrap iron and tin, cardboard, plastic tarpaulins, and old boards; the lean-to shacks teeter on stilts and piles sunk into the water, and one navigates between them via rotted planks. There are no toilet facilities, no running water at all. The tidal bay beneath is awash with garbage (no trash collectors come here), yet the children play at diving from the plank "sidewalks" and swimming cheerfully in it, and here and there an old woman can be seen nestled in her doorway with a crude fishing pole, waiting hopefully. One woman tells me with good humor how she had to jump in a month ago to save her prized possession, a piglet who had decided to swim but couldn't. This coast is regularly pummeled by severe storms during typhoon season, and at least once a year the stilt city is utterly demolished. (Women in the Philippines don't speak of summer, winter, spring, or autumn. They speak of "typhoid season," "cholera season," "typhoon season.") The inhabitants don't move, simply because they have nowhere else to go. So after each ritual flattening of their homes and lives, they scavenge more cardboard, more plastic, more dented tin sheeting—and rebuild.

The women are proudest of their "day-care center"—a one-room hut constructed of boards so flimsy that daylight fills the large gaps; just as well, the women say with philosophic smiles, since the center has no electricity anyway. It is used by those women who have no extended families (for which read, other women: grandmothers, sisters, aunts) to care for their children when they go to jobs as streetcleaners in Davao, or as chambermaids at the tourist hotels. They consider themselves priviledged to have such jobs, to have any jobs at all.

There is a survival wisdom here—dogged, unsentimental, inventive: the women know to a second just when the tide turns sufficiently to do subsistence fishing without catching waste-poisoned fish; they try with a heart-breaking pride to keep their hovels clean; they help one another; they manage to laugh. In the glassless "window" of most shacks, a potted plant, on which great care obviously has been lavished, is lovingly displayed. And on one plank "sidewalk corner" stands a frail bamboo tree in an earth-filled tub. This is the communal tree. It is carefully supported by stakes, and secured against the winds by ropes running in three directions.

These women have managed to rescue that tree and bring it through five typhoons to date.

For the rest of my life, whenever I read or hear of a typhoon striking an Asian coast, the reports of damage will never feel abstract or distant. For the rest of my life, such reports will mean these women and that tree.

The next day, we visit a small women's center just outside of Davao. Up two flights of rickety stairs over a tiny dental office (the two hand-lettered signs outside on the building front proudly proclaim: "Muslim Women's Activity Center" and "Woman Dentist Here"), we find another one-room hive of grass-roots activism. My colleague, Mahnaz Afkhami—herself an exiled Iranian feminist leader marked for death by the Islamic fundamentalists who seized her country—is especially moved by these women. Poor, semi-literate, and devout (they all wear the *hijab*), they nonetheless are involved in both learning and teaching income-generating skills—sewing, knitting, weaving—and basic literacy skills. This has been met with considerable resistance from husbands, fathers, and brothers. Their faces and hopes are poignant reminders to Mahnaz of the women with whom she used to work at home. She speaks with them at a level of intimacy markedly greater than her other interactions, however warm, with other women. Nor has she forgotten that she is, at heart, an organizer: via translations, she is quietly discussing with them—and alerting them to—the perils of fundamentalism. Their dialogue is intense and animated; it ends with long embraces all round. Clearly, Mahnaz is perceived to be a woman they can trust. When we leave, they follow us down to the street to bid us goodby, wearing smiles and new feminist buttons and lofting raised fists. Mahnaz is beaming. I suspect that she would happily spend her entire time in Mindanao with these women, but we are expected elsewhere.

Elsewhere is in Davao City, at the public panel, convened for our visit, which we share with representatives from the local chapters of two national women's groups, GABRIELA and PILIPINA, as well as from SAMINI, the Sisters' Association of Mindanao. There are songs and dances by schoolgirls, and, reflective of Filipina hospitality, juices and light foods. The title of our panel is simply: Women's Rights Are Human Rights. But what is most moving is the audience itself.

Approximately four hundred women have come from all over the island—by car, bus, jitney and jeepney, donkey-drawn cart, and by foot—to attend. A group of six rural women have walked twelve miles to get here. (It is this sort of dedication that makes me highly intolerant of arrogant Western assumptions that "Third World women aren't interested in feminism.") I find that I can't wait for the panelists—however interesting—to finish, so that the audience participation can start. When it does, an at-first surreptitious, then open, passing back and forth of kleenex between Mahnaz and myself begins, because it is impossible to have dry eyes while hearing these women testify about female human rights.

There is the nun who does abortion referrals, preferring to risk imprisonment and excommunication to seeing women bear unwanted children or butcher themselves in the attempt not to.

There is the widow of a union organizer who found

her husband's bullet-riddled body left on her doorstep one morning with a note warning of the dangers of communism, signed by the owner of a local banana plantation.

There is the AMIHAN (Women's Farmers' and Peasants' Association) group, who speak movingly about their own attempts to organize small cooperatives, to break out of the stranglehold of sharecropping for the big landowners and multinationals, to survive the threats and daily terrorist acts, large and small, perpetrated against them.

There are the nurses who tell what it is like to work mostly in the absence of doctors—removing bullets, trying to heal shattered bones, ham-strung muscles, scarred flesh, blinded eyes.

There are the battered women who speak in halting voices about being lightning rods for the rage of husbands and lovers crackling with hatred for the owners who employ them.

And there is the woman, a widow in her fifties, who hobbles up to the floor microphone on crutches, one of her legs amputated, who tells how it happened. Her lovely young daughter had been raped a few years earlier, by a band of local NPA cadres; then raped again, a year later, by a policeman; then, still later, by a foreman at one of the pineapple plantations where both mother and daughter worked. The daughter bore a child after each rape. The third time, the mother went, as she put it, "insane"— and struck back. All she had to strike back with was her belief that now, maybe, since a woman was president of the country, there might be justice. So, against the advice of friends, she reported the third rape to the police. No charges were brought—but the police informed the plantation owner of her complaint. It was his vigilante group that swept through her shack one midnight, gang-raping the daughter, beating and terrorizing the children, and "teaching the old woman a lesson." They cut off her leg with a machete and left her for dead. But she did not die. She lives still, with her daughter, who no longer speaks or moves but just sits and stares, and the three grandchildren she must raise and care for. KMK, the national women's labor group, has managed to gain for her a meager widow's stipend from the packaging factory where her husband had been employed.

This is the woman who, in a gentle voice, thanks us for coming to Mindanao to "give her courage," and who adds that women all over the world *must* arise and win—if for no other reason than to prove the existence of a merciful and beneficent god.

■

Typhoon Ruby hits with full fury while Mahnaz and I are on Mindanao. It is impossible to get back to Manila; no planes are flying, especially not the small inter-island aircraft. So the rendezvous with the rest of the Sisterhood Is Global Institute delegation is postponed for a day and a half. Meanwhile, Marilyn Waring and Madhu Kishwar are similarly stranded in Bacolod, on the island of Negros in the Visayans, and Keiko Higuchi is immobilized by the typhoon in Baguio. Marilyn and Madhu have been in the heart of the sugar plantation area, on a poverty-blasted island complete with obscenely high infant and maternal mortality, and its own "anti-communist" vigilante groups. Keiko is on the mainland, but mountainslides across the one highway prevent her return to Manila, too. She spends her time meeting with local Filipinas by candlelight (since the typhoon has cut power), descending into the mines to investigate the work conditions of women miners, and—as a Japanese feminist—warning the local women about what will *really* happen to them if they believe the Japanese male "recruiters" and become mail-order "brides"; she also networks them with feminist shelters in Tokyo, just in case.

When we all are finally able to meet in Manila, the city

itself is just emerging from the typhoon's aftermath. Almost a mile out to sea from the harbor, the tide is glutted with garbage, the remains of shanties, and the wreckage of small fishing boats. I notice two children, little girls, wading in the debris—their thin, shabbily clad bodies bent, their large eyes hungrily searching for anything of even the smallest value that could be found, fished out, perhaps sold. Dangling from filthy string around each of their throats is a crude wooden cross.

For months after the trip, when I searched back over the weeks spent in the Philippines, I had a strange feeling that something was missing. There had been moments of great intensity, to be sure—of horror and despair, hard-won sisterhood, miraculous cross-cultural recognition, and the joy of being able to be of some small use. But still . . . something lacking. Then, with a shock, I realized what the lack was: in a very real sense—and unlike any country I have been to before or since—the Philippines taught me nothing new about the condition of female human beings.

Its lesson was different.

I suddenly remembered that, years earlier, during a meeting in Jordan with the then-highest ranking woman in the PLO—herself a Palestinian enduring statelessness and persecution as well as misogyny—her housemaid, who brought in coffee, was a Filipina.

I think of the New York subways densely packed with night-shift nurses going to work in municipal hospitals for little pay and less respect, and they are Filipinas.

During the Iraqi invasion of Kuwait, most of the women raped and killed were Asian servants to Kuwaiti households—and most of the Asians were Filipinas. The survivors then spent months huddled in refugee camps at the Jordan border, trying to get home, afraid of going home, no alternative to one form of slavery or another, one form of poverty or another. It was not until 1990 that the Aquino government formally outlawed the practice of contracting Filipinas in groups for labor as "domestics" abroad; in 1988 one could still see the women, each clutching her one suitcase, standing herded together with their "contractor" overseer at the airport, waiting to be shipped like cargo to Europe, Japan, or the Middle East. Now, although "expatriate labor" practices are outlawed, they continue in illegal "black" market fashion. Three million expatriate laborers simply bring in too much revenue to be foregone. And the women go, because they pay no rent as live-in servants and can send home almost every bit of pittance earned—supporting entire families back home by their labor in Bahrain, Saudi Arabia, or the Arab Emirates, by their cooking and cleaning and washing and baby-nursing and serving, and being sexually abused by the men of the house, and having no recourse. All this even before a foreign army invades and rapes and shoots and then another foreign army flies over in great machines and makes the sky look like firecrackers on All Saints' Day, the festival of the dead. All this and the dream of going home someday, and the terror of going home ... And all I can see is a Filipina.

A new edition of the *Oxford English Dictionary* lists as a synonym for "maid, servant, domestic": *Filipina.*

No, the journey to the Philippines taught me nothing new about the complex and brutal enslavement of women, about female endurance, about female hope.

But it so confirmed what I did know that now, whenever I see a suffering female human being, somehow, no matter who and where she is—she is a Filipina.

—1990

Feminist Diplomacy

*Despite all the friendship, comfort, and nurturance that
women give one another as a matter of course—and despite
the fact that in the feminist movement this practice has
been raised to a high art as a matter of sensitized empathy
plus political principle—it is also true that there is a certain kind of mercilessly affectionate criticism the women's
movement reserves for its own. Early communist cadres
termed this "criticism and self-criticism"; drug rehabilitation centers call it "hard love"; couples about to split up
defend it as "honesty." It decidedly has its place, but I also
know (as one who has survived being on both ends of the
stick) that it can mask many hidden agendas, including
ego games, envy, undealt-with political disagreements,
possessiveness—in short, the whole gamut of petty human
emotions. Women are, after all, human.*

*The odd thing, though, is that women usually reserve
real anger for each other—in part out of fear (expressing
rage to a man, given his objective power in a patriarchy,
can elicit dangerous responses), and in part out of respect
(women do tend to respect one another more than they do
men, howevermuch this is denied). There may be no rem-
edy for this imbalance at the present historical moment,
but I do sometimes wish that we sent a little more plain*

courtesy in the direction of each other as women—at least as much patience, civility, and understanding as most women spend on most men. The double standard is still alive and well in our cultural conditioning.

This courtesy becomes all the more crucial when reaching across such divisions as age, race, class, sexual preference, nationality, differing ability, etc. The essay that follows—which in a shorter form became a Ms. *editorial—tries to address that challenge.*

It was Norwegian feminist Berit As who wrote, "A patriarchal state is one rehabilitating from war, presently at war, or preparing for war." So, like everyone else, I find myself emerging somewhat dazed from the Gulf tragedy (still ongoing *in* the Gulf, of course), my attention turning to deferred priorities at home, both public and personal.

Last January, at the height of the war, I turned fifty—a landmark birthday, according to conventional wisdom. Nevertheless, it was a landmark I was too busy to mark in more than a passing manner. Activism, not denial, precluded brooding over whether I was now really a grown-up. But a few weeks ago, at a reception after a speech at a midwestern college, I was asked a question that spun me off into thoughts about age—and "difference," and concepts of "the Other."

A pleasant woman in her mid-forties came up and said, "I was watching you, sitting on the floor with some of my young students over there, all of you laughing and talking. You seemed so at ease, and so did they. How did you do that?"

Her question was flattering, but it stopped me—like the proverbial centipede when asked how it moves its 100 legs—in my tracks. I suppose a cross-generational difference is in its own way as much a distinction as a cross-cultural one; perhaps it *is* a cross-cultural one. But the truth is, I've been privileged to share similar con-

versations, laughter, tears, struggles, and embraces with
women much older than I, as well as much younger,
with women of different racial and ethnic backgrounds,
with women in the refugee camps of the Gaza Strip, the
parliaments of Europe, the favellas of Brazil, the plantations of Asia, and in many other places and circumstances.

"I don't know," I finally answered. "They're . . . *women*,
aren't they?"

It was the best reply I could manage at the time, and
my questioner charitably accepted it with interest. But
since then, I've found myself thinking about what I meant.
After all, on the one hand, as feminists we celebrate our
diversity. On the other hand, we've all experienced how
difficult attempts at dialogue among different women can
be. So what do we mean when we say we "speak feminism"?

It's nothing so sentimental (or arrogant) as presuming
our differences don't exist. But it's nothing so cowardly
(or lazy) as overemphasizing them to the point of justi-
fying not engaging each other across them.

It's a complex, delicate kind of "feminist diplomacy"
that we're still in the process of developing. It involves
respect, courtesy, risk, curiosity, and patience. It means
doing one's homework in advance, being willing to be
vulnerable, and attentively listening to one another. (A
sense of humor never hurts, either.) Skill improves with
practice, and practicing feminist diplomacy is challenging, exhilarating, rewarding—and at times exhausting.

Feminism itself dares to assume that, beneath all our
(chosen or forced) diversity, we are in fact much the
same—yet the *ways* in which we are similar are not for
any one woman or group of women to specify, but for all
of us, collectively, to explore and define—a multiplicity
of feminisms. In other words, our experience as female
human beings in a patriarchy may be the same, but our
experiences of that experience differ.

Feminist diplomacy is, for example, inherent in a wonderful couplet in a poem entitled "For the white person who wants to know how to be my friend," by the late African-American poet Pat Parker: "The first thing you do is to forget that i'm Black. / Second, you must never forget that i'm Black."* It was also demonstrated by the (for her safety, anonymous) Saudi feminist who taught me that the enforced enclosure of the female body by the veil is just the other side of the enforced exposure of the female body in Western pornography.

Feminist diplomacy regards the barriers—of race, class, age, sexual preference, ethnicity, ability, nationality, or culture—as possible bridges. This means that each of us can learn much about herself from a woman she's been trained to think of as Other. (Would war be conceivable if there were no Other?) Because feminist diplomacy is inclusive, it searches out the Self in the Other—and vice versa. There is something infinitely touching and brave about this attempt.

There's also something irrepressible, something of a practical miracle, about it. I think of the Oklahoma farmer who, some years ago, after a meeting at her home about the Equal Rights Amendment, noticed how I looked longingly at her garden, walked me through it, and offered advice on what flowers I could grow on a sooty city rooftop to lure—of all things—hummingbirds. "Good for the spirit, having them around. Now my husband," she whispered conspiratorially, "would never *believe* we're having this conversation." But it was part of our speaking feminism.

And against all rules of reality, the peach hibiscus bloomed.

And a hummingbird came.

—*March 1991*

*Pat Parker, *Movements in Black* (San Francisco: Diana Press, 1978).

The Word of
a Woman

In 1991, the world learned of a recently discovered ancient language devised at least one thousand years earlier in a mountainous region of the Hunan Province in central China.

It was a totally female language.

An Associated Press story by Kathy Wilhelm quoted a China Daily *newspaper report that researchers had uncovered hundreds of stories, poems, songs, and letters written over the past millennium in a unique script invented by rural women for their own secret use.*

"Nushi" ("women's writing") used characters derived from standard Chinese to represent the syllables of the local dialect. Standard Chinese has no such phonetic base; it uses characters pictographically, to represent meaning only. Chinese linguists believe that the women developed the script because they were forbidden to learn standard writing.

Numerous as the remaining texts are, comparatively few survive, because women valued them so highly that they willed the nushi *to be placed in their coffins—so that the cherished writings might be re-read even after death. Such intimacy with and loyalty to the created word may seem bizarre to contemporary sensibilities, relentlessly assaulted as we are by commercial hype, political jargon, trendy buzz words, and a general cheapening of expression. But it may seem less curious once one realizes that for hundreds of years, women used the script to record their hidden emotions and to communicate with one another surreptitiously. As one* nushi *author wrote, "Men leave home to brave life in the outside world. But we women are no less courageous. We can create a language they cannot understand."*

These were the words of a woman who might as well have written, "We shall not suffer in silence." Because this female language was an underground code—an act of rebellion in conception, an utterance of rebellion in content.

The writings gleam with rage at women's lot: at arranged marriages, brutal and vulgar husbands, the right of men to take numerous wives and divorce women whenever they chose; at enforced chastity for women (and required allegiance to one man even if widowed while young); at beatings survived and insults to human dignity endured; at being treated, as the women wrote, "like slaves." But the tone was not always one of suppressed wrath. Some nushi *mourn the loss of a beloved woman friend to marriage; thread-bound books of poems and songs would be given to a bride three days after her wedding: tokens of grief that she could no longer spend time with her women friends, commemorative artifacts of the relative freedom of her single life, and talismanic sources of strength to aid her survival as a wife.*

Apparently the practice of nushi *declined once females were permitted access to education; when scholars began researching the script in the 1980s, they could locate only a dozen elderly women still able to read it; only three could still write it.*

Yet the language had been preserved—alive, intact, and secret—for a thousand years.

It is in honor of these eloquent ancestors, the nushi *authors, that the following essay—published here for the first time—borrows its form from another Chinese tradition. Because it is assumed that author and reader are in dialogue with one another, the margins are deliberately left wider than usual, for "commentaries" by the reader(s). Such commentaries are regarded as more than marginalia or jottings; they are not merely appendages to the printed text. On the contrary, this essay itself is unfinished without them.*

So I invite you to complete this nushi—*these writings— with your own, as another exchange in our millennia-long conversations, as a living metaphor for our interdependence.*

We can create a language they cannot understand.

Letter to a Reader in 2992

Dearest Friend of My Imagination's Optimism:

Dust whispers as you read this, whether from the page, the computer screen, or via some other communicative form beyond current comprehension. Intimate dust: brain cell past to brain cell future.

These are messages from a human being hubristic enough to have faith in the power of words (even those of her own awkward making); mad enough to believe that mind must cease treating matter— and matter stop treating mind—as "Other."

So I dare address you from what they call my time (which is not yet my time), eight years short of a new century and, more dramatically, of a new millennium.

When, as a child, I was taught a meditation entitled "The Lord's Prayer," I wondered why "The Lord" would need to pray, and I wondered who could possibly answer such an omnipotent petitioner. Now, having lived fifty summers and winters, I wonder more simply why I pray, this way, to you—and who you are.

It requires an absurd leap of faith to believe that you are, at all.

If sentient life on this planet survives even the next hundred years—or if sentient life from elsewhere in the universe someday sifts curiously or indifferently through the ruins we leave of the ruins we are—what might be said of us?

It might be said of us:

They lived in a savage time.

They fouled their own home.

They ate flesh, warred on one another, kept slaves.

They believed that the shape and the color of their shells was of importance.

Their politics were even cruder than their technology.

They feared their own intelligence, and so ignored it.

They failed to comprehend the obvious intelligence of their relatives—whether dolphin or cactus, eagle or redwood, monkey, lizard, spider, clay.

Their greatest generosity was in sharing pain.

They did not even understand their own Energy, much less The Field.

It will be a subject of some debate: from

which of two flaws we suffered most—or
perished totally—delusion or denial.

■

So here is a shred of evidence, a testimony, a minority report, a voice from this
epoch in which I (sometimes) live,
imprisoned. These are what they call the
realities of my age.

It is the age of nuclear patriarchy. Our
androcentric world view has become a
life-threatening disease. But it is also—one
way or the other—the age of terminal
patriarchy.

For I am the eve of Adam.

The Four Horsemen of the Apocalypse
canter across our days and nights. War
now goes by the name "intervention."
Pestilence bears the mark of HIV / AIDS.
Famine is euphemized as "underdevel-
opment." Death wears all these masks,
while filtering as well through perfora-
tions in the ozone layer, silting from soil
and river, ebbing and flowing in ocean
tides, entering our lungs and lives through
palpable city smog or invisible radiation.
More humans currently inhabit the earth
than all those who have lived and died
from the beginning of the human species
until the present.

"World economic crisis" is an ethically
bereft phrase, insufficient to describe how
the homeless curl against the dust pil-
lows of Calcutta, squat like revenants in
the Necropolis of Cairo, hunch in cardboard co-ops on the concrete sidewalks
of New York.

"World environmental crisis" is a mor-

ally destitute phrase, inadequate to eulo-
gize the one million species—20 percent
of all species—at risk of extinction, several hundred per day, by the year 2000.

It will be said of us, *"How could they
not know? If they knew, why did they not
act?"*

▄▄▄

How would I answer you, you of the not-
yet descendants or someday-perhaps visitors? How would I answer you so that you
might weep for us in pity and not laugh
at us in incredulous contempt?

Would I whine that we did not really
know the extent of the peril, that we were
kept from knowing the truth? This is true.
But this is also an insufficient response.

Would I claim that there were many
who did know, and some who even tried
to act? This is also true, but this is surely
a special pleading.

Or would I be more honest, and attempt
to explain how most of my species
regarded life, and endured our own existences, as a *trompe l'oeil,* entering with
willingly suspended disbelief into a clev-
erly convincing one-dimensional repre-
sentation of the real thing?

And how would I rationalize that this
was not the result of innocence but of
experience, that this was both delusion
and denial?

How would I justify such a poverty of
vision?

▄▄▄

The unlearned lesson that reality is an
illusion lies at the heart of most major

(even patriarchal) spiritual beliefs of my species. But rarely has this lesson been so painfully inflicted, yet so ignored, as at present.

Jane Wagner, a *nushi* writer of this period, has asked (and answered) wittily, "What is reality, anyway? A collective hunch." Today, however, the hunch is less collective than it is determined by those few who have the power to enforce the credibility of their lies.

For example (and this will be hard for you to understand), in my era the term "ALARA"—As Low As Reasonably Achievable—was applied to "normal" global radiation levels, levels acknowledged by a growing number of scientists to be alarmingly over tolerable limits.

But this is a poison we cannot see, touch, taste, or smell; we sip it in the morning but do not die until nightfall; it vibrates through us, "only probably" connected to the rising rate of cancers, leukemias, lowered immune systems, mutations.

Probability is not considered proof. Like the propaganda of hatred in contemporary racist or pornographic literature, "causality" must be proven. Facts are (try to understand this) actually held more valid than truths, categories are genuinely thought more reliable than connections.

The powerful seek to reassure us. For many, perhaps most, the reassurance works, since it is assumed that the powerful—who clearly believe themselves and their descendants immune to biocide—must possess some secret knowledge of survival. And they alone have the prerogative to prove or disprove, anyway, since they set the standards that define and control proof.

After all, this is an era in which a woman may dance by herself, in public but not on exhibition, only after someone she loves more than her sanity has been "disappeared."

Another contemporary *nushi* author, Adrienne Rich, has written about the necessity of being "disloyal to civilization." She is quite right, of course. But beyond that indispensable, basic disloyalty lies the need for disloyalty to culture itself. And even beyond that, the leap of becoming disloyal to reality.

Meanwhile, the bowl of sky is still (sometimes) a clear, unglazed blue. Tulips push through spring soil to redden the snow. The rain feels cleansing, not acidic.

How, then, can the intensifying danger become vivid enough, soon enough, for us?

How can the ancient law of the Craft of the Wise—"Do what thou wilt, *an it harm none*"—be dredged from our collective amnesia? Especially when those who cry warnings are dismissed as alarmists?

It is not noticed that being Cassandra is a principled choice when there is cause for alarm.

How do we perceive truth despite facts, locate authenticity despite reality—and escape despair?

■

There is a woman named Chhean Im, who might teach us certain things about perception, despair, and what lies beyond.

She is a Cambodian in her mid-sixties, living in the refugee enclave known as Little Phnom Penh in Long Beach, California. She is a survivor of the Killing Fields.

She is blind.

But there is nothing physiologically wrong with her eyes.

Her affliction is called "hysterical" or "psychosomatic" blindness, and she is one of approximately 150 female Cambodian refugees who have lost most or all of their sight (the largest known group of such victims in the world).*

Chhean Im simply has seen too much.

Her village was seized and turned into a prison farm by the Angka, the Khmer Rouge police force that was composed largely of young boys; most of her family were slaughtered before her eyes. She worked an average of 125 hours a week and lived on one small bowl of rice a day. She watched many others starve to death. She watched still more beaten to death or burned alive. One day, she remembers, they picked out one woman and one man and hit them again and again. She began crying again, and couldn't stop. She recalls that "it felt like there was a big needle pushing through my head." When at last

---

*See Patrick Cooke, "They Cried Until They Could Not See," *The New York Times Magazine,* June 23, 1991.

she stopped crying, days later, she could no longer see.

No male refugees are known to suffer from this blindness, although the reasons why are unclear. For one thing, there are almost no male refugees. Eighty percent of the million and a half people killed by the Khmer Rouge were men between the ages of twenty and fifty.

Gretchen Van Boemel, associate director of clinical electrophysiology at the Doheny Eye Institute in Los Angeles, and Patricia Rozée, a California State University psychologist, have been working with Chhean Im and other Cambodian women so afflicted. For years these women, some of them suicidal, had suffered in silence, too terrified of authority to seek medical help, isolated in a foreign culture, prey to hideous nightmares, flashbacks, and traumatic dissociation, and consumed by "survivor guilt" comparable to that suffered by Holocaust victims. Those few who had sought help had been ignored, misdiagnosed, or accused of malingering or conniving to gain disability benefits. Among the approximately 100 sightless women Van Boemel has examined, the commonalities are striking: now between age fifty and seventy, at least half suffer from agoraphobia and dare not leave their homes; all endured forced labor from one to five years in Cambodia and later up to six years in the squalor and violence of Thai refugee camps; almost all had lost family members and most had been forced to watch the tortures and executions.

Van Boemel and Rozée gently and slowly began to interest the women in short-term group therapy and "living skills" training (how to ride a bus, use the telephone). Many of the survivors were too trapped in their fear, and declined to participate. Some even moved away. But fifteen of them agreed to try. Chhean Im was one.

Today, she can see well enough to ride a city bus, go to the supermarket, cook her own dinner, even venture out for a short walk.

On the bus, she must look out through the dirty glass pane at a blur of frowning people who are hurrying through their lives. At the supermarket, she must stand stunned before the bright mounds of oranges and melons, onions and cabbage, the bulging sacks of rice, the tiered tins of soup, the stacked boxes of tea, the piles of plastic-wrapped fresh fish and meat and fowl, the cardboard, the aluminum, the fluorescent lights, the smooth-rolling silver carts, the assault of labels in loud reds and blues and yellows.

One can only wonder, when she ventures out to take a slow, shuffling walk, what Chhean Im sees . . .

▆

If you who read these words still follow the ways of my epoch's logic, then you will misread so much of what I have to say to you as primitive.

But if you exist, I must believe that you have evolved into trust.

If you have not, then there will be so few (or so many) of you, enduring such tormented (or anesthetized) lives, that you will have neither the capacity nor the inclination to read this artifact. Indeed, you will have already erased me utterly for daring to be what I am: a memory of the future.

So I must assume you are not merely the last of my species, but the first of my kind.

To you, then, I will confess several secrets I dared not utter aloud except to one or two others in my own epoch. They are humble secrets, of no great import. But they grow in me toward your birth.

How difficult this is, harder than I anticipated! It is perplexing to find the language with which to speak to you, since I am no longer interested in words for which people have killed and died, and the richness of my epoch's language depends on such utterances. That my eccentricity eliminates such words as *patriotism, wealth, fame, religion, category, revenge, custom, security, authority, zoo, stranger, normal, envy, tradition, conquest, nation, youth, age, tribe, enemy, destiny, race, triumph, alliance, territory, boredom, empire, ambition, ethnicity, ideology, manhood,* and *power* (to name only a few), I count as a loss of little consequence.

That the word "language" itself—not as

communication but as impediment—belongs by all rights on that list, I count as a threat of grave proportions.

What is serious, I admit, is the rapidly expanding inventory of all those concepts I do not understand—although I understood them when I was younger.

For example, I realize that I do not understand "justice." (I would once have said that my life was given over to the pursuit of justice. If so, I'm relieved I got it back.)

*In*justice I understand. Well may you say that this is because injustice has been part of my experience and witnessing. But it is not so simple: *mercy* I understand, and even *fairness* (and I have experienced little of either). *Regret* I comprehend, and *remorse.* Even "righting an injustice" I understand. But "justice"? At best it reeks of bargains, pettiness, hypocrisy; at worst of retribution, vengeance, deals. It pretends that suffering can be weighed and computed, bought off, "made whole." Why would the oath "God give me the wisdom to temper justice with mercy" be necessary unless justice was inherently cruel? It stinks of punishment, of jealous and vengeful Judeo-Christian gods. It is a lazy settling for less than imaginative solutions, ones that might invoke words like transcendence, transformation, grace.

The only justice I can catch a glimmer of is "poetic justice"—but that is really only a two-worded synonym for irony. And (so far) I still understand and retain an affection for irony.

No longer understanding justice puts me out of step with some of the best minds of my era—although there is some comfort in knowing that it also puts me out of step with some of the worst ones.

You see how stupid I am becoming?

Furthermore, "time" is also quite beyond me now. I once thought I understood time in a basic sort of way—clocks, calendars, all those imposed and imposing measurements that we devise to pace off eternity. When I learned that others, far more precociously stupid than I, had realized time and space were identical and indissoluble, I became quite excited. But of late, I cannot grasp time at all, not even in terms of space (how space itself now flies!), but especially not in terms of the singular. That is, I cannot see *time* for all of its variant *times:*

There is, for example, Flying South Time, to the Canada geese. There is Berry Time to the juniper bush. There is Hyacinth Time to the bulb. There is Nova Time to the ageing giant red star, and Dividing Time to the blastula. These lend considerable perspective to such arbitrary notions as "Three-fifteen sharp at the corner of Fifth and Forty-second Street," useful though such a phrase may be.

Yet geese and juniper, hyacinth, sunstar, and cell are never late.

Nor early.

■■

Being gradually divested of vocabulary is part of my problem in addressing you. (Yet were I still encumbered with understanding such words as "justice" or "time" I doubt I would be trying to address you at all.) A side effect, of course, is that grammar—tenses and tensions in particular—sometimes slips through one's fingers as well, along with preoccupations about linear "continuity."

This is why I will have presumed upon your patience with what in my day would have been called disjointed thoughts. Since it is now believed that the brain is less like a computer than like a self-regulating organ, and since every thought was once a chemical—which means that mind becoming matter is a chemical process, as is matter becoming mind—isn't it difficult to imagine how any fresh thoughts could originate as other than disjointed? (Most of my contemporaries would tell me not to mind.) You of all readers know what a strange appetite the brain has, when you let it free to graze . . .

All of which is to say that if the likes of you rise from the ashes of us it will be despite and because of what Chhean Im saw—and sees. Despite and because of what the *nushi* authors knew.

And why should this be so funny if it is so painful? And why should it hurt so much if it is so funny?

And how do we speak to one another in a language not our own? And how do we read one another if we cannot see?

To create our language we would need to go beyond the pictographs of mere descriptive meaning. We would need to enter into the local dialect, as it were, toward the *phonetics* of reality. Toward how reality sounds and feels.

We would need to speak in metaphor.

(Not simile, mind you: that well-meaning but cowardly "like," and "as if"; that middle-of-the-road,   wishy-washy approximation that feels compelled to over-explain itself.) *Metaphor:* the essence of the thing itself—sufficiently tiny, unique, and specific to attempt an implosion into the universal:

——

—If I speak to you from ashes, do I by now already know if fire is the act of burning? Or is fire what it produces: sparks, flame, heat, light, carbon, embers? Is fire not more than the sum of its entropy?

—A (very) short story: As the years went by, she found it extremely difficult to get the caviar stains out of the pillow case. The champagne drops had disappeared, but of course the bloodstains had only faded.

—*Geophagia* is the name for an uncontrollable desire to eat earth. Perfectly healthy, well-adjusted citizens in certain communities around the world enjoy eating dirt or clay. Some become connoisseurs partial to different kinds of soil. Many prefer to crumble it onto a cookie sheet and bake it for a few minutes so as to intensify the pleasure of the crunch.

Less than a craving but more than a preference, this is neither a religious nor cultural practice, nor is it a superstitious
fetish. Earth-eaters are found in considerable numbers in the U.S. agrarian South,
where the phenomenon constitutes a
bond between those blacks and whites
who practice it. When circumstances force
these rural people into urban surround-
ings, they sometimes must content themselves with store-bought starch or chalk.
Only recently have scientists realized that
the particular earth or clay chosen for
eating is rich in dietary nutriments and
may in fact contain natural medicinal
value for a range of ailments from indi-
gestion through ulcers to colon cancer.

All known earth-eaters are women.

—Who invented the question mark?
Encyclopedias are mute on the subject.
Yet the mystery haunts me. Susanne K.
Langer, a *nushi* writer disguised as a philosopher, wrote, "The notion of giving
something a *name* is the vastest genera-
tive idea that ever was conceived." But
surely the notion of giving such an intangible emotion as curiosity a permanent
symbol runs a close second. I think it not
illogical (even in my millennium's rather
cramped sense of logic) to hypothesize
that a woman invented the question
mark—and, for that matter, probably the
question itself. Such innovations spring
from need. If, for instance, you are forbidden to learn to read and write, you
create a means of language. If you are

forbidden knowledge, you devise the question. If you are forbidden both literacy and knowledge, don't you invent the question mark?

Dearest friend of my imagination's optimism, across a hundred centuries I grope toward you; from years of seeing both too little and too much; out of a yearning to dance alone, in public or not, neither for exhibition nor mourning; out of a longing to think in common with my kind.

Because you will have grown beyond justice, you will not need to judge us. You may even smile—feeling something between recognition and respect—in compassion.

But please know, as well, that we were capable of defiance, even of joy.

Know that when they vowed we would never forget their martyred battle heroes, we bent our energies on the heresy of forgetting.

Know that we were no longer able or content to encounter or render surfaces—no matter how tempting their density nor how seductive their luminosity—but were drawn instead to what lives beneath the façade: to geometries of the bone, to refrains of the blood.

Know that we sometimes even dared the grace of laughing at ourselves.

There were more than a few of us, trying to find one another, often in rage and bereavement, sometimes in desire and delight.

It was not simple or easy.

But it was not as difficult as we pretended and feared.

And the miracle that will be was that we who believed this might be buried with us—because we valued it so, because they could not understand it, because it was secret, because it could be re-read only after our death—all these thousand years later, is in your hands: one of the twelve who can still decipher it.

Find the other eleven, and begin again. In Blastula Time.

Index